D1548122

THE VALUE OF WORTHLESS LIVES

THE VALUE
OF WORTHLESS
LIVES

Writing Italian American
Immigrant Autobiographies

Ilaria Serra

Fordham University Press

New York ❧ 2007

Library of Congress Cataloging-in-Publication Data

Serra, Ilaria.
  The value of worthless lives : writing Italian American immigrant
autobiographies / Ilaria Serra.
      p.   cm.
  Includes bibliographical references and index.
  ISBN-13: 978-0-8232-2678-8 (clothbound : alk. paper)
  ISBN-10: 0-8232-2678-6 (clothbound : alk. paper)
  1. Autobiography.   2. Immigrants—United States—Biography—Authorship.
3. Italians—United States—Biography—Authorship.   4. Italian Americans—
Biography—Authorship.   5. Working class—United States—Biography—
Authorship.   6. Women—United States—Biography—Authorship.   I. Title.
  CT25.S47   2007
  973'.045100922—dc22   2007002979

Printed in the United States of America
09 08 07   5 4 3 2 1   First edition

Contents

Immigrants left tears and sweat, but no memories.

❧ GIUSEPPE PREZZOLINI
I trapiantati

Introduction

Nello is buried on a Tuscan cliff that looks toward the tiny island of Giglio, which he left as a young boy in order to emigrate to America. Nello's attachment to his homeland was so strong that he even named his daughter Elba, after the much larger neighboring island. Yet after a childhood on the sun-drenched Mediterranean, he spent the strongest years of his life in the dank, underground darkness of the mines of Scranton, Pennsylvania. The mines earned him a living, but they also left him with disease that plagued his old age with swollen, blistered legs. Late in his life, in the hope of healing him, his daughter took him back to Italy. He longed to see his native island once more, but he died on the coast of Liguria, before reaching his homeland. Nello is now buried on the shore in the cemetery of Manarola, where his tomb faces his beloved island of Giglio.[1]

The story of Italian immigration is filled with such silent lives and deaths—lives that have brought no fame and created no heroes, lives full of longing for their abandoned homelands, lives that have left no record of their stories, neither of their labor, nor their nostalgia. In his 1963 essay *I trapiantati* (The uprooted), after attempting to find some first-person testimonies of Italian immigration, Giuseppe Prezzolini concluded, "Immigration was a great mute tragedy. . . . The survivors do not want to remember." "Immigrants left tears and sweat, but no memories."[2] Prezzolini was certain that after the deaths of their protagonists, there would be no trace of the many immigrant stories. When

I

he tried to find such documents he failed miserably, concluding sadly: "I once tried through the local Italian-language press to gather memoirs of immigration. I got no answer. Nobody preserved memoirs of his own or his parents' migration. Instead, they attempted to forget it."[3]

I can now happily report that this is not true. I have hunted down and discovered dozens of forgotten texts that had been buried in archives and in the drawers of private houses. In those lost places, where no one but family would look, we can find the lives of farmers, laborers, and professionals who did not seek fame, but only wanted to rebel against the silence of a forgotten life. My investigations confirm with overwhelming evidence that many of these humble Italian immigrants did, in fact, write autobiographies—often aided by the sons and daughters, who Prezzolini mistakenly believed did not want to preserve their parents' memories. These uprooted Italians did not attempt to forget their past. On the contrary, they clung to their memories and to their local and national Italian heritages. A remarkable number of proud and moving stories—most stowed away for generations in family attic "archives," manuscript collections, and regional libraries—collectively present such a powerful account of the urge to remember that they beg to be examined as a group. In fact, they disprove Prezzolini's statement so thoroughly that we can now marvel that so *many* immigrants—including those who led everyday workers' lives, those who were unschooled and barely literate, and those who had a difficult enough time moving from job to job, let alone taking pen to paper—made every possible effort to leave their written footprint on this earth. This body of forgotten work that records the hopes, dreams, and stories of this segment of the population—which collectively is so essential to twentieth-century history of Italy and the United States—is largely unknown in these countries. These texts do not record the stories of great wars and leaders, nor are they gifted literary achievements. These simple stories of individual lives slip through the nets of history and literature, but they are invaluable documents for the wealth of information they give us about the strength of the human psyche.[4]

Even though there have been recent studies of Italian American immigration since Prezzolini wrote over forty years ago, the new work has hardly helped to illuminate the real scope of the situation. The most recent work of literary compilation, the large two-volume anthology by Francesco Durante,[5] unfortunately overlooks the phenomenon of autobiographies as a whole. Although it happens to include some autobiographical extracts, they disappear in the crowd of names, because Durante's focus is a general anthology of literary production.[6] The latest monumental historical study on Italian immigration, the two volumes, *Partenze* and *Arrivi,* of *Storia dell'emigrazione italiana,*[7] unfortunately do not include a chapter on the autobiographies of immigration (only a few are mentioned by Caterina Romeo). This is unfortunate, because this would have given personal insight into this historical phenomenon. Preserving the testimonies of these individual experiences from permanent erasure gives another face to history, as it represents the actions of so many people at such a critical point. As Antonio Gramsci, a scholar of the people, summarized, "Autobiography certainly has a great historical value in that it shows life in action and not merely as written laws or dominant moral principles say it should be."[8]

The great waves of Italian immigration to the United States (from the end of the nineteenth century to the period after World War II) were not intellectual migrations.[9] For the few Italians whose words have been published, as Jerre Mangione and Ben Morreale observed, "it was in the realm of fiction, rather than poetry or autobiography, that Italian American writers began to gain a foothold in the literary mainstream, but that was not to happen until the children of the immigrants were old enough to take stock of their bilingual situation."[10] To find the voices of the real protagonists of such an important historical phenomenon, we have to examine material that is generally considered to be second-rate. These works are truly "autobiographies from unexpected places," to borrow a phrase from Martha Ward, who has studied autobiographies of women.[11] These immigrants' stories enlarge the genre of autobiography to provide a truer cross section of the immigrant population and their individual histories, struggles, and dreams. Including works by "illiterate" or "unliterary" authors is necessary if, to borrow again from Ward, we want to "describe a wider spectrum of the ways and means by which people in the twentieth century speak themselves into textual existence."[12]

In this volume I examine these histories of such inconsequential people, "undistinguished Americans" as Hamilton Holt called them in 1906, a moment when the immigrant wave was rolling into full force.[13] It was only in 2005, after a century of optimism, that Scott Sandage admitted, in his study of unsuccessful people, "Deadbeats tell not tales, it seems"—although he went on to show how these sources are all too common, if one can only bear to listen to them.[14] Holt and Sandage are in tune with an important premise for my study: we are so accustomed to reading remarkable tales about brilliant lives and fortuitous chains of events. In the immigrants' stories I have examined we are faced with the ordinary and the mundane, and we see examples of people who have plugged through bad and worse luck, and whose day-to-day decisions—or lack of power to make decisions— sometimes seem to have worsened their situations. Yet these tales reveal a compelling human endurance and resilience.

There is an insistence among these largely unlettered immigrant workers to *write* a *book*—for many of them the naive approach to their project is what makes this phenomenon so telling.[15] With a shaky hand, Giuseppe Previtali, an immigrant doctor, scribbled *"il libro"*— "the book"—on scrap paper while on his deathbed as his last word to his son. And other authors, less acquainted with books than Previtali, are almost obsessed with creating what must appear to them as an object of intellect: a book, a story, a literary work. In my researches, I have personally met immigrants who wanted with all their strength to see their writings become books, and I have found such little booklets published by vanity presses or in provincial typography, perhaps read only by their relatives and close friends. Especially in recent years, when technological means make it so cheap and easy to produce such volumes, it is impossible not to notice the determination of these writers to have their lives contained in a book. It seems that immigrants who come from a productive, material background need the objective, material form of paper and cardboard covers, however simple and homemade they look. Holding a book is a subversive action for ordinary people, a performance of protest against anonymity and oblivion, a gesture that would seem to escort one to the next class. In the margins of the polis, the book is a rhetorical tool, a powerful means of persuasion with which the unempowered can break into history.

I found these texts in private houses, libraries, and in three archives: the Immigration History Research Center in St. Paul, Minnesota; the Staten Island Center for Immigration Studies; and the Archivio Diaristico Nazionale of Pieve Santo Stefano in Italy. I have translated passages into English in a style that corresponds to the grammatical (in)correctness of the original. Many of these authors had just as much trouble with formal Italian as they did with English, and I sought to preserve the character of each of their voices, even at the expense of passages that can be difficult to follow.[16] No matter how important learning English was to these writers, when it came to their autobiographies, they almost always chose to write in their native language. Even Joseph Tusiani, who is an accomplished translator and poet in both languages, wrote his autobiography in Italian. Yet even in our age of multiculturalism, it is still marginal to have American literary production in a language other than English.[17] But this choice of language is important: it belies any supposition—which has long been the perceived wisdom—that all immigrant autobiographies are stories of Americanization.[18]

In a time of globalization, it is more important than ever to emphasize language as an author's chosen baptism. Twenty years ago, Werner Sollors's influential *Beyond Ethnicity* introduced for autobiography the concepts of ethnicity by "descent" and "consent," terms that have now become part of the standard vocabulary of ethnic criticism.[19] He opposes the importance of consent that tends to lump all ethnic people as one homogenous group when they accept becoming Americans. He observes that American ethnics are more similar among themselves than to the same ethnic that remained in the old country. "Descent relations are those defined by anthropologists as relations of 'substance' (by blood or nature); consent relations describe those of 'law' or 'marriage.' Descent language emphasizes our positions as heirs, our hereditary qualities, liabilities, and entitlements; consent language stresses our abilities as mature free agents and 'architects of our fate' to choose our spouses, our destinies, and our political systems."[20] Thus, *descent* and *consent* are key terms when discussing why ordinary Italian American immigrants choose Italian or English for their memoirs.[21]

The first part of this book consists of a chapter explaining the historical context of autobiography and why the set of subgenres—Italian American autobiography, autobiography of ordinary or unlettered people, and immigrant autobiography—presents such a compelling case for study. I show how autobiography is the privileged expression of immigration because both are built on the discovery of the individual and the separation and trauma that accompany migration. Lives of first-generation immigrants, mostly of a subaltern social class, present a special case, since their experience of migration from a land that kept their families tied down for centuries seems to trigger their need to write. This individual is different from the protagonists of traditional autobiographies of outstanding Americans, such as Benjamin Franklin or Lee Iacocca. As I see it, our authors have what I call a "quiet individualism"—they are aware that their lives are not spectacular and they don't present themselves as models, only as examples of those who survived the personal traumas of immigration. Finally, Italian American cultures offer special rhetorical styles and conventions that must be acknowledged in order to provide more insight into this genre and its use as evidence in history, the social sciences, and other academic disciplines. Many of these narratives fall between worlds of nonliterate oral traditions and literacy, as these relatively uneducated writers use vivid rhetorical storytelling devices such as proverbs, colloquialisms, and appeals to the listener in folk manners of both Italy and America.

Part two of this book presents digests and discussions of the immigrant autobiographies, organized by five general types: the working-class writer, including those with political or poetical presentations in their autobiographies; artist immigrants; immigrants who answered a spiritual vocation; women; and the immigrant who has achieved traditional "success" in the new world—the college graduate, doctor, or businessman who becomes perfectly integrated into American society. My discussion of these types is somewhat general, and one could identify many overlaps in these somewhat arbitrary categories. My analysis is not intended to provide any rigorously systematic division, as some scholars have done; it is only to get a handle on some of the immigrant issues that are not only of interest to the general reader—many of whom will see their grandparents or great-grandparents mirrored in these pages—but that also would be helpful to future scholars who might be inspired to probe more deeply into aspects of this rich treasure. I have summarized or excerpted passages from fifty-eight individual accounts, and their rich diversity belies the only sparse observations and rash generalizations that have been made in past scholarship about Italian American immigrants' writings and lives.

Still, these groupings show that there are many similarities and themes that run through them, even though the writers settled in different American cities, took various careers (or, for most, odd jobs), and experienced mixed luck and fortunes. From this cacophony of dozens of immigrant voices we can start to hear the destinies and undertakings of their inner and outer worlds, their adversity and satisfaction, their unassuming voices in the narratives of history. Taken together, the autobiographies are evidence of the importance of these texts not only for various aspects of history, but for a study of the strength of the human psyche. These documents contradict the clichéd tales of heart-wrenching departure that are often associated with emigration from Italy to America.[22] And for many Italians and Americans, these stories can be treasured more subjectively, as they are moving documents that preserve the simple hopes, dreams, fears, cultural struggles, and quiet individualism that our own families, and past generations like them, have faced. These diverse texts share universal themes. They are stories of transformation, survival, and a desire for recognition—however modest their authors' dreams may be. My research shows that we have come a long way since Giuseppe Prezzolini made his observations in the epigraph that heads this introduction: in fact, immigrants left tears and sweat, as well as many memories.

PART 1

1   Autobiography: The Literary Genre of Immigration

If a novel lays out an imagined immigration, and poetry offers us a distilled and rarefied immigration, autobiographies provide us with the most real and sincere account of the process and effects of immigration that we could have. Letters also contribute an important voice, but since they are addressed to relatives and friends in the heated immediacy of experience, they don't offer the comprehensive perspective of autobiography. An autobiography speaks of the wholeness of the experience. It is there that we find the image of the entire person— already shaped, metabolized, and pondered. Immigrants have not only lived the whole experience in first person, they have reworked it into a coherent image of self. Moreover, as the Italian writer Antonio Gramsci maintained, autobiography is the unfiltered product of "people who act," a point he uses in his critique of Italian intellectuals who are detached from the people.[1] Finally, autobiographies appeal to our curiosity: there the intimate communion between the writer and reader is hard to resist, for as Roy Pascal has written, "we are won over simply by being admitted to his intimacy."[2]

Definitions of Autobiography

Autobiography is a broad genre, and the debate over its limits is contentious.[3] Etymologically, the word is a sum of three concepts: it is "the description (*graphia*) of an individual human life (*bios*) by the individual himself (*auto-*)."[4] That would all seem straightforward enough. But its use in scholarship has had a sequence of evolving definitions that bears reviewing here.

In 1960 the critic Roy Pascal's seminal book *Design and Truth in Autobiography* marked the critical rediscovery of autobiography in the United States. With his modernist obsession for a hierarchy of values in literature, Pascal can be characterized as an elitist who sees autobiography as the ancient and venerated genre of *uomini illustri* (illustrious men), of the earthly and saintly heroes. Pascal considers only few autobiographies as worthy (the Florentine Mannerist sculptor Benvenuto Cellini, Jean-Jacques Rousseau, Saint Teresa of Avila, William Wordsworth, and J. W. Goethe)—those that speak of "the whole man," that document great deeds, and that rise to a symbolic level as "a search for one's inner standing."[5] He narrows down the field of true autobiography to include texts written "by men or women of outstanding achievement in life," and those of higher spirit: "the value of an autobiography depends ultimately on the quality of spirit of the writer."[6] The rest of us, alas, are unworthy. Looking down with diffidence at the multitude of autobiographies of average people, he counts their shortfalls—from "vanity, complacency, self-indulgence" to "self-distrust."[7] V. S. Pritchett has called this deficiency "the cliché of having lived": "There is no credit in living. . . . Not every bucketful of our lives in the conveyor belt from cradle to grave is valuable."[8] As we can well imagine, Pascal's great expectations allow for only a meager harvest, and many autobiographies—those lacking literary quality, even if dense in content—are but the chaff.

For James Olney, living and philosophizing are the same action, for which he uses a suggestive word play. In his *Metaphors of Self* (1972) he coined the verb "to self": "Each is selving in its unique way an inclusive 'Self' of all things."[9] Seen in this light, the story of a life is a philosophy of its own, realized as a metaphor of self, "something known and of our making, or at least of our choosing, that we put to stand for, and so to help to understand, something unknown and not of our making."[10] Following Olney, when the old immigrant looks back at his life, he is unifying it through a metaphor and making it "thereby fit into an organized, patterned body of experiential knowledge."[11] The metaphors of self used by the immigrant *I* to represent his or her life could be as concentrated as the building of the perfect house or finding a place in the world, or as loose as "making oneself" or "surviving."

Olney's concept of autobiography as the way we know the world is valid for most of our immigrant writers. Even though the authors were certainly not thinking of writing their own philosophy in their autobiographies, we cannot fail to notice that much of their work addresses some kind of moral lesson, and if there are not individual sections devoted to it, the whole text takes on that tone. We can ascribe that partly to an entitlement of old age, but we find that out of their collected lives surfaces a sense of optimism against all odds. Perhaps, following Olney, we could call this the "immigrant's philosophy." These immigrants live an experience they call *"fare l'America"*— "making America"—which can also mean making oneself there.[12] This linking, the idea of gaining control of oneself while one gains control of the new land, is made explicit in one of our autobiographies, when the terrace maker Pietro Toffolo parallels America with the immigrant growing within it: in Long Island he sees "so much open space with the signs that something was growing, and then really grew, and I grew with it."[13]

The French critic Philippe Lejeune revalued the relationship between writer and reader in his definition of autobiography, couching it in legal terms as the "autobiographical pact"—what writer and the reader agree to consider an autobiography. The pact is sealed by the signature of the proper name, "the only mark in the text of an unquestionable world-beyond-the-text, referring to a real person. . . . Exceptions and breaches of trust only emphasize the general credence on the type of social contract."[14] In his *On Autobiography* (1989), Lejeune chose a grammatical standpoint to explain the boundaries of the genre. He might be considered by some as simplistic, naive, and modernist (as opposed to postmodern) in his faith in author and reader and the pact he sees established between them. Nevertheless, he offers the most useful clarifications for my study, not least because his naïveté is shared by the autobiographers in this volume. In this book, I have accepted his much-quoted definition of autobiography: "A retrospective prose narrative produced by a real person concerning his own existence, focusing on his individual life, in particular on the development of his personality."[15] Lejeune's definition reintroduces a lost element in literary criticism, the notion of trust in the author's existence, apparent intentions, and language. In its integrity and in the confidence it places with the authors, Lejeune's definition offers the perfect starting point for my study of Italian immigrant lives.

Autobiography as a Historical Document

Postmodernism has done much to scar the reputation of autobiography as a historical document.[16] Paul John Eakin recognizes the genre's ambiguity—not trustworthy enough to be read as fact, but not literary enough to be considered fiction.[17] James Olney believes there is never a guarantee of objectivity, since we are always subjective.[18] And Robert Elbaz goes so far as to say that even objective history is a creation: "history, science, or for that matter any meaningful statement, in no way duplicates reality: they construct it. . . . One does not report, duplicate, or verify the truth: one makes it."[19]

However, that is just one swing of the pendulum of opinion. "The fact that a source is not objective . . . does not mean that it is useless," asserted the Italian historian Carlo Ginzburg, who relies on nonobjective sources to make a history of mentality[20] and who is one of the leading proponents of the school of microhistory that emerged in the 1970s—a school that values autobiography as a dignified historical document. In England, the social historian David Vincent uses working-class autobiographies to write about the Industrial Revolution, and shares this same faith in the value of autobiographies as historical documents: "more than any other source material, autobiography has the potential to tell us not merely what happened, but the impact of an event or situation upon an actor in the past."[21] Olney admits that it is this subjectivism that is so valuable: "what one seeks in reading autobiography is not a date, a name, or a place, but a characteristic way of perceiving, of organizing, and of understanding, an individual way of feeling and expressing that one can somehow relate to oneself."[22]

In this book I study autobiographies as documents of this internal view of history to show how immigration has been lived within its protagonists and how their experiences capture the scent of an era and a way of seeing the world. These stories reveal the immigrant's philosophy of hard work, a melancholic optimism, homesickness, and will. I hold that in the end it is not so important to distinguish between fiction and reality in autobiography, because we expect the author to present him- or herself along with some measure of self-censoring memory and fiction. As long as their stories present themselves as autobiographical, we can be sure that the will of the author is to be remembered as such.

The density of the *imaginaria* of emigration—a complex tangle of collective imagery and self-representation—can be invisible and impalpable, yet absolutely real.[23] The same fact of finding autobiographies in the homes of unschooled workers tells us that immigrants were so concerned with their self-image that it propelled them to portray themselves, rather than passively accepting representations and clichés by others. It demonstrates that first-generation Italian Americans did not only work constantly, they also found the time and motivation for literary pursuits, as humble as they might be. Finally, it offers proof of the deep humanity of first-generation immigrants, who have been often seen as mere working beasts, through insulting nicknames and deviant stereotypes.[24] In sum, autobiographies are always a document of the set of historical conditions that made them possible. It is this same conviction that has allowed historian Diane Bjorklund to build her study of autobiography: history shapes the self, and it is thus directly related to one's story of oneself.[25]

The autobiographies quoted in this book testify to a self-realization having taken place in the Italian immigrant's consciousness. Sifting through their words, we find certain values belonging to their generation, their age, and their existence as Italians and Americans. These values fall into our hands like golden nuggets: the value of the self-made individual that situates these works in the optimistic climate of turn-of-the-century America; the value of age and experience, which

authorize the speaker to command an audience; the value of self-abne-
gating work, family, and patriotism.

Finally, for these writers, autobiographies not only recover history,
they recover the presence of the man or woman who is seldom heard,
seldom queried for opinions, and who seldom speaks out. According
to the linguist Emile Benveniste, without uttering that "*I*"—the ego,
the linguistic foundation of subjectivity—a person cannot exist: "it is
inside and through language that man is constituted as *subject*; because only language creates in reality, in *its* reality that is the reality of
being, the concept of 'ego.'"[26] Thus, the recovery of these immigrants'
autobiographies is an existential act. We are reclaiming the existence
in history that they fought so hard to assert. These texts, as we will
see, are indeed historical documents, but their richness can best be
appreciated by the awareness that they are much more: they record
personal changes that stem from sets of cultural standards of a historical era.

Scholars of autobiography are generally divided between those critics who approach it from a philosophical point of view and those who
see it from a historical one.[27] But it is also important to take into
account just who is writing their story. For it is the subject of autobiography, the voice, that after all is trying to be heard. So let's now turn
to what influenced our subjects.

Immigration and Autobiography

Georges Gusdorf identified the birth of autobiography in the age of
the Copernican revolution, which destabilized the sense of mankind
into a mere particle of the heliocentric engine of the universe.[28] After
such a period of upheaval, a reassertion of a sense of individuality, an
enlightenment that could honor the mere mortal, if in a transformed
way, was a necessary self-sustaining movement.

Immigration and autobiography have several connections. Immigration works as a kind of Copernican revolution that destabilizes an
individual's sense of self: one is severed out as a single particle from
the rest of the universe of countrymen; that individual is no longer at
its center. The effect is a new sense of loneliness and responsibility.

Pushed to their limits, immigrants are called to act with a stronger sense of responsibility as well as a growing sense of individualism. Immigrants also discover their identity or the wholeness of their egos once they are destabilized. Their discovery is a natural reaction to keeping balanced, as instinctive as crouching down or retreating into oneself at the prospect of something frightening. It is as though the immigrant feels the ground shifting under his feet, and autobiography becomes the tool to build his or her centrality and identity as a particle of this chaotic universe.

Trauma, the Impetus of Autobiography

Autobiography appears after times of crisis, after an earthquake of any sort gives birth to a new individual, a fragment severed from the constellation of a population. The trauma of immigration triggers the human individuality that is the subject of autobiography; it separates the immigrant from the masses; and it enriches the person with cultural capital, if not economic capital. At the same time, autobiography provides a healing effect to the trauma.

Immigrants recapture the wholeness of their ego after this destabilization: their discovery is a natural instinct after their loss of equilibrium. The immigrant's autobiography becomes the tool to rebuild his identity in the chaotic universe of his new world. It becomes the "revenge on history," "the final chance to win back what has been lost. . . . The task of autobiography is first of all a task of personal salvation."[29] Indeed, the works of the immigrant writers featured in this book are pacts of reconciliation with their own lives, little revolts against a suspicion of having lived in vain, of having forsaken kin, friends, and homeland in name of a personal pursuit.

Some of our autobiographers—Elisabeth Evans, Elvezia Marcucci, and Pietro Toffolo—pointedly try to therapeutically clarify the fragmented thoughts of the immigrant. In her study of limit-cases of trauma, Leigh Gilmore, in her study of autobiography, asserts that "language is pressed forward as that which can heal the survivor of trauma,"[30] but she warns that trauma often erases memory. An autobiography about trauma is therefore a forceful paradox: "for the survivor of trauma such an ambivalence can amount to an impossible injunction to tell what cannot, in this view, be spoken."[31]

In our autobiographies, the trauma of immigration is sometimes sublimated in devices such as name changing. The first name is extremely important for the autobiographers, and its change is always noted in their writings.[32] The stone carver Oreste Fabrizi described his name change in surgical terms: "The change to the actual Fabrizi happened, not requested, when they gave me my American citizenship in 1934. For a mistake of transcription in the certificate my name resulted amputated of its 'o' vowel."[33] In the same way, postman Michael Lamont was renamed against his choice, and he sarcastically ended his autobiography with a lapidary: "Michelangelo Lomanto now known as Michael Lamont due to circumstances beyond my control. Thank you."[34]

The autobiography is the *sutura* for the split identities of those who are essentially foreigners. Pietro Riccobaldi, for example, found two words to indicate this painful cut in his being: "straniero indesiderabile" (undesirable foreigner), a phrase he used as the title of his memoir, which frames the immigrant as a foreigner terrified of being discovered. Thus Riccobaldi is extremely sensitive to the scrutiny of other people: "We were scared of everything. We didn't have any document . . . men in uniform frightened us; maybe they were only postmen, firemen, or road sweepers; for us they were all policemen looking for 'undesirable foreigners.'"[35] The essence of this being extraneous—the sensation of *straniamento*—is felt by any immigrant, as historian Emilio Franzina emphasizes: "Seen with the eyes of those who watch them arriving, in fact, the immigrants are immigrants even before they really become so, and therefore are all potential or actual enemies. They are, in a word, foreigners with all that follows."[36]

Moreover, immigrants are doubly foreigners: they are Italian to Americans, and *americano* to Italians. The poet Joseph Tusiani translated this loss of identity into nihilism: "You see my friend, you come back to your own land after almost forty years and how do they treat you? Like a dog. They almost tell you you're not Italian anymore. And over there they tell you you're not American. So you're nothing. Believe me, if you leave your country for more than five years, you're lost, you don't belong anywhere."[37] Antonio Margariti, in his simple language, explains the vexation of his split identity through an anecdote: a woman in Italy "sat by my side and told me, you are American, I was born in these towns in America they call me Italian here they call me American."[38]

Autobiographies also work as a *sutura* of the familial tissue. The earthquake of immigration not only shakes the individual, it rifts the extended family apart. Autobiography mends the broken ties of a family divided between two continents and draws together generations that speak different languages. "All I have written, a sum up of my memories, is written as a remembrance for my children because they are interested in knowing about their descent," wrote Lorenzo Musci in his short, plainspoken autobiography.[39] The immigrant writers who are perhaps the most conscious of the importance of autobiography as a hinge fastened to past and present generations are those who also speak two languages. Born in Ramazzo (Bologna) in 1878, Humbert Tosi worked as a recording representative in Boston and founded the Tosi Music Company. After 1911 he worked for the Edison Company, where he met the famous inventor himself.[40] At the age of ninety he compiled a short typescript autobiography with a dual-language title—"My Memoir. Le mie memorie"—and he elegantly bound the pages between two white cardboard covers. His identity is double: he was a border-crosser, but he chose English as his preferred language because his goal was to become a bridge between the past and the future, his family in America. His autobiography also includes a genealogical tree: Tosi is fully aware of his duty to keep the memory alive and the family together after the cataclysmic experience of immigration: "The family genealogy offers information that should be appreciated by relatives. To-day with more families scattered than ever before since informations should help preserve sacred family ties."[41]

Immigration and autobiography even share the same narrative discourse. Immigration is a physical journey through space in a specific quest for a place. An autobiography is basically an immigration of the soul. One of our autobiographers, Dr. Michele Daniele, asked himself autobiographical questions that are also those of any immigrant, whether expressed in their autobiographies or not: "I wondered what all these months and years, since that cold, gray December day [when he arrived in New York City], what have they really added up to in the great ledge of life? To success? To failure? To happiness? To lasting, meaningful accomplishment? Had I moved forward? Backward? Or merely stood still?"[42]

Finally, autobiographies connect to immigration in that they add individual relief to the anonymous immigrant masses described in history books. As immigration historian Michael La Sorte has explained, since the very beginning of the exodus, immigrants were treated as animals, as a herd, as lacking individuality: "An Italian was not an Italian. He was a wop, dago, duke, gin, tally, ghini, macaroni or spaghetti bender. He was also Hey Boy or Hey Youse, or he was given some generic name: Joe, Pete, Tony, Carlo, Dino, Gumba. 'Do you know why most Italians are called Tony?' 'No.' 'Because when they land in New York they have cards on their caps that say: To NY.' Most of the terms were obviously meant to dehumanize and to degrade. Others were simply ways of addressing a worker by someone who felt no need to indicate individual identity."[43]

Autobiography as Remedy

Writing autobiographies, where the authors are distinguished by first and last names, is a remedy for such anonymous dehumanizing degradations. Through their autobiographies the immigrants achieved their own voice, their identity, as Joseph Tusiani illustrates in the description of his picture: "The first on the left is a young serious man whose thoughts only I know."[44] Only immigrants can tell how it really is, as Michael Lamont says of his friends who don't write down their biographies: "it's too bad because the tales they will tell will die with them, it's a shame because they really tell it how it is."[45]

Sometimes we even discover a new truth hidden behind numbers and records, or official stories. For example, the miner Antenore Quartaroli, who wrote a memoir of his experiences being trapped for eight days in the Cherry Mine disaster of 1909, through his rudimentary Italian spelling and grammar, proposed his own history, and denied the "high" version written by a priest when he polemically noted in his awkward syntax: "So the reader if he had read the book about the Cherry Mine Disaster written by F. P. Buck that on page 124 Father Hanney, St. Mary Church, tells that the Catholic priest of Mondota was the one who walked 3,000 feet from the well to the exit to come to help us and instead this is not true we walked until 50 meters before this blessed well and nobody else sacrificed for us."[46]

Constantine Panunzio also announces to the reader that he has to rectify the official history: when he was unjustly arrested in Vermont he used his new Italian-American name (which was easier to pronounce), and thus left a distorted trace of himself in history. His autobiography now clarifies the mistake: "I presume however, that somewhere in the records of the state of Vermont, my name, alias 'Frank Nardi,' is to be found; along with thousands of other unfortunates, some of them doubtless as innocent as I. Doubtless also, somewhere the careful student of criminal tendencies of the foreign-born people of this country has counted my name along with the thousands of others in his impersonal statistics of the criminality of the immigrant group in the United States."[47]

Social critic Giuseppe Prezzolini lamented exactly this lack of flesh from the arid statistics of migration when he wrote: "The huge majority of Italian immigrants in the United States did not have the time to write their autobiographies. And we do not have a trace of them if not in arid statistics: how many came, how many children they had, how many died, how many went to prison, how many filled the asylums, how many returned won, how many conquered a certain well-being; but the reality of their miseries and their triumphs remains without story. . . . They are really lost generations."[48]

In reading their autobiographies, in giving a name and even a nickname to each immigrant, in listening to their personal stories, in perceiving the tone of their language and the vibrations of the chords they strike, we can for once flesh out the sterile lists of Ellis Island. We can gaze into the eyes of those mute black-and-white pictures and give a face and a personality to the blurred immigrant masses that silently move about in old photographs and history books. Far from a shadowy image of a herd, we can start to identify their individual dignities.

Autobiography of the "Other": Ethnic and Minority Voices

A significant number of scholars now study autobiography of the "other"—women, homosexuals, immigrants, and minorities.[49] The study of ethnic autobiography has begun only recently. William Boelhower dates its birth to 1911, right after the peak of the new migration from Europe,[50] with Italian American autobiography situated as a subgenre of that.[51] Italian American autobiography is still a relatively uncharted territory. Only Diane Bjorklund includes one Italian American in her wide survey of autobiography, but the subject is hardly typical: Lee Iacocca. The problem is not only the lack of immigrant testimonies, but also the devaluation of those few existing ones. The disparaging look at the Italian American production has been evident since the beginning, coming not only from the American observer but also from the Italian one. Our autobiographies share the longtime contempt destined to Italian American literature. It is testified by Giuseppe Prezzolini's condescending scorn of the production of Italian immigrant poets in the library of Italian immigrant works in the Casa Italiana of Columbia University, which he describes as a "literary tragedy," as he describes a typical author there: "when the poor fellow tried to express things he may have been feeling, but certainly did not know how to express, then he could but repeat things that he had been reading."[52] We cannot deny that we are dealing with mostly works of poor literary quality. William Boelhower also alluded to this "text-type which has traditionally been written off as aesthetically poor,"[53] but this did not keep him from recognizing in immigrant autobiographies the birth of the "modern self and condition, the American condition *par excellence*" that is represented in the "composite self" of these writings.[54]

Boelhower's *Immigrant Autobiographies* (1982) is the only book completely dedicated to Italian American works. It treats four texts as the representative examples of a fourfold structuralist model.[55] However, my much larger sampling of autobiographies—I evaluated fifty-eight texts, most of which are my original discoveries, plus twenty-one that have been commented on by scholars in previous studies—proves Boelhower's structure to be very unsatisfactory. It is far too rigidly schematic in its binary opposition of Old World versus New World and ideal versus real. His four examples fit the corners of such a schema, but my fifty-eight examples prove that there are innumerable variations and multiple oppositions.[56] Moreover, his literary stand-point and structuralist framework are not attentive enough to sociolog-ical or historical reality, which is crucial to my perspective. His fourfold model does not take into consideration the multiple position-ing of the *I* and subjectivities in historical contexts: there is the *I* of the immigrant, the *I* of the wanderer, or the *I* of the returned immi-grant; the *I* of the immigrant of 1900 and that of 1950s immigrant; the *I* of the rich and that of the poor; the *I* of the educated and that of the uneducated; the *I* of the immigrant woman; the *I* of the fugitive from Fascism, of the Anarchist, and of the Italian Jew; the *I* of the southerner and that of the northerner; and so on, with many cross-overs among them.

The other important critical study on Italian American autobiogra-phies is Fred Gardaphé's *Italian Signs, American Streets* (1996). He gathered here some recent autobiographies and suggestively inserted them in Giambattista Vico's division of the three stages of history—poetic, mythic, and philosophical. According to him, three of our authors—Pascal D'Angelo, Constantine Panunzio, and Rosa Caval-leri—fall into the "Poetic Mode" (the Age of Gods) of immigrant auto-biography, being characterized by the large presence of *vera narratio*, a strong consciousness of the divine, and a direct affiliation with the Italian oral tradition. In reality, I would argue, this description can only partially fit them. If they do come from the poetic tradition (found in its genuine form in the oral culture of peasant Italy), they eventually leave this tradition when they start writing (or telling) stories about themselves. They keep the formal structure of the Poetic Mode, espe-cially in their preference for the realism of style that shies away from the figurative and symbolic language, but their contents are already Heroic. In fact, in keeping with Vico's definitions, D'Angelo, Cavalleri, and Panunzio, along with the other writers in my research, live the shift from the cosmic consciousness of the Age of Gods to the self-consciousness of the Age of Heroes. They urbanize by leaving the country villages of their Italian youth to settle in American towns.

They are individuals who detach themselves from the folk culture of origin, from the "gods" of Resignation, Trust in God, Fortune, Providence, or Malocchio (the evil eye), and from all those transcendental forces that may govern people's lives. And they become the heroes of their own lives. They make up their own personal tale, and not the tale of their people.[57]

Histories of Ordinary People

Our writers also can be seen within a larger movement of histories of "ordinary" people, the study of whom in recent years has had an important place in historical writing in tandem with branches of "other" history. This branch of history studies various disenfranchised groups, especially in Europe, where the autobiographies of ordinary people have been elected as reliable source of such "other" history. Several European institutions are devoted to this study: the Italian Archivio di Scrittura Popolare gathers autobiographical material of peasants and housewives; the British Mass-Observation Archive of the University of Sussex preserves the lives of twentieth-century workers of industrial towns; and Philippe Lejeune energetically works in France with his Association pour l'Autobiographie.[58]

Diane Bjorklund has looked at ordinary people's self-published autobiographies and observed the phenomenon that, starting from those nineteenth century, self-published autobiographies became so numerous that one critic complained in 1826, "England expects every driveller to do his Memorabilia."[59] Ann Fabian dates the origin of "plebian narratives" of one's life to even earlier, around 1700, when "converts, captives, soldiers, sailors, beggars, murderers, slaves, sinners and even wounded workers" became writers in the United States and were ultimately absorbed into a larger cast of social and moral types.[60]

Most pertinent for my approach to this material are studies by David Vincent and Philippe Lejeune. Vincent's *Bread, Knowledge and Freedom. A Study of Nineteenth-Century Working Class Autobiography* organizes 142 autobiographies thematically, touching upon their sense of history, their love and family relationships, their childhood, and their schooling and pursuit of a "useful knowledge."[61] He also coauthored *The Autobiography of the Working Class*, which collects an astonishing 783 previously scattered working-class autobiographies[62] with an aim to see the shifts of the Industrial Revolution from the perspective of its most humble protagonists. This approach coincides with my entirely comparable intentions to view Italian immigration from inside and below. Although my study is smaller in scope, I share with these authors their problems in cataloguing material by heterogeneous authors. Most important, both our autobiographies and the British ones spring from a kind of seismic trauma: in our case, immigration, or, for British workers, displacement: "oral history was now under threat. It was partly a result of the disruption of communities as the population moved into and around the expanding towns."[63] In France, Philippe Lejeune also studied autobiographies by proletarian writers—"honest" people, "some very average people, clinging to their lives"—that have not survived in mainstream culture.[64] Lejeune takes some distance from the field of social history, because he claims to be doing something different: "I look at these autobiographical texts not as *documents* containing information about the author . . . but as *social facts* in themselves, in their reality as texts."[65] For him, the presence of these writings are signs of a change of consciousness in peasant society.[66] For us, this phenomenon signals a change in the immigrant consciousness that accompanies the journey across the ocean.

To my thinking, Lejeune's work goes to the heart of the real significance of our Italian American immigrant autobiographies, whose study can't be limited by viewing just facets of a single discipline taken by most historical, critical, or literary scholars. These humble writings were never intended to be historical or literary, as the Italian Jew David Yona asserts from the opening of his story: "My dear grandchildren: I decided to write this story of my life not because I, at any time or under any circumstance, had any part in the development of what happened in the world or because my actions had any influence on the life of any important segment of humanity. On the contrary my life was *quite common*, and only my family could in any way feel that my actions and attitudes had any bearing on my closest surroundings."[67]

The First Generation
I concentrate on first-generation immigrants in this study because I believe that the key impetus for this phenomenon of average men and

women writing their autobiographies was the trauma of their journey. As border crossers, these men and women attained a unique perspective of knowing both worlds.[68] Their compelling narrations, which bring us from one world to another, entice the reader with some of the oldest forms of narrative: tales of bravery, adventure, and exoticism. These men and women might be simple, but they have experienced emotional and sociological complexities that few people—not even more affluent world-weary travelers, whose peripatetic lifestyle is by choice—have had to face. Another reason for considering only works by first-generation immigrants was for the sampling it offered: in my study I recognized that extremes of selection—Boelhower, with his four texts, or Vincent, with hundreds—each had unfortunate drawbacks. Finally, my focus had a personal element: I have lived as an Italian American border crosser, and this group of writings struck a sympathetic nerve with my own experiences with shifted homes, languages, and cultures.

The voices of this forgotten critical sector of our culture and our past are on the verge of falling into oblivion. These are the revered founders of Italian American culture that crowd so many third-generation Italian American writing and film production.[69] But they almost never speak directly—in fact, oral communication has been one of their downfalls. Their children speak another language (the preacher Constantine Panunzio quotes a mother in his parish: "as soon as they learn English they will not be my children anymore"[70]). Reading their autobiographies is thus like giving a voice to the mute grandmother that Helen Barolini described: "When I asked my mother why Gramma looked so strange and never spoke to us, I was told, she came from the old country . . . she doesn't speak our language. She might as well have been from Mars."[71]

Finally, I found that past studies have confused the issues by grouping multiple generations of Italian American writers. Every generation has distinctive characteristics and should ideally be treated separately, just as does every success level—the lifelong manual worker or the immigrant who advanced financially.[72] First-generation immigrants are a special class of writers and their autobiographies are the most self-justifying. An important distinction can also be made between those who write in Italy, after returning to their roots, and those who write in America, as their chosen home. The autobiography's point of view is important: as a comprehensive view of a person's life, it enables the writer to see a unity: "the beginning is in the end," said a sibylline Roy Pascal, who explained that "it is his present position that enables him to see his life as something of a unity, something that may be reduced to order."[73]

The main difference between immigrants who returned and rooted immigrants is that the former are more likely to write what amounts to a travel book, where the experience of immigration closes with the return to Italy. An entirely different situation is presented in the autobiography of the rooted immigrant, for whom the act of permanent immigration is the totality of the life experience, the quintessence of life, the metaphor of life.

Class

Class also enters further into our subject. In Pierre Bourdieu's ideological screen, art and cultural consumption are "predisposed, consciously and deliberately or not, to fulfill a social function of legitimating social differences" and writing is also predisposed to distinguish between classes.[74] Bourdieu sees a trap of exclusion and self-exclusion, according to which those who feel incompetent, unentitled, and impotent are also indifferent to art, culture, and writing.[75] If we were to follow Bourdieu, our authors are not presumed to engage in pure aesthetic enjoyment, which requires high taste and detachment from the necessities of life. This relegates them to a social class that is poorer in cultural capital, and they are not supposed to exit from it. Also, for Bourdieu, personal opinion is a bourgeois invention that reflects participation in some privileged groups having higher educational and economic capital.

Our authors strike pickax blows to the fragile determinism embedded in Bourdieu's locked societal distinctions. They absolutely do cross all these lines when they feel entitled to produce a personal opinion—indeed probably the most personal of all opinions: their own version of their life. They make Bourdieu's boundaries seem more like a wobbly wicker fence than a stone wall. These immigrants are also unorthodox by their act of appropriating literacy in the most productive sense: writing.

In doing this, our immigrants reverse the concepts of magical comprehension that, as has been observed, has been practiced by their class for centuries. Italian peasants and lower classes often suffered from what social psychologist and activist Paulo Freire calls a "magic consciousness" that "simply apprehends facts and attributes them to a superior power."[76] For Freire, those classes are powerless because they live and accept a worldview constructed from above. However, literacy can gain them back the possibility of their agency. But there is a passive literacy, which enables people to read while it keeps them in the same subservient position, as well as an active literacy. For scholar William Covino, true magic is the real rhetoric: "action that creates action, words that create words."[77] Our rooted Italian-American authors must also jump a double hurdle of class and ethnicity. By taking writing in their own hands, by daring to produce a *book* (the insignia and accessory of a superior cultural class), by becoming subject and not object of a productive rhetoric, our authors again cross cultural boundaries.

Treating authors who are nonwriters—and nonwriters who record their average lives—I am in need of a new terminology to critically comment their works. The categories "autobiographies of conversion," "success stories" and "autobiographies of Americanization" —preexisting catch phrases of immigrant life and autobiography— simply do not adequately describe these cases. For Boelhower, immigrant autobiographers must either comply or confront themselves with the model of the immigrant in the process of Americanization. Yet his model satisfies only the few "autobiographies of Americanization" (such as Panunzio, Orlando, Massari), but would leave the vast majority of our authors unexplained. According to Boelhower, the immigrant writer must only follow the behavioral model already provided and "re-elaborate" or simply "re-write" it.[78] In the same way, James Holte regrouped three ethnic autobiographies and asserted that they can be distributed among types of stories of conversion, linking them to the American tradition of Puritan moral autobiographies, and ultimately to Benjamin Franklin's autobiography.[79]

These theories simply do not prove out. Our autobiographies are not merely repetitions of the success story or the transition to Americanization. They are only marginally narratives of conversion, and many of our authors care little for the model of Americanization. In our autobiographies there is also little reference to prejudice and racial discrimination; to be sure it is far from being a significant concern. Why? It is possible that they have suppressed this past pain and in the protected space of their autobiography they are secure and immune from outside criticism. In fact, the writing of these immigrants concentrates on individual achievements and adventures. They are completely self-absorbed in their *own* immigrant model, their own standards, their own particular story of immigration. My investigations conclude that their ethos is that of the quiet individual who survived history.

Quiet Individualism

Our authors open up an entirely different perspective on the history of individualism. As we have seen, all critics agree that autobiography is the product of a society that believes in the individual, in which the individual is thought to rise above or apart from the mass of humans.[80] This explanation does not entirely explain our writers, who are not exceptional individuals, but common people with nothing to boast but their decency, and they have lived inconsequential lives. Miner Pietro Riccobaldi expressed a typical sentiment of our immigrants: "I was returning after twenty years. I did not gather big fortunes, but I felt I had behaved well, I had kept faithful to my origins and my family's teaching. I felt a certain sense of pride."[81]

But any individualism at all is noteworthy among this group, because Italian culture is hardly known for individualism. The sociologist Edward Banfield defined the almost perverted sense of unity of the Italian family as "amoral familism." According to his study of a southern Italian community, the nuclear family is the dominant social unity that absorbs all "material short-run advantages" to the disadvantage of the individual or the enlarged community.[82] The novelist Giovanni Verga gives a literary description of this kind of familiar philosophy in a metaphor of the fingers of the hand, and dramatizes the individual's helplessness in his *The House by the Medlar Tree*. Scholar Joseph Lopreato also finds this lack of individual identity in Italian-American families is "closely knit together and disciplined to the idea that the major decision of the individual's life ought to be made in accordance with the aims and the good of the group as a whole as defined by the oldest active member of the family."[83] Patrick Gallo's psychological research on the political alienation of Italian Americans also remarks the closeness of the Italian-American subgroup: thanks to the persistence of a tight family structure ("father dominated but mother centered"), they are "structurally unassimilated" and this "structural separation of the Italians results in the retention and solidification of an Italian identity. It also causes the Italian subsociety to persist."[84] And when we look at Italian stories we only rarely see the individual as the center of narration: Fred Gardaphé maintains that if there is a strong storytelling tradition in southern Italy, its center is almost never the self, but some more or less cautionary story. "In the Italian storytelling tradition," he explains, "the self is suppressed and is not used as a subject in storytelling. . . . Traditional stories served both to entertain and inform the young, while reminding the old of traditions that have endured over the years. Personal information was expected to be kept to one's self."[85]

In our autobiographies there are many examples of this attachment of the writer to his people, *"la gente,* or common folks, to which we belonged," wrote preacher Constantine Panunzio in his autobiography, while the pick-and-shovel poet Pascal D'Angelo always used the pronoun "we" to describe his immigrant adventures. Terrace maker Pietro Toffolo spoke of "my people" (*la mia gente*) in Italy ("my people hadn't changed, they fought and worked only to remain poor. The world was poor and sad then, but my people were not sad; it took little to make them happy! They had the ability to accept")[86] and miner Gregorio Scaia never really separated his figure from the crowd of Trentini that conquered foreign lands. When there is an emphasis on individualism, it is always expressed as an American discovery: for Panunzio it is the "mental awakening" to individuality of the immigrant in America; doctor Previtali remembered his first return and his American transformation: "I believed it was American to be more assertive and bold;"[87] and Toffolo asserted that in America, "the identity of a man consists in his individuality . . . and he doesn't have to shine while he walks to be noticed."[88]

We therefore need to identify a different mode of individualism to fit autobiographers who are neither exceptional nor individual heroes. I call this "quiet individualism." Quiet individualism is conducive to a narrative about the self told *sottovoce* rather than shouted in triumph. Rather than a sharp tale of adolescence (typically American, according to Sollors), these are buffered tales of mature years. Rather than the individualism of the fighter, these are of the fought, of those who had been tamed by life. Looking at their past stories, our authors do not flaunt them, but they protect them, they bury them under a sheet of earth as the servant of the parable with his master's talents—exactly like people who are accustomed to defending themselves from the blows of fortune, rather than those on the offensive line. The archetype of this mode of writing is the autobiography of Elisabeth Evans: she wrote the story of her life longhand, in pencil, not an assertive pen, as if whispering her individuality, as if apologizing to exist.

Quiet individualism is an intermediate conception of individualism. It is valid for most of the immigrants who are not entirely successful, even if they "made it" in their own smaller world, and who are decent but who do not stand out for admiration in American society, and who, more often than not, are scorned for their accents and ethnicity. These immigrants have learned the meaning of individualism because they have detached themselves from the mass that remained at home. Yet they are still common people: they do not put themselves on pedestals. Unlike, say, Lee Iacocca, they cannot claim they have been the best. Writing for their family and not for the general public, unlike autobiographers Benvenuto Cellini or Henry Adams, they cannot invite you to sit down and read a life that is far more interesting than your own, or that of anyone you know. They focus on what they did in the past and do not give a prescription for future generations' success in the future, as Benjamin Franklin's story does. To the exceptionality of the individual they substitute the normality of experience, to the representative life they substitute a common life, to the listening audience they substitute the few interested ones. Thus, they seem to say: *Here is my life, I've made through it, I have endured many storms but I'm still here, I worked hard and I made it well. Listen to me, you my children, and the few who can be interested in my small life. Store it in your memory, enclosed in a book, I'm not asking you to use it as a gospel or a manual for action, but keep it on your shelf.*

But while this characterization fits Italian immigrants, it does not fit all working-class immigrants. Virginia Yans-McLaughlin and Victor Gioscia have introduced the terms "history of self" and "self in history" in their work on narratives in immigration studies.[89] Drawing a comparison between the oral stories told by Jewish and Italian laborers in New York, she observed different senses of self and different senses of history that distinguished Italian from Jewish immigrants. Yans-McLaughlin maintains that Italians hold an "atomistic" sense of history that "does not perceive the self or society as an unbroken, linear development."[90] For the Italian immigrants, fate, not will, dominates, and resignation, not fight, is the remedy. This atomistic sense of history is a motif through many of our autobiographies: the texts are a succession of facts, and these facts push the person to act and decide his or her actions, not the opposite. As is evident even from the summaries and excerpts later in this book, in many of the biographies I have studied, the author will mention a wish or dream they had, only to conclude, "but it was not meant to be."

This particular mode of quiet individualism is clarified by the comparison between common Italian immigrants and the Americanized autobiographers who tell stories of self-made men who fought and succeeded against all odds—as with the exceptional cases of Jerre Mangione, Leonard Covello, Lee Iacocca, Angelo Pellegrini, Edward Corsi, and Frank Capra. As James Holte indicates, they adopt Franklin's individualism and claim their success because they exercised the virtues of labor, frugality, strong will, and tenacity. Americanized authors do share the American sense of history where the self, not history, prevails: events do not happen *to* them, rather *they* make them happen, as the successful public-relations figure Guido Orlando affirmed: "Nobody gives you ideas, Guido, you just reach out and get them."[91] On the contrary, common immigrants are filled by a sense of self where history, not the self, prevails. Theirs are stories of the "self in history."[92] While successful immigrants tell the adventures of the self as rising against the background of history, common immigrants tell the misadventures of a self constantly wrestling with history.[93] Luigi Barzini stresses the importance of history in shaping the Italian behavior: "[The Italian] is powerless to deflect the tides of history. He can only try to defend himself from their blind violence, keep his mouth shut and mind his own business."[94] Even in our day, a journalist such as Beppe Severgnini notices this profound difference between American individualism and Italian historicism, when observing today "a nation of optimist self-educated people, convinced that happiness is first of all an act of good will. It demonstrates that Americans refuse the idea that success can arrive without explanations and all at once (thanks to chance, a saint, or a relative)."[95] Chance, saints, and relatives are instead daily companions of Italian lives.

I would even suggest that such a different sense of self is rooted in the different history and space of America and Italy.[96] The Italian American professor Angelo Pellegrini notices the spatial dimension of this difference: "It was the vastness and the freedom and the impersonality of what we saw that seduced and bewildered and troubled us. . . . The fields we had known were but garden plots in comparison. Diminutive areas hedged in by grapevines supported on willows. And stone houses and teeming humanity everywhere. . . . And a visible end to everything. . . . Is it any wonder that we were seduced and bewildered and troubled by what we saw, and that we felt that we ourselves had been released from narrow prison walls, into a freedom the immensity of which frightened us a little?"[97]

The past of the United States is ideologically drawn by a people who construct themselves out of victories against history, out of conquering the "empty" space, destroying pre-existing populations, wiping out enemies, and domesticating the environment to their will. On the contrary, the Italian has grown to live in a dense milieu, elbow-to-elbow with other people, in a tight social structure, fettered by centuries-old hierarchy of classes and foreign governments.[98] Therefore, the history of self cannot be true anywhere else but in the United States, where the mainstream American, white, male, successful, "uncommon" man is born. It is in America that the self cuts through the flow of history, pushes against the limit of things, like a battering ram against the walls of reality; while the Italian, ethnic, marginal, common man slips away in history, through its cracks, balancing on its ruins, jumping over its ditches or harsh edges. This is the "self in history" we find in most of our autobiographies.

The "ethos of the survivor" is another key phrase in this research. It is shared by all social classes, especially the poor ones, and refers to the sensation, nourished by the individual in history, of having escaped from destruction, having survived through the stampede of history. Immigrants normally feel it because they have escaped the bites of hunger and misery, but often also specific events, like earthquakes, wars, Fascism, the Quota Act of 1924 (which establishes a fixed number of entries per nationality), or accidental deaths. They all feel it. The ethos of the survivor is perhaps particularly strong in unskilled laborers, those who "made it" or not, but who surely had to struggle against destiny or a social structure that already framed them as a lower class. They have survived America itself and a deterministic social structure for the purpose of making themselves. John Podestio notices this characteristic of the humble immigrant writer in his introduction to railway builder Giovanni Veltri's autobiography: "Veltri was a simple man, uneducated and uncultured. His recollections are those of a pragmatist, free of ideology, who looked at the world as he found it. He used all his resources to survive. Part of the value of the *Memories* lies in its being a very simple record of the achievements and failures of an immigrant, a marginal man who had to cope with an inimical, if potentially rewarding, New World."[99]

These characteristics—pragmatism, survival, marginality and simplicity—are shared by almost all our writers, even those in the upper classes. From the poor worker who survives the explosion of the Cherry coal mine disaster of 1909, Antenore Quartaroli, whose struggling ethos is obviously the high point of his memoir ("Yet we had to fight until the last moment even if sure to die");[100] to the physician Michele Daniele, who also adopted the ethos of the struggling immigrant: "The truth of the matter is that I shall be quite content to be able to say about the years to come what I have been able to say about those that are past: *I lived through them.*"[101] The engineer David Yona, who escaped misery and death as a Jew in Fascist Italy, strengthened the feeling of having made it through history with his Jewish identity: "My life covers a period of very deep social and political turmoil, with so varied and in many cases horrifying experiences . . . I was an exceptionally lucky man."[102] In Yona, the immigrant's survival complex is superimposed on that of the Jewish survivor: "*I slipped through all those crushing events*, it is true: more than that I was never involved in any of the experiences that crushed millions and millions other men. But why am I a witness of those events, instead of being their victim? I cannot even thank any superhuman entity for my deliverance: how could I do that, knowing that many other men, more intelligent than me, more worthy than me were drowned in a blood bath?"[103]

Textual Considerations

We have already seen how immigrants' writings have generally been dismissed for their lack of literary quality. However, there are significant textual formats, styles, and tropes that strongly come to the fore with a sample of texts as large as ours. While some of these can have parallels in other ethnic autobiography or storytelling, the strongest of these qualities link them to specifically Italian traditions, especially those of less-educated classes, whose local customs are hundreds or, in some cases, thousands of years old.

Parallels in Merchants' Autobiographies
In earlier sections I have discussed how the mere fact of surviving the traumatic event of immigration in many cases was the impetus for telling one's story. These humble authors' matter-of-fact, plainspoken styles can be defined as "material"; I use the word to indicate the concrete, even monetary, approach they show toward their lives. Because so many of them are manual workers, they identify with concrete objects, such as the beautiful house to build, or the store to open. Without the financial secrecy or deception of a more sophisticated social class of writers, they do not refrain from giving the exact price or the exact prize of their migration, in monetary terms. Many of them carefully disclose the facts and figures of their earnings, their savings, their debts.

This ledger-book character ties our texts to an old and little-studied genre of Italian merchants' autobiographies, dating at least as early as the Middle Ages, which were also "literary" exceptions in a time of non-individualization. In particular, merchants in medieval Florence recorded the salient moments of their lives, recounting perhaps births and deaths or other major events we would consider more crucial and narrative, but mixing them with financial calculations from their trades. Medieval autobiographies are little known, because they do not belong to artists or others whose lives historians have traditionally wanted to research, rather they were compiled by common people. They contain the seeds of the bourgeois individual, evidence that autobiography comes from a bourgeois state of mind. These merchants needed to write because of their monetary interests, because they need to establish their property, calculate their earnings, and pin down their individual life achievements. They are also a surprising phenomenon from an age that traditionally has been seen as suffocating the individual.[104] According to scholar Christian Bec,[105] there are thousands of these documents in Florence's archives, titled "Le ricordanze," Il libro di famiglia," "Ricordanze di Donato Velluti," "I ricordi di Giovanni Pagolo Morelli (1371–1444)." Authors such as Lapo di Giovanni Niccolini (1379) and Bonaccorto Pitti (1354–1432) intersect their financial adventures with their personal life events, such as deaths and journeys. In his "Libro degli affari proprii di casa," Lapo Niccolini recorded his life's events in a way that has remarkable similarities to our autobiographies, both in the dryness of his style and the factuality of his tone.[106] When his son died, for example, he wrote: "he was acute, virtuous, and generous, but too much a waster of his and others' money, who cared about nothing if not following his desires and wills, and he gave me many hardships while he lived in this poor world."[107] Lappo wrote in 1379 of feuds and business agreements gone wrong in a way that has parallels with many of our texts, as if to be a record or warning for the family, or to set a dispute straight: "And then this said lady Antonia started a litigation about a house that I had bought from the said Messer Francesco."[108]

Among our autobiographies, the clearest example of a descendent of this very old tradition is Gioanni Viarengo. He was probably born in 1839 in the province of Alessandria in Liguria, and is the author of the handwritten notebook "Memoriale di Gioanni Viarengo." This is hardly an autobiography, but it is a true immigrant version of the *libro dei conti*. It gathers some events, especially of his migration in Europe and his call to the army, but when he gets to his emigration to America, the autobiography becomes a mere bookkeeping: "I started to work with a macaroni producer for nine dollars a week plus room and board."[109] He bought a "stendio" (an Italian American hybrid word for "stand") on Market Street; he rented a room; "I started to work as a carpenter on my own."[110] He especially annotated the exchange of money, advancements, and debts of his associates, and the profits and expenses for his *grosseria* in St. Louis in the 1860s and '70s. For example, his net profit for the year 1874 was 735 dollars. In 1877 he opened a society for the "groceria," and, through his father, he bought a villa with meadows and vineyards in Annone.

This aspect of the literary and historical tradition of these texts refutes even more the assertions about literary quality and form that we encountered earlier in this study, such as Roy Pascal's insistence that the only worthwhile autobiography was of illustrious men, or Giuseppe Prezzolini's scathing criticisms of the literary quality of immigrant writing. These works are in a tradition of a rich, centuries-old genre of relatively practical writing, and one that would seem to have survived with little mutation for dozens of generations in regional communities. Although we would assume that account books or diaries of major life and accounting events would be more personal, and thus written, and outside of an oral tradition, we can imagine that similar information was transmitted—at least to certain people— orally as well, in normal forms of bragging, complaining, or gossip, through familial channels or among loquacious merchants or neighbors. So even in the ledger-book-like passages of these autobiographies we can see a certain oral tradition in these writers' willingness to make public the varia of their debits, credits, spats, and milestones.

Style: Authors Between Orality and Literacy
The oral poet Homer called words "winged words," and the Romans used the expression *Verba volant, scripta manent* (words fly, writing

remains): the instability of spoken words has been a constant, even in mainly oral societies. Even the oral tradition in its most elevated form—epic poetry—was known among the peasant classes in Italy. The time-honored literary form of *poemi cavallereschi,* whose most famous masterpieces were Torquato Tasso's *Gerusalemme liberata* and Ludovico Ariosto's *Orlando furioso,* were still memorized in the Tuscan countryside three hundred years after they were written. A witness of those times, Giovanni Giannini, attested that many average people knew the *Gerusalemme liberata* by heart, as well as *Orlando innamorato, Orlando furioso,* and Homer's *Iliad* and *Odyssey:* "I found a shepherd who every evening would read the *Divine Comedy* to a group of lowly people, helping himself to interpret it with the comment by Camerini."[111] In rural Italy, not only those masterpieces, but also other long Renaissance courtly romances "exercise a strong attraction for these country people that often borrow from them the names for their children."[112] As Maria Berdinelli Predelli has described, "in the Renaissance chivalry genre we could find values that, progressive in the moment they were conceived, become then vastly common until they reach the lower strata of the population (individualism, research of one's own advantage, disposition to discovery and adventure, prevalence of love, reason and nature on social and ideological constrictions)."[113]

It has been said that Italian immigrant autobiography descends from the oral tradition of peasant Italy.[114] In our autobiographies we find evidence of at least one genuine practitioner of the oral tradition: Francesco Ventresca remembered that among the railroad workers there was the storyteller who each day would tell a piece of "the long drawn-out story of the Royal House of France (*I Reali di Francia*) . . . without a hitch . . . to me unconsciously it was an inspiration which was to bear fruit in future years."[115] The returned immigrant is also an inexhaustible source of tales: Agostino Stagi, who immigrated to San Francisco between 1899 and 1908, tells numerous stories to his granddaughter while repeating: "tales? . . . but what are you saying, little fool? Tales are that your mother tells about the Befana. My tales are real facts."[116]

Our authors come from an oral society, and like winged words, they have experienced the instability of immigration. Once settled and matured, it was time for them to stabilize themselves, as immigrants and as stories. The decision to write an autobiography, to pass from the voice to the pen, should not be taken for granted. They were often the first in their families to have learned to write, and they lived in an environment where writing was used for its mere instrumental value (to keep record of expenses or to write occasional letters. Their decision to write is therefore significant, not only because it bridges the oral and the written cultures, but also because it involves a larger shift of consciousness.

Walter Ong reflects on such a shift provoked in the human mind when orality becomes literacy and when literacy of manuscripts becomes that of printing, and then of technology.[117] First of all, says Ong, the alphabet is a democratizing script, it is easy for everybody to learn, and it soon becomes available for all. Writing is a democratizing act because it gives poor people a tool to contribute to "history" usually written by the powerful. Immigrant Antonio Margariti reacts to the elitism of history written by the few: "The life of the big people is written by the great historians and it remains in History, but for me who is nothing but a little grain fallen from the space and outside my neighborhood, nobody knows I Exist."[118] Second, the technique of writing moves internal mechanisms when it calls for an enhanced introspection of the individual. The necessities of writing—silence, time, meditation—bring about an inward turn of the writer, as Ong underlines: "the evolution of consciousness through human history is marked by growth in articulate attention to the interior of the individual person as distanced—though not necessarily separated—from the communal structures in which each person is necessarily enveloped. . . . Writing is consciousness-raising."[119] In this light, we could see the genre of autobiography as a direct child of the writing technique, since it is an individual act that favors a lonely meditation on the self. Besides, only in writing, and not in the instability of spoken words, do we find a stable construction of the story into a self-contained unit, where there is a closure between the three stages, beginning-middle-end, and there is no possibility of modification. It is therefore the perfect medium for revisiting and wrapping up a life.

Our authors demonstrate stylistic qualities of both thinking and narrating. Especially the less-educated writers often translate onto paper their oral tonalities, such as repetition, redundancy, and direct appeal to the reader. The weighty oral tradition still tilts their pen in different ways. David Vincent noticed the same in his research on British working-class autobiographers who "write as they spoke. Punctuation is disregarded, syntax owes nothing to the grammar books, and spelling is determined by the accents in which the authors conversed with his family and neighbors."[120] As ours, they draw from the oral tradition, thus "we must look not for the author and his pen, but the narrator and his audience, whether it be his children, his workmates or his drinking companions."[121]

In fact, our authors still maintain the strong feeling of the presence of a listener typical of orality, by directing their speech to the young ones or addressing the readers directly. They often break the fourth wall and seem to be looking at the reader in the eyes, and say "But I will tell you about that later on . . ." or "You must remember the story I told you . . . Remember?"[122] The farmer poet Antonio Andreoni wrote his epic of immigration in eight-verse stanzas like the knightly romances he heard orally repeated in the Tuscan countryside, and thus addressed his readers by calling them "listeners": "Here, O listeners, a day of happiness / here, O listeners, a day of consolation / here, O listeners, the biggest contentedness / that a man can feel before his death."[123] The same happens to the unskilled worker Tommaso Bordonaro, who at the end of his written memoirs thanks his "listeners": "Thank you for having listened to my story."[124] Even the most educated writers, like David Yona, speak to their grandchildren: "again please do not laugh at me; those times were tremendously different from the one when I write these notes, and probably even more from the ones when you may read them."[125] We find this habit, says Ong, even in many nineteenth-century novels that continuously intone "dear reader." This is because "both author and reader are having difficulties situating themselves. The psychodynamics of writing matured very slowly in narrative."[126]

Our autobiographies make use of formulaic expression typical of orality. The oral poets (Homer is the example) had a large list of formulas to use as it fitted their metrical verse. This habit remains with our authors, even if they do not have to obey any metric rule. Some formulaic expressions remain to punctuate the discourse, and perhaps to give it an internal rhythm. For example, we find phrases such as "the harsh destiny of the emigrant," "hard life of the immigrant," "working as a horse," "real facts" that sound like refrains and seem to reflect the repertoire of themes and formulas available to describe a specific hero. As we have "pious Aeneas," "swift-footed Achilles," and "wiley Odysseus," we find our own sets of stock epithets for the immigrant.

The postman Michael Lomant inserted many oral sayings such as "believe it or not ripley," "don't get me wrong," and even the exclamation "boy." Construction worker Emanuele Triarsi finished his digressions with statements such as "let's go back to the macaroni." He even closed his booklet of memories, morals, and poems with the formulaic expression that ends all Italian fairy tales: "Larga è la foglia, stretta è la via, dite la vostra che io ho detto la mia." For Triarsi this is: "I think it so. The others can think it as they like."[127] The ice-cream maker Calogero Di Leo colored his narration with oral expressions such as "seeing is believing" or "there are more days than sausages" and with many proverbs: "we say who lives hoping dies in despair," "the old proverb does not err that the satiated does not believe the hungry," "the old proverb says if there is life there is hope," "you know the old proverb everything is good for broth," and "an old Sicilian proverb says the jug brings the water until it breaks." The Sardinian Giovanni Arru doesn't refrain from adding an obscure proverb in his incomprehensible dialect: "if when the wind blows you don't clean the wheat in the courtyard, then you'll have to wait who knows how long"—in other words, "do not postpone." Proverbs are also present in a more educated writer, the printmaker Carlo Dondero: "There is more time than life," he writes, hinting to the immigrant's fear of not having enough time to pursue all the opportunities. Elsewhere he adds: "Young as I was, this saying of wisdom occurred to me, 'as a hound returns to his vomit, so do fools return to their folly.' As my good mother had often demonstrated to me, my motto was 'that a bird in the hand is worth two in the bush.'"[128] These autobiographies maintain the characteristic of oral speech as being additive rather than subordinative, and making large use of "and . . . and . . ." or short phrases typical of paratactic prose. Let's take for example this passage from Antonio De Piero's fantasy of his trip before his departure. "Sleep didn't want to come, many things were crossing one another in my brain and I closed my eyes to see them better, the first was the bitter departure; the train that had to take me to Paris the Ship, the sea, North America with his treasures, the big bay of New York the big metropolis, The colossal statue of liberty with her right arm raising a big lit torch, symbol of protection and liberty for all the peoples; and it dominates majestic on the sea at the harbor's entry. In front the colossal city with its restless traffic with thousands of cars and trucks a deviled noise, with his titanic buildings called cloudscrapers for their immense height, I see also the numerous Factories Mills Farms with their ponderous chimneys all smoking everybody works, everybody lives, and well, and here we die of hunger."[129] It is a long list of short events and flashing images. As the oral storyteller, this narrator does not edit, but blurts out his thoughts just as they come to him.

The structure of these autobiographies keeps a temporal movement, from the beginning to the end, along a mostly linear itinerary. This attachment to a traditional storyline is the natural form of the narrative structure of oral expression. Only a few of our autobiographies jump in time, and those are mainly by more educated authors. Even when there is time shifting anyway, it is of the most basic form: a few flashbacks or flash forwards, and a few examples of beginning in the present tense, at the time of writing.

Almost all our autobiographies avoid abstract interpretations, an approach that Ong finds to be typical of orality. To explain the unknown, they choose images of the known world, of their job or their rural world. They conceptualize "their knowledge with more or less close reference to the human lifeworld, assimilating the alien, objective world to the more immediate familiar interaction of human beings."[130] We find this tendency in their use of metaphors derived from the life they lead, images drawn from their works, or their animals. The shoemaker and postman Lomant describes people with concrete details that his eye catches, for example: he was "the best teacher I have ever had and the first who wore rubber boots." We can compare these with Vincent's example of his British farm worker, who writes "I was as fond of my wife as a Cat is of New Milk."[131]

Especially among the least educated autobiographers, we find more the description of external events than stages of development in the character: "I was born, my son was born," or "I did this, I started that" is the normal sequence. The assessment of the character comes more often in practical terms: their success on the job or their accumulation of belongings substitute for their internal evaluation. Ong observes that in oral cultures, external facts are more important than internalized ideas: the question "are you happy with yourself?" might inspire this answer: "I need more land and sow more wheat."[132] This is comparable to how, in many of our autobiographies, the appraisal of a life is present alongside a financial or material computation.

The attachment to facts is a characteristic of the rhetoric of these writers. They dip their hands into the bucket of "nonartistic proofs," as Aristotle calls them: they bring facts as their testimonies, real facts, "fatti veri," as Calogero Di Leo says repeatedly. The stress on the veracity of their words is always strong. For their artistic proofs these authors naturally appeal to logos, ethos, and pathos. They create their ethos of the immigrant, the unlucky struggler, the fighter against an adverse destiny. Then, they make large use of pathos: their stories drip sufferance and hardship. Pathos is their first source of ethos, because their lives of sorrow make them heroes. Finally, the kind of logos these writers create is drawn in great measure from folk culture. They rarely use enthymemes or syllogisms, but often play with maxims of their youth, and retell examples from the oral tradition, stories of the past that everyone in the village knows. Maxims and examples give to their stories the flavor of eternity, the echo of timeless knowledge.

Words and Punctuation

Style and content are often strictly connected in these works. The unfamiliarity with writing of these autobiographers often reveals a "sweat of writing" ("fatica di scrivere," says Antonelli) where style is strictly intertwined with content. The fatigue of writing is heavily present in the many almost incomprehensible pages that are filled with Italian American slang, but exude the writer's will to tell. An archetype of the immigrant working man, barely literate but still wanting to leave a written trace of his accomplishment, is Giuseppe Camilletti's autobiography.[133] His style is a succession of bare facts that build his life in the American mines: "I worked very hard that in the evening my back hurt and my ribs . . . with a tiredness I could die."[134] His entire life he has been a "leba," the Italian correspondent for *laborer* in his own language. Camilletti uses "mina" for mine, "jiobba" for job, "bosso" for boss and "bordinbosso" for boarding boss, "lo storo" for the store, "piccare la sletta" for pick the slate (even if the translator interprets it as "pull the car"). Many of the phrases, if not all, are sing-song verses, a characteristic that is completely lost in the translation by Robert Scott, but that seems to derive directly from the oral tradition. This difficulty of writing becomes a principal characteristic of this autobiography (like in Antonio Margariti's work) where the hard work and the hard life are conveyed almost primarily by the style than by the content. Reading this autobiography in the simple but ordered English into which it is translated makes it appear like an easier life, really another life.

The outer appearance of these humble writings is a hodgepodge of English, Italian, and dialect, with seemingly random capitalization and punctuation. Among the first observers of this strange Italian American patois was the journalist and immigration inspector Adolfo Rossi. In his *Un Italiano in America* (1907) he offered a short but complete dictionary of new Italian-English words.[135] Such an idiolect is not a real pidgin or creole because it is primarily made of short insertions of another language in the primary language of choice.

The tailor Pio Federico interspersed his writing with Italian American words such as "la fattoria" for the factory, "argomento" for argument (*litigio*), "renditai un appartamento," conjugated like the Italian for "to rent" (*affittai*). Calogero Di Leo's language is reinvented at every sentence, coming from a vocabulary of "not good Italian and perfect Sicilian and twenty English words" and includes such New York places as "Rigivud Brooklin" and "an avenue called Nichibacher," all written in a text filtered through Sicilian dialect, titled "Mai Biuriful Laif."[136] He also remembers the misunderstanding due to mispronunciation: "One evening we were playing cards I lay an ace [*arso*] she heard *arso* and started to laugh and she couldn't stop, *mamma mia* what did I say this lady laughs a lot then she told me that the word *arso* in English means ASS I didn't know it, *arso* is written ACE and is pronounced *eis* and the lady it's clear she had to laugh when I threw an ass on the table true facts."[137]

Sometimes these immigrants make up their own words that are rich with meanings. Pietro Riccobaldi's resentment of American business and money inspires his noun *la Malamerica*. One of the most meaningful words invented by our immigrants is Tommaso Bordonaro's *spartenza*. This original term, translatable perhaps as "dis-departure," gives all the idea of the upside-down world of the immigrant, forced to leave in a way that does not make sense to him, that is unnatural, a negation of the natural law. "Painful and heart-wrenching has been the *disdeparture*, but finding all the opposite of what I thought. I could not imagine what I have found," he writes with disbelief.[138] Like in Camilletti or Margariti, Bordonaro's style has been defined as "wild," and it is perfectly adherent to its content as "syntactic pain" or "linguistic pain." A harsh style is the perfect tool to describe a working life: as a naked succession of facts (often disgraces) where descriptions are almost absent, in part because such a busy life doesn't allow time to rest, look around, and brood.

Decorative devices of not only a rhetorical, but also a typographical nature play a large role in these writings. Perhaps for their unfamiliarity with words, these authors mold written signs as they would mold hot iron or carve a piece of wood. Antonio Margariti, for example, otherwise incapable of expressing irony, inserted a sequence of question marks, giving words visual importance; many other authors use capital letters or underlines for emphasis. Perhaps out of his unfamiliarity with writing, Margariti made almost a sacred alphabet, a system of hieroglyphs in which all signs have a private meaning. Punctuation is a gimmick to shape a conversation.

These authors seem to be aware that the literary "ugliness"— grammatical mistakes, spelling errors, structural formlessness, and inclusion of some tiresome detail that would be tedious even to their families—will keep their works from being treated as history, as evidence of a social or personal mentality, or as forms of any narrative genre. But after this analysis of the context and form of these texts, it is possible now to continue to summarize extracts of these biographies with an open mind to the qualities that they do reveal about the history, psyches, and narrative heritage of their authors.

PART II

Follow me in the world with no people:
It will feel good to say, even as dead:
I was there!

❧ G. PASCOLI, *Inno degli emigranti italiani a Dante* (1911)

2 The Working-Class Writer

Most of the autobiographies reviewed in this section are characterized by how central work is to the immigrant's life. Often the person chose to migrate out of the desire to find or change jobs. Indeed, "work" is an American value that these immigrants have internalized; for most American autobiographies personality alone is not enough to warrant a book. It is the accomplishment, the grand story that provides the impetus to write, and it is the sage advice on how to reproduce such a grand story that provides the reasons for writing it—just look at the extraordinary case of Benjamin Franklin.

The immigrant in America identifies with his or her work, as the poet Joseph Tusiani observes in his autobiography: "I did not have *la giobba,* the job, and therefore I was nothing in this land where only those who work are somebody."[1] He explains that for the immigrant, "if the work ends, America ends—and what remains? The illusion remains, the babble of a foreign language. . . . a painful sensation remains, the sensation that America does not need you anymore, your Italy does not want you either, where if you decide to return after many years nobody recognizes you."[2]

The ethic of the worker was often planted into the minds of young immigrant children, as Peter Mattia demonstrated in his typescript autobiography.[3] He recounted an episode from youth when his father prohibited him from thinking about sculpture and drawings and pushed him toward manual work: "One time he gave me a piece of

49

paper and said. 'Can you draw a picture of a pick and shovel?' 'I'll try.' 'Do it!' I did, and he looked at it. 'Very, very good. That's what you use to make a living. Now go and learn what you like, but remember that I am not spending any money on crazy ideas. You have a home, but as far as buying clothes or paying for anything else, no!' "[4]

The journalist Giuseppe Gaja, an observer of Italian emigration at the turn of the century, points exactly to that immigrant work ethic: "All those who migrate with the courage of ancient Spanish adventurers with dreams of the Golden Land across the ocean—real sons of Christopher Columbus—should not be ashamed to say that—in order to honestly make a life—they have really agreed to do anything."[5] The concept of the self-made man is key in our autobiographies, and will and work are in the forefront, superceding any attention placed on education. Our writers brush over their childhoods quickly and emphasize their work experience; and they shorten the story of their families to emphasize the importance of the self.

The Working Man's Sense of Self

The immigrants presented in this section define themselves mainly by their labor. Hands become the metaphor for the immigrant worker.[6] The novelist and immigrant autobiographer Camillo Cianfarra (whose life story seems to melt too easily into a novel to be studied among these texts as a genuine autobiography),[7] explains the simple truth: "my hand could not be ready to write when it had glued labels and moved barrels for ten hours."

MICHELE PANTATELLO ∾ The calloused hands of Michele Pantatello can be seen as a metaphor of these working-class lives. When Pantatello was able to leave his office job and go back to being a blacksmith, he looked at his reddened and blistered hands and rejoiced: "in one week my hands would regain the old glory of my craftsmanship."[8] He regretted having played in the stock market instead of simply earning his money through the sweat of his brow: "Temptation is a bad thing and those who look for luck should know that the best way is work; idleness is the father of vices."[9] Born in Oppido Mamertina (Calabria) in 1894, Pantatello's first uprooting was from Calabria to the northern region of Friuli, where he served in the army during the World War I and met his future wife. At the wedding he experienced an exasperated *campanilismo* in the prejudice of his uncle's family against his wife. At the dawn of Fascism he worked in an office as a clerk but he felt he was betraying his working-class ethos: "I looked at my hands and thought, what a metamorphosis for the war. For three generations, skilled artisans from father to son, and now me with clean hands. . . . The day after I gave my resignation."[10] In 1922 he arrived at Ellis Island; in New York he worked as a mechanic in a factory that made soda fountains. But he struggled against hard times, the strikes on the job, and the suffering of his wife who returned to Udine. He was a recipient of the Home Relief program during the Depression that undermined his eagerness to work: "I was starting to lose my patience, I was disgusted by America, we had to work like horses to earn a living. But destiny wanted so. Fascism was stronger and I could not return home, unless I accepted to bow my head, something which I would never have done."[11]

"Destiny wanted so." Not the self-made immigrant, but the self-preserved immigrant is the main character of these autobiographies. They slip through the obstacles of fate like eels through the crevices. "*L'ultimo immigrante della Quota*" is the epithet he gives himself: he slipped through the immigrant regulations and was lucky to be the last one entering before the Quota restrictions for Italian immigrants in 1924. He delineates his ethos of survivor of Fate from his very birth: "November 13th 1894 is the date of my birth. For some the number 13 brings good luck and works against the evil eye, others thinks it is catastrophic. For me, after three days, November 16th when a strong earthquake shook our city and villages around it with incalculable damages, I could survive, and I can call myself lucky. . . . I reached the age of 72 and I beat the evil eye. 'Foolishness, superstition' said Benedetto Croce, 'but it is always good to be aware.'"[12]

In the hardest moments of his life, Pantatello did not praise his own courage and initiative, but the help coming from above, a theme that we will see is common among our authors: "An old saying goes

'God tries but does not abandon you' "[13] and in fact, "in the moments of sadness and anguish a higher hand arrived in my help at the right moment, incredible!"[14] Even when he succeeds he does not present himself as a hero but as a ram with his head down: "In this country whoever is not able to make way with his elbows always remains in the back."[15] Pantatello built his life with hands and elbows, failure after failure: for example, he organized a society for soda fountain machines workers only to discover that soda fountains were disappearing in the wake of the new vending machines. Nevertheless, he resurfaced every time: "America is the land of opportunity, today you're poor, tomorrow the opposite, a strange combination can make you rich, without going to look for it, it happened many times."[16] He was finally able to build a house for his wife and his daughters married "intellectuals."

Sadness creeps into Pantatello's description of his triumphal return to Italy. Even if economically satisfied, these immigrants know the price of their success. His 1960 trip back to his hometown is done to renew a family tombstone and to honor the disappearance of his entire family "to remind the future generations, always, the name of a family disappeared from the Village, for the circumstances of life."[17] In his final paragraph we find the main characteristics of the immigrant autobiographer: the sheltering gesture toward the family and the act of writing a name, not accompanied by trumpet sounds but by the soft whisper of death.

GIOVANNI VELTRI ∾ The same idea is present in Giovanni Veltri's autobiography, marred by the prospect that his Italian name will be lost: his two grandsons in Canada have inherited the anglicized name Welch: "Finally I built a decent chapel in the cemetery where I hope my bones will be laid to rest. However my soul is tormented by the thought that my name will end with me because there is no one who will pass it on."[18] Called John Welch in America and Giovanni Veltri in Italy, he lived his identity as a worker with intense pride. He not only worked for himself, but through his railroad company, the Welch Company (founded with his brother Vincenzo), he started a chain migration from his hometown of Grimaldi in Calabria: "a ghenga e Veltri" (Veltri's gang) was the common name for these laborers. The two left in the 1880s, directed to the American Northwest. Giovanni, the storyteller, was ninety years old when he dictated his memories to his niece in Italian.[19]

Veltri's *Memories* span 1867 to 1954, and with the ability typical of an oral history, he remembered hundreds of names. Born in 1867 "into an excellent family with honest parents," "at fifteen I decided to emigrate to Africa."[20] In Algeria, working in railroad construction, he lost contact with his cousins and friends, and the contacts of his first immigrant all-male community crumbled. He decided to go to America to build the Montana railway from Helena, where he faced alienating isolation. After six years in Italy for military service, marriage, and the birth of his first child, he returned to America in 1895. He worked as a miner and witnessed a great explosion that left his workers dying in his arms: "more than 2,000 people came to view the explosion site, but the tragedy saddened everyone, us more than the others."[21] After work in various mining towns, he returned to Italy for two years, then in 1905 went to Winnipeg with his brother and first-born son, Raffaele. Veltri experienced the harsh face of immigration in the cold of Canada, living in tents that left him frostbitten, fighting with slush, snow, black bears, and the drunkenness of men. He saw storms with "trees of various sizes being hurled through the air like twigs," that left him "trembling with fear." His work ethic was always intense: "We bought more horses and soon started working. It was wonderful to see how well we worked in that sand with the horses and equipment we had."[22] In 1913 his brother died of peritonitis, and for Veltri it was a tragedy that he overcame with the resignation: "my grief was overwhelming, but I had to resign myself to the will of the Lord. This was my poor brother's destiny."[23] When his wife and daughters reached him in 1924, they did not adapt to the life in North America. He was thus forced to go back with them and leave the company to his sons, another tragedy for Veltri, who all his life moved around the world from one job to the next. Without work, he is bitter, but he still bows his head to destiny: "Accustomed as I was for nearly 40 years to journeying the North American continent from the Atlantic to the Pacific, to scouring the immense prairies and to plowing the length and breadth of the Great Lakes system, it was not pleasant to be confined in my primitive native village, Grimaldi, a town which has only a few thousand people. It had been my desire to be buried next to my brother in Canada, but I let destiny prevail and went to end my days away from the land where I had spent the best years of my life."[24]

EMANUELE TRIARSI ∿ A carefully chosen tomb and an autobiography were the last gifts of the construction worker Emanuele Triarsi to his wife: "Nino, Antonietta and I went to buy your last gift, your eternal home. Where we went we did not like anything, so we went somewhere else and we found what we wanted for you, and so I bought the last palace for you and for me."[25] Triarsi's goal in life had been to build the perfect house for himself and his wife, and this became the metaphor of his life as an immigrant. When his wife reached him in New York he saw a silent disappointment on her face: "I would have liked to give her a castle but I had nothing else than this finch's nest. And looking at this situation I silently promised myself that if God helps me I will build the house of her dream. With time, I did so. With the help of God I built our home."[26]

Emanuele Triarsi was born in New York in 1922. Brought back to Sicily when he was only one month old, Triarsi came back to the United States in 1949, and was joined by his wife and son in 1950. Today he is a "snow bird" who migrates from New York to South Florida every winter. His autobiography spans from his birth to the death of his wife.[27] Like Pantatello, he felt the pride of being a working man, and no job was too humble. In America he accepted all kinds of jobs with a light heart, even working in a sewer: "I can't tell you the dirt, but anyway we were working and we felt good even in the 'shit'."[28] Triarsi's immigration is colored by work all his life: "America is good if you work, but if you don't work it's troubles and bad ones."[29]

The authority of our humble authors comes not from their education, but from the sincerity and the value of their firsthand experience. At the end of his booklet, Triarsi sighed: "Ah, if I were a writer!" but he has made up for the lack of education with his sincerity by testifying that this book is written with his heart. "I do not have instruction and so I cannot write a novel, but only a little story, the best I can."[30] The effectiveness of his prose is not marred by his roughness. He also gave a testimony of Sicilian culture, a culture made of cactus figs, old customs, recommendations, friendship ties, and favors to obtain what was needed. He remembered the Littoriali, a Fascist contest that he failed. He annotated his economical transactions down to the last lira, because large part of his youth was spent to pay a debt of 36,000 lire for some land. He remembered the "hunger, black hunger,"[31] and meeting his wife. His descriptions portray the love dreams of a young Sicilian shaped on novels and movies, but crushed under the stiffening Sicilian tradition that prevent the lovers to meet alone, to talk about love openly, and to sleep together even on their wedding night. The migration to America was not necessary ("To tell the truth, I could not complain in Italy"),[32] but motivated by ambition. His physical appearance changed in New York, and he cut his Sicilian moustache when he heard that it made him look like a thug. He shared the beliefs of the immigrant philosophy, its resistance ("Passing through all these episodes and always raising to the surface in each difficulty, I am convinced that God is behind me and helps me,")[33] and its resilience in building the house of dreams against the difficulties of life ("but even in that discouraging situation I nevertheless went on").[34] In the end, he measures his happiness in material terms and carefully describes the hand-made details of the famous house he is able to build for his wife in Yorktown Heights, especially the floor.

ALDOBRANDO PIACENZA ∾ If the perfect house is the metaphor of Triarsi's immigration, a clay reproduction of his village is the allegory of nostalgia for Aldobrando Piacenza. When he shapes the block of clay to create a miniature version of Saint Anna in his yard, he finds a visible allegory for his identity and his Italian roots: "Seeing that I could not go to Italy so soon, I thought of bringing Italy to Highwood . . . in small shapes I built the Church and the Campanile of my town of Sant'Anna and by them I built the house and the hut of Casa del Colle. I had it photographed and I sold a lot of postcards and I still do."[35] Piacenza is a retired tobacconist and school janitor (he had too many jobs to be easily defined) who at sixty-eight spent his time in the company of an old typewriter in the suburbs of Chicago writing his memoirs, which describe his life and his six trips to the United States from the Apennine Tosco-Emiliano. The difficult uprooting of his first departure as a boy of fifteen, in 1903, is achingly present in his pages, where the orthographical mistakes take nothing out of the intensity of his writing style, nourished by the books he loves to read: "Approaching the departure, after I felt the pleasure of being satisfied to Emigrate that was my biggest desire, and then one day return with a nice suit and the golden Watch, also I could not think of the pain of departing from the people I loved and from my Village that even if poor still conserved my most precious memories. I was not to hear the melodious sound of its Bells and the sacred functions, the murmur of its Rivers and the Singing of Birds, I felt a deep bitterness. [My parents'] sacrifices that they made for me . . . created a strong determination in me that I would do anything possible to give the deserved consolation to my dear mother and dear father. . . . I departed with that Company, with the most bitter pain I can remember from my dear Father and mother and sisters toward America. . . . Many times even in the far America when I thought about that departure I would bitterly cry, and when sometimes people surprised me while crying I would say it's nothing."[36]

Piacenza vividly remembered his first impressions of America ("mixed through the Mist I saw the Skyscrapers and the Grand Brooklyn Bridge, with the huge iron constructions, I can't deny I was filled with Wonder"),[37] the different sense of space in the American vastness between New York and Chicago ("Infinite Prairies, Woods and immense agricultural land immense Rivers Lakes that seemed like Oceans. We traveled for hours without seeing the trace of a House . . . . All very different from what I had seen in Italy").[38] He loved both countries, but his writing suggests that his heart was in Italy while America had his gratitude. His love for Italy pushed him to sell Italian newspapers and books in his shop, and this cost him the accusation of being a Fascist spy. The police even interpreted the clay reproduction of the church of his town in his yard as a reproduction of a Fascist palazzo (he defended himself less than honorably by giving the name of a drunkard, who was not even Italian, as a Fascist).

Yet the work was always honorable: "With honest work I built my decent refuge here in America."[39] He eventually set up a tobacco and

newspaper shop in Highwood, in the Chicago area, "with no l.
little school, and no apprenticeship";[40] he worked in a biscotti ι
a pastry shop, selling strawberries in the street. He chose his wι
Italy based on her strength as a worker but "without much
mance,"[41] and in fact she never complained and worked with him. Hι
entire migratory effort was dedicated to rebuilding and owning Casa
del Colle, his family house on the hills of Modena. He went back many
times, hoping to restart his life, but the economic situation always
forced him to leave. He gave up his family for the desire of owning
that house: "If all these years that I spent in America to ransom Casa
del Colle and rebuild it, and then finally I cannot enjoy it, and I feel
offended, perhaps it was even better if I were not the Owner."[42] As an
economical man, he included many financial details and the whole
dispute over that house. Money matters define his life, and in the 1959
postscript to his autobiography he asserted that he wrote it to deny the
myth of his wealth: "All the people in Italy and in America would say
how much money has Aldobrando Piacenza. But the true fact is that
if I wanted to go to Italy now I would need to borrow from the Bank."[43]

PIO FEDERICO ∾ The tailor Pio Federico put his apology at the
beginning of his autobiography:[44] "In this story I will try to describe
in the best way possible all I remember of my past, from childhood
till now. . . . this is a simple story written by a man who is sixty-
nine, a tailor, with minimum instruction of fifth grade. Therefore I
am grateful if I won't be teased."[45]

He was born in San Valentino in Abruzzo Citeriore in 1891 and
came to America as a mustached youth in 1909. In 1960, at sixty-
nine, he sat down in his house in Los Angeles and started to write his
life story. In 1966 he resumed writing and covered those six years.
Federico described his life in his little town, where he was ashamed
that his father had been jailed for debts. At twelve, he learned the
crafts of carpenter, dyer, and tailor. In the tailor's shop Pio first encountered the dream of America, through the owner—Tranquillo
Placido—who would be Pio's passport to emigration. Pio stated it mat-
ter-of-factly: America seems to be the natural option in Abruzzo for
him, and Placido: "since he could not go on as he wished, he thought

of migrating to America and so he did. Before leaving he promised he would call me as soon as he reached the right condition. In 1909 he maintained his promise sending me the ticket for the ship."[46]

When Placido sent for him, Federico could not find a loan for the famous *cento lire* for his departure: "For a hundred lire I could not go to America."[47] This expense held such importance that it even decided his future relationship with his family and friends, for it was the mayor who lent him the money, which Pio returned as soon as could pull it together once in America, writing to him first, before any of his family. His arrival in America was a drama that becomes familiar to us from its many variations, told by many of our immigrants: "At the exit, I did not know where to go with that suitcase and that bag that weighed more than me."[48]

Federico's life in New York was marked by hard factory labor from morning until eleven at night. When he married, he did not even take time off for his honeymoon.[49] Eventually he opened a little shop with two friends: "I took a sewing machine from Tranquillo that he had in his house, I went to a place where they sold secondhand machines, I bought an ironing machine, tables, chairs, and irons we had in the place. So I prepared my first factory, with six people."[50] His failures never ended, even when he moved to California, supposedly to recover from too much work: after not sleeping for five days to finish 287 blazers, "we sold the goods, the factory, with a loss of six thousand dollars, all work and time spent without earning a cent."[51] "The Italian immigrant is always pushed to do more and better, since the first day he left his land." This was Federico's pride and the cause of his downfall. His health became unstable and he acquired a stuttering problem.

With this long list of failures and some successes, Federico is the perfect example of the quiet individualism of the Italian immigrant autobiographer. Destiny and the hand of God are as important as his own initiative. "We started [the business] with three and so we have to remain,"[52] and later, "$80,000 would be in my pocket had I been alone, that's how it cost me to maintain the promise I made."[53] Even Federico's marriage was decided by fate. In 1913 he met Lillian, an embroiderer: "Lillian's mother had lost her first daughter of my age, and with my name, her name was Pia, and she said that the Lord had sent her another one to replace the loss. She loved me like a son."[54] Life appeared to him to be a mountain of obstacles, yet, "I thank the good Lord . . . I always did everything by myself with my arms and my brain, without anyone's help, only to one person I am grateful: Tranquillo Placido, this was his name."[55]

If in the immigrant philosophy work and material success are the measures of life, inactive old age is a defeat for the working man, who is reduced to being puppet, as Federico describes himself in these bitterly poetic words: "What is it worth to pretend to be alive when one has already been dead for a long time? When you are not in condition to create a family, a new factory, to speculate in the buying and selling, to go the sea or the mountain, to enjoy the pleasures of life, how can you say you are alive? What is worth living long if this is all in the past? . . . all that remains is a dressed doll."[56]

GIOVANNI ARRU ∾ Resignation had been daily bread for Sardinian Giovanni Arru ever since he was a young boy, when a disgrace struck his home. Arru wrote twelve pages packed edge-to-edge with tidy handwriting, pressed by the fervor of telling.[57] Born in 1890 and writing at eighty, he remembered the rigid social structure of the town of Pozzomaggiore at the time of his birth: "To clarify the well-being of my family then, the town was divided in three categories: Signori, Messeri, and plebeians. My family was considered Messeri, it was a family considered as well-off."[58] Arru remembered his father as a hard worker who sustained the family, but he had a tragic accident one day when he saw the fruit of a fig tree reflected in a fountain pool and fell while trying to retrieve it for his family. The family spent all their money in search for a cure, but in vain. His mother started working as tailor and embroiderer; his sister did farm work, while Arru brought home the bundles of wood and worked many other odd jobs. After a childhood of hard labor to help provide for the family, he went to America to look for work, where he took various jobs and returned to Italy after two years. He immediately regretted his decision, and when the war was over, he surmised that "in Sardinia there was nothing to do, only dig stones, I thought of returning to America since I had a free trip. In America it was winter and there was nothing to do but go to shovel snow on the streets."[59] His situation improved when he started selling bananas on the street for two Sardinian grocers. Working for five years, from eighteen to twenty-four hours a day, he was nevertheless successful because he made his stand beautiful, arranging fruit better and making it appear more yellow than the others.

He returned to Sardinia and triumphantly invested his money in building a house, despite the interventions of envious *signori*. He opened a bar and reinvented himself as the civilizer of his little town: "Without showing off, I have to say that my arrival in Pozzomaggiore from America brought a little civility, not only because I opened the coffee shop . . . but also [bought] the first car, the first radio, and the first TV."[60]

ROCCO CORRESCA ∾ The biography of Rocco Corresca was published at the turn of the century as an exemplar of the model hardworking immigrant.[61] Being a worker and performing useful work was the key to assimilation, the deserved award for all the immigrants who could contribute to the building of America. While many such stories were told to and rewritten by editors, Corresca's story does not seem to be one of them.[62]

Corresca wrote a rough story on the theme of rags to riches. He started with the description of his horrifying childhood as an orphan reclaimed by an old man, who presented himself as his grandfather and made him work as a beggar in the streets of Naples. He lived a life of Dickensian abjection, putting up little scenes with his accomplices to get money from foreign tourists, sleeping on the floor, eating little, because fat beggars would not get money, and was regularly beaten by the old man. He escaped from the hands of this man the day that he heard him speaking about crippling the boys to get more money. From then on he lived the adventures of a vagabond boy with his friend Francesco, who eventually worked with him in America. Corresca's image of the country was mythic: "I had heard things about America—that it was a far-off country where everybody was rich and that Italians went there and made plenty of money. . . . One day I met a young man who pulled out a handful of gold and told me he had made that in America in a few years."[63]

He worked in New York as rag- and bottle-picker for a *padrone,* from whom he eventually freed himself, and with a friend became *padrone* of their destiny: They learned English from Irishmen and in exchange taught them to read and write; they opened a shoeshine station in a basement. Rocco described it as his personal life realization, annotating all expenses as in the tradition of medieval merchant autobiographies and showing his understanding of the ways of the market: "We got a basement on Hamilton Avenue, near the Ferry, and put four chairs in it. We paid $75 for the chairs and all the other things. We had tables and looking glasses there and curtains. We took the papers that have the pictures in and made the place high toned. Outside we had a big sign that said: THE BEST SHINE FOR TEN CENTS. Men who did not want to pay 10¢ could get a good shine for 5¢ but it was not an oil shine. We had two boys helping us and paid each of them 50¢ a day. The rent of the place was $20 a month, so the expenses were great, but we made money from the beginning. We slept in the basement, bought our hot meals at the saloon until we could put a stove in our place, and then Francesco cooked for us all. That would not do, though, because some of our customers said they did not like to smell garlic and onions and red herrings. I thought it was strange but we had to do what the customers said."[64]

Corresca's story is a succession of facts without dates or comments. His "cumulative" style of telling his accomplishments is typical of the humble immigrant's autobiography. He wrote as a young man of nineteen, in the prime of his strength and dreams. Rocco became "Joe" for his clients: his Americanization was in full progress. He often repeated the lesson of assimilation: "We learned." "We were very ignorant when we came here, but now we have learned much."[65] He saved 700 dollars, Francesco was twenty-one and had 900 dollars: "some people call us 'swells.' Ciguciano said we should be great men."[66]

George Guida sees in Corresca an Italian Horatio Alger novel, specifically, the only novel with an Italian protagonist, *Phil, the Fiddler* (1872): "Corresca takes cues from Horatio Alger in his pioneering development of complex, fully human Italian American male selves."[67]

He tells the same story of a slave-boy and his adventures with *padrones*. According to Guida, Franklin is also the model for Corresca's story, especially in the telling of his apprenticeship and finances. It may seem surprising that a bootblack really had read both these works by Franklin and Alger, but it is possible that he was imbued with the model of the self-realization story that was raging in the post–Civil War era.

TOMMASO BORDONARO ∾ One of the best-known working-class autobiographers is Tommaso Bordonaro.[68] His work ethic is reflected in his style, the succession of facts with little description, quickly passing from one disgrace to another, and never resting to brood or look at the landscape. Bordonaro was born in Bolognetta (Palermo) in 1909, the first of eight boys. He started school in first grade and he worked as a shepherd with his uncle; his father had emigrated to America. Bordonaro traced back his family history to the Greeks, thus honoring the memory of an ancient glory, now completely evaporated: "my origin comes from Greece from a noble family of the first period after Christ who settled in Sicily in the time when Dionysus was the governor of Sicily. But when I was born my family lived in a low condition, poor and almost miserable."[69]

After his military service in Liguria he tried to leave Sicily for the first time, but his mother's tears stopped him: "my mother had tears lining her cheeks, my smaller brothers did not have any courage. . . . For my mom I was ready to give my life."[70] Bordonaro married a poor girl, his first love: "I preferred love to self-love and respect, and sincerity to well-being."[71] He started working and was able to build a little house. When his young wife died, he was desperate, but he married an older woman who had been dishonored by her lover, and since she was born in America, he started thinking of emigration. In 1947, at thirty-eight, with five children and his second wife, Bordonaro started his series of trips to America.

His years there are marked by various jobs, in a macaroni factory, in the public works, and even in a cemetery, a place he had always avoided with fear: "my first job in America was burying the dead to earn a piece of hard bread and nourish my family, dig holes and bury the dead."[72]

Bordonaro's greatest blow was the death of his twenty-one-year-old son in a fire when he was a volunteer in the army. He received ten thousand dollars' insurance and spent it all on the funeral and on building a chapel in his garden with a Venetian mosaic in it, "to show the unknown people that I did not need to lose a son to live."[73] Tommaso was obsessed by people who watched him and judged him.

Bordonaro never became really American, like his children and grandchildren. He knew that America was his "last motherland," but he couldn't ever forget Sicily. He undertook numerous trips back to see his parents, and he never could really depart from his family. Each time he went back to his town he found happiness in the reconnection with the earth and its fruits: "I had so much pleasure eating the special fruit, and gathering the almonds from the trees I had planted 30 years before and that were now old."[74] In Tommaso Bordonaro we also find the ethos of the survivor who, even if without luck, has made it through life. His story is far from a success story: "I've always been unlucky in my life, in my business, in my work, even in love."[75]

CALOGERO DI LEO ❧ An untranslatably unique language characterizes the autobiography of the last working man in this section, Calogero Di Leo.[76] This is a fresh piece of writing by a sixty-three-year-old author who looks back at his accomplishments and defeats with sarcasm, evident in his autobiography's title: "Life of a Millionaire Immigrant Tourist." Di Leo's prose vividly spans from a long reconstruction of his youth in Lucca Sicula (Agrigento) to his work in England, New York (1965), and Florida (1982). His dreams of America started at a very young age, thanks to the packages sent by his immigrant relatives that were opened with a reverent enthusiasm that Di Leo recreates in the stream of consciousness of his memories: "As usual, all around the package to open it, as if we had to open a treasure, we open the packages . . . mom exclaims, o they are beautiful brand new, Four shirts, oh, how beautiful for you Giuseppe, three packages of spools: thread needles and pins o how beautiful, Four women's dresses, these for me and for you to my sister, a piece of sugar in little cubes this for the coffee, a little suit that says in a piece of paper attached to the suit this is for my nephew Calogero I jump in the air and I shout thank you Saint Anthony, a beautiful suit of wool color pale milk and coffee, brand new the size was perfect as if Don fifi had been taking the measurements when I wore it I looked like a model I had never seen a complete suit, always two pieces shirt and flannel pants and the more I grew, the shorter the pants. He is really a Saint, that man, long live America, long live zio Antonino, long live spaghetti and long live meatballs, I start [to think] how to go to America."[77]

The immigrant philosophy is shaped in Di Leo's words, on this conscience of the weakness of the unarmed immigrant who does not have a voice in any matter and must only absorb the blows: "the one that suffers is always the poor immigrant," and "the immigrant bears many injustices and humiliations and sometimes he cannot defend himself."[78] He has to close both his bars because he is not as strong as the corporations: "All the other shops that are big chains like tacco [Taco Bell] viva Sbarro pizza, Japanese, Chinese, etc. . . . there was no problem they are big fishes, I am a sardine and with a family to maintain and sick and paying always the rent on time and responsible in everything."[79] Nevertheless, this sense of resignation is softened by an undying optimism: "going directly back to Italy I have to die of hunger. I say no, Calogero, be brave because who endures wins."[80] Yet, as in many other testimonies, compared to Italy, Di Leo finds America a land of abundance. During his visit to the California vineyards he saw the enormous quantity of grapes that remained on the picked branches: "With all that remains on the vine you can load trucks and trucks of grape, seeing is believing. . . . I remember when we made the big vintage on the two hundred vines that grandfather Calogero Bacino had in his vineyard, not even a single grape remained on it, what a difference."[81]

The immigrant defines himself as a simple worker in these autobiographies, but from this ethos these writers build their humble greatness, as humility and dirty hands elevate them to the heroic. These gravelly stories are facts, softened only by time. But they retain the harshness of what they have been: the roughness of the snow shoveling or the excavation of dirty sewers, the fatigue of sleepless nights sewing jackets or the sore acceptance of their business failures. The survivor, the quiet individual who digs his life out of hard soil or urban labor, appears here in his simplest form.

The Politics of the Working Man

In this section I discuss the authors who have a clear sense of the worker in society, their rights, and the quality of their living conditions, and those who see themselves as workers in a political sense, with anarchist or leftist views and a "proletarian nationalism."[82] The following two groups are the real "philosophers" of the working class.[83]

ANTONIO MARGARITI ✎ The working man springs forth in all his rage from Antonio Margariti's 1983 autobiography, *America! America!*[84] Margariti, born in Ferruzzano (Reggio Calabria) in 1891, departed for America in 1914 when he was twenty-two and worked in Rochester, New York, as a stonecutter in canal construction. He went back to Italy for a short time and then returned to America, where he settled in Willow Grove, near Philadelphia, where he worked in an automobile plant. After the last member of his family died, the need to defy oblivion pushed him to write a masterpiece of literature of the impoverished. His broken Italian is a rough yet powerful tool to express his pointed ideas of history as seen from below. Margariti is an anarchist who openly defended the two Italian worker-martyrs Sacco and Vanzetti. His tone is witty, ironic, and cutting. He is one of the few autobiographers (with leftist Pietro Riccobaldi, anarchist Carlo Tresca, and the martyr-fisherman Bartolomeo Vanzetti) with a mature political conscience that we could define as leftist. He is an activist, and denies the typical Italian immigrant disinterest in politics and passive acceptance that we see in the story with bootblack Rocco Corresca's experience. We can easily imagine Margariti yelling in public meetings as a vociferous member of a community or labor organization.[85] His fascinating world is clearly divided between "thepowerful" (*ipossente*) and "thepoor" (*ipoverette*), as he coins his terms [86]

Margariti is in search of well-being, liberty, equality, and dignity. He left Italy unwillingly, forced by the hopeless situation that remained there for him. He regretted that his brother Peppino, who also emigrated, was swallowed by oblivion in the United States.[87] His America is not the land of success, but one of bitter injustice: "I came to this far land in 1924 when I was 22, and here I found a completely different life and also here INJUSTICE exists also here there is who works and has not much or nothing and other who do nothing and have everything and they are the padroni."[88]

His strong political consciousness pushed him to gain a space in history: "the life of the big people is written by the great historians and remains in history, but for me who am nothing else than a little grain fallen from the space and outside my neighborhood nobody knows I Exist and perhaps one can think I write for Ambition without Ambition one can't do anything."[89]

GREGORIO SCAIA ❧ Gregorio Scaia is also conscious of cutting out a space in history, not only for himself, but for his entire immigrant group. Scaia, not openly partisan, pays tribute to the itinerant Italian worker.[90] For this worker-writer, the rhythm of life is given by the calendar of the occupations in the fields, as the tale of his birth suggests: "born in the summer time when the wheat was being cut, the night of Saint James on July 25 1881, in the town of Prezzo in Giudicaria Valley, Tirolo."[91] Gregorio lived in Australia, Alaska, and California, before settling in Seattle, in 1909. He wrote his memoirs in 1953, at seventy-two. "I believe this is the only book to this day written about our foreign colonies, the only and unique reason of writing this book is telling and informing . . . our people and future generations, the works and obstacles and struggles that our Trentini had to fight in their trips on land and sea."[92]

His use of the word "colonies" reverses the perceived wisdom: he was not a poor immigrant looking for work, but one of the glorious founders of Italian colonies around the world. He saw the world as centered on the little Val Giudicaria and honored the imperialist impulse sprouting from this unknown Alpine valley. In his introduction, Scaia told of the generations of his heroic fellow villagers who, with their tools on their backs like mules, were guest workers in Lombardy and Switzerland. His political conscience did not derive from any specific party, but he held a social agenda: he wanted his own group of men to gain weight in history. He was not urged by an egotistic need to justify his own life, but inserted it in the local community of men coming from the same tiny valley in the Italian Alps.

BARTOLOMEO VANZETTI ∽ Caught in the mortal net of politics, Bartolomeo Vanzetti was a fishmonger from Piedmont who gained his fame in history, with Nicola Sacco, a shoemaker from Puglia, for their unjust 1921 trial for murder and their execution by electric chair. Theirs was the most famous case of the United States of America versus anarchy, work subversion, and immigration. He was arrested with Nicola Sacco, accused of having taken part in two Massachusetts robberies, one in Bridgewater and one in South Braintree that included a brutal double murder. The two Italian immigrants were found with anarchist material in their car. Sacco was indicted because a bullet in the body of one of the victims matched his gun and Vanzetti was "recognized" by eyewitnesses even though he did not resemble any of their original descriptions.[93]

The case of Sacco and Vanzetti is the infamous example of a trial guided by prejudice against Italian aliens who were seen as subversive. The fairness of the trial is still questioned, to a large extent because of testimony of their alibi. For Vanzetti, it is worker politics that hastened his accusation: "I am suffering because I am a radical, and indeed I am a radical. I have suffered because am I an Italian, and indeed I am an Italian."[94] The story of Sacco and Vanzetti resounded through Italian America, in both political and apolitical circles. The writer Wallace Sillanpoa remembers his grandmother spitting on the floor of the car every time she drove in front of the white mansion where Judge Thayer, who condemned the pair, lived.[95]

While in prison in Charlestown, in 1921 Vanzetti, who mastered only mangled English, wrote a short autobiography in Italian.[96] Curiously, it did not focus on his self-defense; instead, he simply appealed to his situation as a working man and immigrant, as if this was enough to find justification for his life and the false accusations. He painted himself as a good, willing young man who suffered much in his life, first for the early death of his mother and then as an immigrant. Work is the main dimension of his life: he was born in 1888 to a life of toil, and as a boy loved to study and imagined being a lawyer, but then his father "read on the *Gazzetta del Popolo* of Turin that forty-two lawyers had all applied for a position paying 35 lire monthly."[97] He then began working in a pastry shop fifteen hours a day, until he fell sick and had to quit, and he eventually left for America: "That period was one of the happiest of my life. I was 20: the age of hopes and dreams, also for those, who like me, run quickly through the pages of life."[98]

When he met a young boy "poorer than me," they decided to leave New York and look for a job in the countryside. They found temporary jobs as farmers, brick makers, and stonecutters in Connecticut. He ultimately went to Massachusetts, where he worked as an unskilled laborer and a bricklayer. Eight months before his arrest, he bought a boat and worked as a fishmonger, hoping to raise the money to go back to Italy.

Vanzetti's story is a defense of the humble worker. He finds dignity in the proletariat, and he calls a friend in Piedmont "nobile popolana," the "noble proletarian."[99] His political conscience illuminated his life. His informal education had an important place in his growth: schooled until he was thirteen, he read and found inspiration in Socialism in Turin among his coworkers. In the United States he found solidarity and generosity among humble people who were often poorer than he. To the explanation of his political belief in Socialism, fraternity, and universal love, he dedicates only one fervid page and the postscript.

PIETRO RICCOBALDI ∾ The Communist miner Pietro Riccobaldi was a fervent admirer of Sacco and Vanzetti. Riccobaldi was an immigrant who returned to Italy and never went back to America, where he spent his "strongest years." He originally went to America to escape Fascism, but he was never really integrated into the United States. As a member of the American Communist Party, he participated in the anti-McCarthyist efforts to save the Rosenbergs. His political leftism and his being a clandestine for the first years of his immigration made him a *straniero indesiderabile,* an undesirable foreigner—the qualification he chooses as the title of his autobiography that won the Pieve Santo Stefano Prize in 1987.[100] His autobiography, written when he was seventy-three, covers the years between 1912 and 1973 and tells the adventures of an immigrant who strengthened his Communist beliefs while working in the mines of the United States. Riccobaldi was born in Manarola in the beautiful but poor Cinque Terre of Liguria in 1901. He had a fair amount of education, and his style was polished; when he describes leaving Liguria, he quotes the well-known Italian novelist Alessandro Manzoni: "I saw the mountains of my Liguria getting far; I thought about the piece of the *Betrothed* and mentally recited it."[101] In his pages it is also easy to find echoes and references to progressive newspapers such as *Il Progresso Italo-Americano* and the *Daily Worker.*

Riccobaldi saw Italy as a battlefield where life was at stake. When Fascism ("black plague") spread through Italy, he was forced to leave, threatened by the sticks of the town's Fascists. He decided to go to America, even if this is the final shame among his people who considered migration as a defeat, the last capitulation before death: "Migrate, looking for a job outside was considered a declaration of surrender. So almost everyone remained attached to their own vineyard, proud to be the owners, and to work on his own."[102] The wish to change his life, to become independent from the stingy land, was deep in his soul. He described life in Italy as a debasing coexistence of people and animals: cats, goats, hens. He recounted the gruesome details of a tug-of-war between a cat and a man over food, and of a woman who died after eating a goat that had been buried some days ago, and of his own psychological fight against gnawing hunger: "I swallowed without chewing so that I could say:—Enough, I am full, I've had enough; I never succeeded. I swallowed everything and digested everything; I would have digested rocks too, like the hens."[103]

Being anti-Fascist he could not obtain a passport, but with five thousand lire he embarked as a clandestine on the old ship, where he worked in the boiler room ("If Hell exists, it is the pipe room!").[104] "I was always thirsty, hellishly thirsty; I was always attached to the water barrel: drink, drink, drink and the more I drank the thirstier I was. I sweated and drank and felt always weaker . . . all those burning grease drops sticking to the grids were falling at my feet."[105] Entering the Mississippi River was for him the beginning of a new life ("I became so happy I did not know what I was doing. I washed myself, I shaved and I prepared my soul for this jump into a new life").[106] On the train toward Scranton, he felt reborn, and as a twenty-four-year-old, he left his grueling past behind.

A miner in Scranton, Pennsylvania; a speakeasy bartender during the Prohibition; an apple and detergent salesman during the Depression; a dishwasher and waiter in New York; Riccobaldi also defined his life in terms of his work, where he discovered the truth of socialism and the rights of workers, as well as his own self-respect.

Until the end, he remained attached to the foreign identity associated with being an immigrant. When he was allowed citizenship because he married an American, Elba, "those were the happiest days of my life. I could not believe that it was true until I hugged Elba . . . I wasn't 'undesirable' anymore, but only foreigner."[107] Yet when he finally settled down in Italy for the sake of his father-in-law's health, he continued to remain an undesirable foreigner for his politics: "Many years have passed, and I have never gone back to America. Some years ago, I was already 73, I felt like taking a trip there as a tourist. I had left some friends in New York and a piece of my life; I hoped that the laws had changed and that my age could be seen as a warranty, but the forms to obtain the visa, so full of questions. . . . Too many inquisitions, too many moral vexations; I would have had to tell too many lies, I lost courage, I gave up. Since a few years I had come back to be an Italian citizen and therefore more than ever 'undesirable foreigner.'"[108]

CARLO TRESCA ∾ The anarchist intellectual Carlo Tresca was a leader, a defender of the working class. He was involved in the major episodes of working class protest, such as the strike in Lawrence, Massachusetts, in 1912; the textile strike of Paterson, New Jersey, 1913; and the strike of the Minnesota mining district in 1916.[109] He wrote an autobiography of a protester, a dissident, a radical, or as he says, "a fighting spirit." It is an atypical story of immigration in that he skipped over most of his personal life to speak about his political action, enumerating the steps of his *autocoscienza* and his fight for freedom and against Fascism.

Born in 1879 in Sulmona, Abruzzi, into a rich agricultural family ruined by the wine war with France, he showed his face as a rebel early on. He attended high school for two years, then technical school, but neither study nor the idea of being a clerk appealed to him. Revolt had been in his mind ever since he was young, a transference from his attitude toward his father, who "sowed the seed of revolt in my head. I could not rise against him. So I turned my unconscious feeling of revolt against anyone who exercised authority."[110] At twenty he was already attracting groups by speaking in the park, and it is clear this recognition gave him satisfaction: "I was no more a buoyant, exuberant, impertinent boy. I was a man, a man of command, of action."[111] He edited the Socialist newspaper *Il Germe,* and soon started thinking of America, a place of ideal liberty for the worker: "Strange name of cities, mysterious voices of a distant, unknown land came to me from America. The workers of the United States felt themselves free from that form of slavery and serfdom that was so detestable in the small town they had left. . . . I looked toward America as a wanderer in the desert looks for a drop of water when thirst grabs him by the throat. America! America! America! I went on fighting in the small towns but dreamed of a better, a bigger field of action; looking forward . . . toward America, the land of the free."[112]

He was arrested and "there was nothing else for me to do: go to jail or into exile."[113] After an unhappy start in New York, Tresca started to feel at home in America only when he found his enemy—after all, a revolutionary with nothing to protest is dead. He started investigating the exploitation of immigrants. He disguised himself as a lower immigrant and headed to find the men working on the railroad tracks of Hoboken, New Jersey. "The terrible odor of their bodies; their scornful approach on the question of love, their sexual perversion, their supine obedience to every command of the boss in the job, the beastly, arrogant attitude of the 'boss' toward the men, did produce in me a sense of hopelessness. I felt as if I had been submerged in the depth of the sea of human degradation."[114]

He began his sharp attack on employment agencies, white slave traffic, and prostitution. He lived with the miners in Pittsburgh, and there launched his accusations against the indiscretions of members of the Church. While in jail in Philadelphia, charged with libel, he learned of the strike in Lawrence, which aroused his activist spirit: "to me Lawrence was the beginning of a new era; with Lawrence I joined the army of revolutionary American workers for a real and greater struggle."[115]

Tresca's autobiography is a large mass of unfinished notes, without an ending. But his life had a tragic conclusion: after receiving numerous death threats he was killed in New York in 1943 by Carmine Galante, a professional killer, but whoever gave the order was never found. It was perhaps a Mafioso who killed him for non-political reasons, or even a crime of passion. Nunzio Pernicone ventured to hypothesize that the most convincing hypothesis could be that Galante was paid by Frank Garofalo, ex-Fascist Mafioso, with the silent blessing of another ex-Fascist enemy of Tresca, Generoso Pope. Now almost forgotten, "not the kind of individual usually included in history books intended for general consumption,"[116] Tresca remained a symbol for many Italian Americans, like Efrem Bartoletti, an immigrant poet of Scranton who dedicated the poem "Ricordando Carlo Tresca" to him: "And you deserved another destiny, / a honored old age / a quiet sunset and not a death / violent and undignified."[117]

Poetics of the Working Immigrant

Another group of autobiographies of workers stands out for being more introspective and poetical than the rest. Poetry and emotion mainly stem from these writers' pride for their working-class ethos and their strong immigrant nerve.

PASCAL D'ANGELO ∾ Perhaps the best-known and best-written autobiography of a first-generation immigrant is Pascal D'Angelo's *Son of Italy*, the story of a boy who comes of age in a masculine society of workers who "stick together like a swarm of bees from the same beehive."[118] Born in Introdacqua (Sulmona) in the region of Abruzzi in 1894, D'Angelo described his timeless land as a "peaceful" place and "my people" as "a people of seers and poets. We believe in dreams. . . . We have men who can tell the future and ageless hags who know the secrets of the mountain."[119] He arrived in Ellis Island in 1910 at sixteen.

D'Angelo never denied his existence as a pick-and-shovel worker, but his personality had a distinctively poetic cast, and he strongly cultivated the idea of being considered a poet, partly by continuing his education. He started by memorizing Webster's dictionary, reading poetry and magazines, and writing jokes to tell his friends. He became the topic of his friends' speculation: Will he always remain a laborer because he was born one? Will he advance in the world? Can he become a foreman? He aimed high, to a literary career, and he left his job to pursue it. He spent his days in the public library and nights in a malodorous former chicken coop that flooded with each storm and was reachable through the toilet of ten families: "At least if my body was living in a world of horror I could build a world of beauty for my soul."[120] He succeeded in his literary pursuits when his poems were finally accepted and published by Carl Van Doren, the editor of *The Nation,* who then awarded him with the magazine's poetry prize.

D'Angelo wrote as a poet and inserted poetry into his autobiography, yet he did not shy away from his laborer's roots. He never denied his work ethic and his humble origins, and he stressed his struggles, not his successes, barely giving a page to his literary pursuits. At the end he praised his triumph, but this again is shown though the eyes of Italian working men: "But more sincere and dearer to my heart were the tributes of my fellow workers who recognized that at last one of them had risen from the ditches and quicksands of toil to speak his heart to the upper world. And sweeter yet was the happiness of my parents who realized that after all I had not really gone astray, but had sought and attained a goal from the deep-worn groove of peasant drudgery."[121]

For D'Angelo, writing his story was the last effort to symbolically uplift himself and step into the upper world. Even if it didn't bring money, for D'Angelo writing was what made a man a man: "Who hears the thuds of the pick and the jingling of the shovel. All my works are lost, lost forever. But if I write a good line of poetry—then when the night comes, and I cease writing, my work is not lost. My line is still there. It can be read by you to-day and anyone else to-morrow. But my pick and shovel work cannot be read either by you to-day or by anyone else tomorrow."[122]

ANTONIO DE PIERO ∾ The bricklayer Antonio De Piero was born in the small town of Cordenons (Pordenone) in Friuli (northeastern Italy) in 1875; he worked in Germany and Canada before settling on Staten Island with his oldest son.[123] He was self-taught, and his writing is filled with mistakes in spelling and syntax that enliven his vivacious tone. He described his decision to emigrate to his wife: "I had just finished this meditation, I entered the house my wife asked me about my preoccupation, I answered her immediately. Listen, Catina, I said; our savings are melting like snow in the sun our dreams are disappearing, no house, no fields, and if nothing changes also the little money we have will go, and soon we will remain in the blackest misery."[124] De Piero describes with his disjunctive, poetic personal style the anguish of his immigration: "I took the sack on my shoulders, got lost in the darkness . . . the howls of dogs awaken by the noise of the poor travelers. Resigned with rhythmic steps, with bowed head under the weight of my bag, starting to fight against destiny, the way was opening toward . . . the unknown."[125]

De Piero explained his decision to work with the quarantined immigrants on Ellis Island and reported his remuneration: "a hospital of diseases, infective typhus, smallpox, scarlet fever, yellow fever, they send them all here for the fear the disease can spread in the city and the epidemic widens. So it was necessary to be brave, what do you think? But the clean hundred dollars a month made me brave."[126]

CARMINE IANNACE ∾ A hymn to work is sung by the unskilled laborer Carmine Biagio Iannace, who wrote his witty and unpretentious autobiography in 1966, at seventy-five, two years before his death. His is such a poetic style that it does not seem to come from the pen of a man with a third-grade education. This is how he describes the importance of work: "But the most important element, which is the touchstone between the American and the non-American, is the idea of work as a dignified activity. In coming to America, one enters a new dimension if, consciously or unconsciously, he accepts the idea of work as a vital opportunity to express himself, as a hymn to life and the physical and mental possibilities of being productive, as a means of communicating with others and with the new society. It is a fusing of one's own sweat with the great American experiment, it is feeling oneself different and equal, creature and creator."[127]

Born in 1890 in San Leucio del Sannio (Benevento), he came to the United States at sixteen in 1906, eager to discover his America. He found a job with a gang of *paesani* on the Erie Railroad and worked as an unskilled laborer, a factory handyman, and a gardener. His story describes the duplicity of the immigrant—dream and reality, cross and delight, Italy and America: "It was like living a double life; not two different or opposing lives, but one having double value."[128]

Back and forth between his two countries, he ultimately chose to be an immigrant: "You have tasted the air of America and sometimes you are here and sometimes you are not. You're like a bird out of a cage. Have you ever observed your blackbirds when they are left out of the cage? They sing more than the others. They flit about more than the others, they hop, they rub their wings in the dust, but they refuse to go away. They're free and they're not free' . . . Agnesella was right. Had I not considered that time an intermission, a period of wiling away the time, I would have died of a broken heart. I had to return to America. It was as if there I lacked air."[129]

Iannace's Italy is a bucolic place where song resonates in the air, peasants sing to each other, and boys and girls flirt from the neighboring hills—serenading under the balconies and singing in the bars. "We drank out of the crystal pitcher that I had brought from America. . . . and the warmth multiplied in their eyes was reflected in the thousand facets of the pitcher. And the wine made the picture laugh. . . . 'This is America,' they said, passing the pitcher and holding it just at eye level."[130] He associated the pleasure of America and the pain of leaving, as he describes a decision to again leave Italy: "I tormented myself night and day. There had to be a way out. . . . My departure was set for October 15. Like the first time I had left, neither my father nor my brother accompanied me to the station. This time, however, it made me happy, almost as if America began there, with that violent separation from my family. "[131]

PIETRO GRECO ✵ Pietro Greco's unpublished and apparently un-finished autobiography gives as much importance to other immi-grants as to his own life.[132] Chapters of his book are dedicated to the descriptions of the evil foreman Michele Carbone, the blacksmith Don Ciccio, his beloved Elvira, and numerous other characters who are part of his immigrant family. Greco had a third-grade education and worked all his life in Kenyon's military clothing factory in Brooklyn but, like Pascal D'Angelo, he was fascinated by the world of culture and strove to find his place in it. He tried to publish his poems in New York's Italian newspapers (*La Follia* published one) and organized a theater group with his fellow immigrants.

Born in 1889, in the little village of Sant'Andrea Apostolo sullo Ionio (Catanzaro), Pietro Greco, the son of a tailor, emigrated at fif-teen. A boy so paralyzed by shyness he couldn't even bear to deliver the clothing to his father's clients, that shyness cost him endless frus-tration: "My brother judged me from my shyness! He never thought it was fruit of an excessive sensibility and it had nothing to do with imbecility."[133] In New York, Greco found soul mates in his coworkers, who shared his love for poetry. These factory workers took advantage of their free time to read poetry aloud, seated on bundles of war uni-forms: "Since this was allowed, my friend Procopio and I would lie down on the huge stacks of jackets and coats lying on the floor like rags, without respect for those soldiers that would wear them, and we would read aloud Stecchetti's poems, trendy at the time, surrounded by a group of merry and beautiful girls, in their years' prime, fresh and fragrant like May roses who loved poetry and the way Procopio and I read it."[134] Greco's immigrants created a community of their own: "No other factory hired a larger number of Italians who spoke only exclusively Italian in it. . . . It was as if I were in Italy."[135]

Greco's Little Italy is the picturesque neighborhood transported from Naples or Palermo with its typical colors and sounds. But he also cut out a cultural space distinguished by the language. He described the crowded evenings in the little theater Regina Margherita, where immigrants applaud Lina Baccigalupi and Rocco De Russo (whose autobiography is treated in this book). He founded a group of young immigrant actors (Filodrammatica Virginia Reiter) that lasted five years. He tried to publish a magazine in Italian. He organized a successful evening of poetry and song called Piedigrotta della Canzone Napoletana. He met Riccardo Cordiferro, editor of *La Follia,* and described the cultural scuffle that took place in his office, a scene contrasting with the usual descriptions of violent Italian knife fights: "In the office there was a little man who was fighting and wanting Cordiferro to publish his sonnet. 'You don't know who I am, I am Professor Alberico Torquato!'—'A plagiarist, says Cordiferro,' and he picked up a poem by Foscolo from which he had copied." When the professor read it and looked surprised, he knocked his head with his finger: "Oh, 'we met with Foscolo . . . I didn't do it on purpose. We just met, that's all."[136]

Pompous in tone, the seventy-six-year-old Pietro Greco provides us with his own immigrant philosophy. Greco's quiet individualism preached resilience against adversity. Surviving is the goal of the quiet hero: "The man who has been hit must resign, if he doesn't want to die. Let him keep the flame of hope lit and smile at life! Let him create a new existence! Let him gather the broken pieces . . . react to pain . . . live, even if forced to adapt into modest limits, but live!"[137]

Greco's cultural "Piccola Italia" finds its highest moment in his description of Mastro Gaspare's barbershop, which became an unexpected kingdom of poetry. "Mastro Gaspare's poetry was not put on paper to be preserved; it had the lifetime of some combinations of clouds that appear beautiful and suggestive in the blue immensity of space, but a sudden wind destroys and dissolves, and they only remain in the memory of those who saw them."[138] "In the shop of Mastro Gaspare everything seemed to be tied to poetry and governed by its rhythm, all harmonized: from the slow dripping of the small water basin in a corner, to the monotonous slow ticketing of the clock on the left. In that small barber shop all was poetic and musical!"[139] Greco recognized the poet in a barber that others see as "an bald old donkey."[140] He significantly leaves his autobiography unfinished on the tomb of Gaspare.

GABRIEL IAMURRI ∞ Gabriel Iamurri, who wrote his autobiography when he was sixty-three, was a worker gifted with rhetorical strength.[141] He studied two years in a seminary, then at the Extension University of Chicago, La Salle, but worked all his life as a road builder and, after his marriage and after fighting in World War I, he ran a small confectionery store. Here he finds happiness because he was able to write "on almost anything that my imagination could have conceived; and painting between times for change."[142]

Born in Carpinone (Campobasso) in 1880, Gabriel Iamurri started his life with episodes of survival, when his parents twice took him for dead. Iamurri immigrated to America in 1895 as a boy, dreaming of American fairy tales and stories of Columbus. In New York, "I felt like one who is carried somewhere into the woods blindfolded knowing where he is but not knowing where he came from nor where to go to get out."[143] Even the Statue of Liberty, comfort for many, was silent for him: "she could not speak, she was mute, could not tell me where to go or what to do about it."[144] In Iamurri we not only find a survivor, but also the concept of the immigrant as a man in history. Iamurri was sure that personal talent alone is never sufficient: "in order to succeed [one] not only has to have certain talents, but also the soil wherein they can develop, where they can grow to their full size, for if not they will die with him and nothing will ever be known."[145]

He also described this concept with a comparison between the different conditions of the American pilgrims and the Italian immigrants: "The former didn't have to learn a new language, didn't have to adapt themselves to a new custom, didn't have to go through the trouble to understand new laws and a new way of living, besides, the Pilgrims, as soon as they set foot on this Continent, soon became the owners of it, if not of the whole land, at least, as much as they then needed. Their main struggle was mostly with the elements, the Indians were no match for them. . . . The same cannot be said of those who came later; their main struggle was with man-made elements. They landed not only on foreign soil but had besides to learn a new language, the worst stumbling block of one's success."[146]

Iamurri's obstacles in America were many; he recounted numerous misunderstandings of the language and tales of horrible working conditions that run through many autobiographies: "no man can either paint it with the brush or describe it with the pen, for the human mind can never conceive or grasp how hard they worked us."[147] "A shovel, a pickaxe, any kind of tool had more value for them than one of us; for if a man lost his life for them he could soon be replaced without any cost to them, but if a shovel or a pick was broken, it was a different story, it cost them something."[148] "Nothing is ever recorded of their suffering, their tears, of their hunger, and, especially of the injustice they suffered at the hands of their employers. They are indeed the forgotten man, the unknown soldier who gave much for the prosperity and greatness of the country but received very little in return."[149]

In the last chapter of Iamurri's autobiography, he tells of sitting on a bench, "disheartened on account of an article I had written which the press did not accept," when he saw a grasshopper trying to get out of a steep sandy hole. "He made thirty-six attempts but failed, the thirty-seventh he succeeded—got out of it. I clapped my hands several times in an expression of admiration for him, for his determination not to surrender. . . . And here I am, I said to myself, an old buck, exhausted, depressed, dejected. . . . The classic lesson imparted to me by the grasshopper was salutary, for it spurred me not to give up but keep on trying until I would succeed."[150]

PIETRO TOFFOLO ∾ A terrace maker and mosaic decorator with an excruciatingly divided soul, Pietro Toffolo was a returned immigrant who wrote his story in 1977, before his final return home to Friuli.[151] Toffolo was born in Heidelberg, of immigrant parents, in 1911. His story is written in broken English, Friulano, and Italian; his sisters, who found his notebook after his death, had it translated into Italian. Toffolo's writing is directed inside his soul, and aching, he describes his split identity after fifty years of living in New York. His images in describing his immigration are extremely poetic. In New York he described himself with the imagery of a mountain boy by depicting himself scared like a pursued deer. Toffolo's New York is described with a mountaineer's mind: "New York in 1927 wasn't like today, but to me it seemed so new, so big, from the subway to the skyscrapers similar to the Alps but man-made. Those buildings so much taller than the campanile of my church scared me and made me dream, dreams of riches, of being able to return and bring grandfather across the Ocean and show him all the wonder of this new world as he had shown me our small world."[152]

Toffolo has a particular touch in describing the inner life of the immigrant. When he was detained in Ellis Island for a period, he described the familiar view: "I remember well that dinners I would never tire to watch the lights of New York, the flame in the hand of the Statue of Liberty, the silver sparkles on the harbor's water, the ferry-boat lights sliding to and from Staten Island and all this wasn't a dream!"[153]

Yet through the years he went back and forth, like a bird, and feels split between the two lands: "Which half will decide to join the other? Or has destiny already decided my end, and the end of these two loves of mine that only death can erase?" "In October of 1969 I was back home again. It should have been forever, but my heart was divided in two, not only marked. Leaving the United States would have been worse than death. I lived there forty-two of my 58 years of life, since I was 16, there I had learned to live, a way of life that I wish for my people and all the people of the world. Because to consider well, despite its deficiencies and mistakes, in the United States any man can live in liberty and human dignity, if he wants it. His identity consists in his individuality, not in a number, and he doesn't have to produce sparkles when walking to be noticed."[154] Eventually, especially after World War II, old views and people of Friuli are no longer the same, and Toffolo inconsolably wrote about the loss of his nest: "HOME is no more."

CARLO DONDERO ∾ Carlo Dondero was a man of Risorgimento, infused with 1800 Italian rhetoric even if a humble immigrant. He worked as a stonecutter and then as a typesetter in San Francisco, contributing to the local cultural life. His grandson helped him edit his papers and publish his autobiography when he was ninety-one years old.[155] Dondero played an important yet silent role in the history of California behind the scenes of history: he was the typesetter who printed the first issue of the *San Francisco Chronicle* and a stonecutter who provided marble to build Stanford University. Dondero is the prototype of the Italian immigrant who, without being successful and remembered, is behind many great enterprises. If his name will be never immortalized on a plaque on the wall, he is nevertheless the one who provided the very substance of history's "marble." This awareness and the pride that he poured into his construction work is evident when he notes that his marble work survived the 1906 earthquake: "the museum came through being the only building that remained standing with all its marble walls still intact as they are today."[156]

Short in stature, with a typical nineteenth-century triangle of a beard and strong moustache, Dondero was remembered in his grandson's preface as an old man sitting under the knotty grape arbor of his home in a typical Italian American and patriarchal setting—the very grape arbor he sat under to write his memoirs. He appears in his autobiography as a romantic man, full of patriotic ideals of political freedom. He was always in contact with intellectuals and journalists; he wrote some articles of his own, such as one he included in the book in defense of Italians. He was editor of *Rassegna Commerciale* of the Italian Chamber of Commerce in San Francisco, where he worked as a secretary. In his late years he was pro–Italian American, but against the Italian American yes-men of the Church and the monarchic consul. Naturally, his idol was Giuseppe Garibaldi. He himself gives the interpretative key to his book, as he describes in his introduction, "a great moral and educational Italian-American narrative, of drama, of pure, immortal Washingtonism and Lincolnism, and tasting of sublime Italian sacrifices and love, written for the family, for the school, for the patriot, for the sincere churchmen of all creeds and for all the good souls of the world. . . . [where] the pioneers are not essentially admired for the shining pile of their luck, but for the nobility of their individual traits and the merits of their loftiness of heart and mind. Woman is honored as the supreme beauty of creation . . . I gave the best part of my life to a true and unselfish Americanism."[157]

The immigrant of Dondero's autobiography is a pioneer seen in a romantic light. He painted his self-portrait as an idealist who, refusing the lure of money, prefers ideals to coins: "I never knew a lust for gold nor greed and my glory was fulfilled with a host of friends and many wonderful children."[158] "To me, my life in California has been a great story, one of the opportunities offered people who want to prove themselves capable of doing many things."[159] His own immigration had an epic beginning that was not uncommon among our autobiographers: "one fatal, dark evening, while feeding the livestock on his farm, my father was bitten by a viper hiding in the hay. He died a horrible, agonizing death within a few hours."[160]

Dondero's initiation to American labor started in the street of New York, where chance takes him into a printing shop, like Benjamin Franklin. It was again the hand of destiny: a snow blizzard forced him to enter the first door he found open in the street, a printing shop, where he was hired as a typesetter for *L'eco d'Italia*. He went west during the gold rush of 1859–62 with his friend Jack De Martini, a bread maker. As in a children's tale, he found four diamonds on the ground, droppings of some illicit activity, and with them bought a marble quarry that he calls "Carrara." In San Francisco he opened his own printing shop, and worked as a writer of love letters for voiceless men seeking Italian brides: "Many brides came to San Francisco as a result of the love letters I had written."[161] He became the brother-in-law of Andrea Sbarboro, founder of the Italian Swiss Colony Winery and a banker, with whom he printed the textbooks for the School of English for immigrants, thus contributing to the integration of the San Francisco colony.

EMANUELE CARNEVALI ❧ On the far side of the spectrum of the poetical working man, we must insert Emanuele Carnevali, who understands that America means work, and he hates it for this. A poet of some fame ("I am nothing but a pot full of lilies, a noise, a wind, nothing more"),[162] Emanuele Carnevali wrote his autobiography on his deathbed, vexed by an illness that made him tremble and shake, in Italy. He was an unusual immigrant who died in secret during World War II.

Carnevali did not give any dates, but brushed over his life in impressionistic sketches. He described his illness-ridden youth in different cities (Biella, Pistoia, Bologna) where his crazy mother took him; he was expelled from military school; he decided to leave for America as a rebellious adolescent.

When he arrived in New York he experienced "one of the great disillusions of my entire unhappy life. These famous skyscrapers were nothing more than great boxes standing upright or on one side, terrifically futile, frightfully irrelevant, so commonplace that one felt he had seen the same thing somewhere before."[163] He lived like an impoverished immigrant—begging for jobs, living in shabby places, and eating the city's free meals with "men like me who carried rage and hunger through the streets for New York, walking, walking, until human strength was practically extinguished."[164] It is work and the search for work that he found particularly degrading: "the JOB, that damnable affair. THE JOB. Nightmare of the hunted, THE JOB. This misery, this anxiety, this kind of neurasthenia, this ungrateful, this blood-sucking thing. THE JOB, this piecemeal death, this fear that grips you in the stomach, this sovereign lady who leaks terror, who eats the very heart out of man."[165]

Carnevali, who had never worked, found himself hired in grocery stores, restaurants, and hotels as an errand boy, a waiter, and a cleaner. He was fired each time, but always fought back. He survived by scraping bread crusts and cleaning them under the water, picking up cigarette butts on the streets. He never once saw his identity reflected in his working and earning a living, as other working immigrants. His employment was instead a curse: "enough of the places where I worked! I curse them all! I never had a single hour of joyous labor, not one hour, unless I was drunk, as frequently happened."[166]

Immigration crushed him and he eventually returned to Italy as a "shipwreck—my sick body, / and this feeble candle-light—my soul."[167]

RAFFAELLO LUGNANI AND ANTONIO ANDREONI: VERSE AUTO-BIOGRAPHIES ∾ Very unusual autobiographies were written by two farmer-poets, Raffaello Lugnani and Antonio Andreoni. Without knowing about each other, they each wrote their autobiographies in verse once they returned home in Tuscany. These two poets demonstrate the regional strength of the rural storyteller tradition discussed in part one of this book. The verse form of *ottave* (eight-line stanzas) for Andreoni and *sestine* (six lines) for Lugnani descends from *poemi cavallereschi*. In fact, Andreoni's family has names that are found in these famous poetic legends—such as Solimano, Clorinda, Orlando and Achille.

For these two immigrant writers, then, it is only a matter of donning the hero's clothes, to "move their experiences into the model of the extraordinary adventures of those literary knightly heroes."[168] It is possible at times, especially in Andreoni's high-sounding verse, to be reminded of the folly of Don Quixote, who transforms his unromantic adventures into knightly epics. The great enemy of these immigrants' tales becomes immigration itself.

Epic genre is perfectly congenial to these stories of immigration. It offers the mode of individualism needed by the farmer, who has strengthened his identity mainly through his travel. Just as autobiography is the perfect form for life stories of immigration, these epics correspond to the writer's needs. The narrative form of these epics responds to the oral tradition of peasant culture: "the dimension of creativity has remained essential in all popular cultures, where it manifests in different genres and forms, in the measure in which living conditions give good occasions of space and time."[169] The presence of the narrating voice "is perfectly congenial to the narrative practice of a rural milieu."[170]

A short moustache over a sarcastic little smile, a raised eyebrow, and a hand clutching his traveler's sack: this is how Raffaello Lugnani, ready to leave, appears in his photograph. He has a mandolin, a jolly nature, and a curiosity that prevents him from being content with what he has. He seems bitten by the tarantula, he cannot stop nor rest in his constant fight against misfortunes that end up crippling his body. Born in 1881 in the province of Pisa, he left for the United States when he was twenty-two; in 1902, he would return again in 1906 and 1923.[171] He traveled all over the country, as far as Alaska, unable to stop, unable to find peace. Surely he escaped from a familiar situation that he did not like: he married the daughter of a rich farmer who after only one week resented his leaving and his return without money.[172] Not only did he come back penniless, he was also afflicted with Parkinson's disease. He started to write his memoirs during his third trip and finished after he came back in 1935; he died silently in 1952.

Lugnani's book is exceptional. His son has his original manuscript, written in a long and tilted handwriting on a plain book of days with a leather cover. Ornamented with drawings that had a documentary value, this is the story of thirty years of emigration, written by an uneducated miner, in over a thousand six-line stanzas, sometimes in irregular hendecasyllable (eleven-syllable verses). The rhyme is AB-ABCC, and it is usually an easy rhyme, often made with infinitives (*-are*, *-ere*, *-ire*). The drama of migration is thus lightened by the music of its verse. This harmony transforms his experience into a legendary enterprise, epic and heroic, but enjoyably airy: "It will be fun for the readers / who will put the spices in the sauce."[173] He also ends his story with the moral of an oral tale: "this is true, I give you my word, / that I still have its fishbones in my throat,"[174] Readers who know Italian will want to read the original version here in the notes, but even those who can't understand will appreciate the charming music of the original words.

Lugnani's "immigrant I" is characterized by a strong optimism that permeates these verses. The poet feels to be a hero whose life has been a constant resistance against the blows of destiny. Having lost almost everything, he is still able to smile back. Lugnani is an ironist of failure ("we tried to change destiny, / we'll be satisfied with having tried,")[175] a cheerful storyteller of tragedy ("America took my best years, / little money it gave me, and many diseases").[176] This farmer-poet does not refrain from echoing Dante's *Divine Comedy*: "that strange mountain,"[177] "it looked like a devil, / of those born before the Messiah,"[178] "I saw all the stars and Paradise"[179] "among strange people in far lands."[180] Curiosity moved this pilgrim. His thirst for novelty was his way of being fully human. Like Dante's Ulysses, moved by his arrogant curiosity, Lugnani is moved by his understanding of what being a man means: "my walking cannot be intimidated / we are men and we have to face, / nothing in the world can frighten us."[181]

In addition to the echoes from Dante and Ariosto, the literary precedent of Lugnani's storytelling is perhaps in the tradition of the *epica maccheronica*, an oral production since the Italian Middle Ages played by the lower strata of the population. In response to the high epic of knights and kings, the epic of macaronic verse featured ragamuffins and chicken thieves. They are antiheroes who nevertheless live big adventures between their cabbages hurlings and battles with pots and pans. It was the epic for the poor, for those who did not have courtly poets to sing their dynasties.

Lugnani's epic reflects this genre mostly because his adventures often end in failure. His first arrival in New York in front of the Statue of Liberty was antiheroic, as Liberty resembles the siren of the Odyssey: "that woman makes you dream if you watch it: / it seems she wants to erase your fear, / she teaches to find freedom, / to the poor ones that go to adventures, / but those who think so, are deluded: / here a free man becomes a real slave."[182] He crossed America en route to San Francisco, where he was part of a colony of Massarosa people. He worked in restaurants and in the fields, where his poetry (sounding like Ariosto) described his job trimming the trees: "the sun now kissed that land that he could never see, / full of love; even the grass, previously hidden by the shadow, / regained the prime morning dew, / part was reborn, part was relieved, / full of ardor the sun kissed it."[183]

Lugnani's verse speaks of both the hard and the funny sides of immigrant life. His difficulty with English is ironically explained: "English is a nice language to listen, but you can understand fish for flesh."[184] We learn his jobs: pounding spikes on the railroads, gardening, keeping the animals in various stables and pens. He also includes tragic moments, like the death of the young immigrant with typhus, or his own nostalgia for home: "You can imagine what a flowery age / I spent, so far from my parents, / so soon sacrificing my life / like the fall sacrifices the color of flowers, / but it was my destiny to face, / I could not go back."[185] He hit bottom when he was hired as a shepherd in a isolated cabin in California, and was scared to death by its loneliness and the contact with Indians. It was an impossible life for an Italian peasant used to living elbow to elbow with other people— "tranquil in my bed I would fall asleep, / knowing I was in town among a hundred people."[186] The wilderness was too inhuman for him: he is advised to kill anybody who comes close and leave him there.

Lugnani survived the 1906 earthquake during his second trip, and when he traveled to Alaska to work in a mine, he found a horrifying reality of ice and sorrow. Inhumanity is his memory: "I always walked ahead with courage, / thirty miles of iced lakes, / only in the company of all the saints, / always careful to look in each direction. / We do not remember who we are; / life there is desperate."[187] He saw a friend mauled by a white bear; he shot at an Indian; he survived fires and mine explosions; and he even had a Boccaccio-like adventure in a convent, where he pretended to be castrated in order to work, and escaped the day of the doctor's visit.

In sum, Lugnani speaks of emigration as both a blessing and a trap of destiny. Immigration is a constriction to change and to hope, and for him hope is the worst enemy of the poor because it makes him restless. Lugnani in fact seems to love change itself. Like Don Quixote, he is never content with a quiet situation once he finds another one, craving for mutation. More than once, he refers to immigration as a "dream," not death, but worse than death: "It seems like a dream, if you think about it, / I who say the truth assure you, / that having to leave from everyone, / can seem a mystery to those who don't know; / some think death is the same, / but instead dying ends all evils."[188] When time passes and he is not able to raise money, his comments become bitter, such as this one against Italian rumors: "many in Italy make their comments: / they say it is easy to work here in America, / instead we have to pass certain moments! . . . / I would like to see them trying, / certainly they could then say / how much we have to suffer here."[189] Nevertheless he was proud of having worked and seen America, unlike other immigrants who only worked as brutes: "They saw America only from outside, / they have lived inside a sac, / they only worked as possessed by the devil."[190]

Antonio Andreoni was a farmer from the countryside of Lucca, born in 1859, who came to the United States between 1903 and 1906. He looked for jobs wherever life took him, even in far and lonely regions: he traveled through Chicago, Missouri, and Montana, where he worked for the Northern Pacific Railroad. He returned home with just enough money to fix his farm for his seven children; he died in 1945 and is buried in the cemetery of Capannori. His work, *Passaggio di Andreoni Antonio nell'America del Nord,* was despitefully refused by the local school teacher as deserving publication, and thus remained to gather dust in the attic of his farmhouse until his great-granddaughter, Maria Berdinelli Predelli, found it and published it in 1997, adding a deep critical apparatus that shows its literary influences.[191] Many of them jump right at the eye, like the *captatio benevolentiae,* the incipit addressed to the Muse, the appeals to the reader, and the many poetic similes.

Andreoni's life epic is pinned on the truth of facts at the very beginning and end of the narration. Like Lugnani, in his opening Andreoni resorts to the feast metaphor, comparing his narration to a lavish dish with "true" ingredients: "Friends of mine, if you'll listen to me, / I want to tell you a true fact, / and I am sure you'll remain satisfied / as with a big dinner."[192] At the end, he appeals to witnesses—names and last names—to prove the truth of his story.

The sadness of Andreoni's departure is rarefied by his verses: "merrily arrived at the station, / an echo of joined voices resounded, / but I, poor and suffering, / was thinking of the big wounds / I had in my heart, / since I left there a crying wife, the sons and the games / I played with friends and relatives, / and my heart was in big torments."[193] He describes the storm during the trip as a fight between Titans, like in a knightly romance: "certain waves so tall came toward us / and they lost their shape and their wave form, / now the ship raised to the stars / and on the clouds it seemed to be raising its sides."[194] As a man of survival, Andreoni does not forget to thank his Savior: "I thank Heaven with all my heart, that now that tempest has passed."[195] In the same way, when he remained miraculously alive after a mine accident, he says: "this is the second time / that the infinite Goodness saved my life."[196]

His lament over the working conditions of the immigrant is loud and clear. In America the immigrant becomes a brute, a sweaty animal: "we arrived there sweating like oxen / with certain faces like assassins."[197]

Andreoni described some funny episodes of life among workers, jokes, and friendships, but most of all he stressed the difficult aspects of immigration. His work on the railroad is always bestial: "It is true, / when the cat is present, / the mouse can't do as he likes: / and there being all our superiors, / we had to work like oxen."[198] His work became a prison because he was forced to work. Thus, with his companions, he became a strike-breaker ("And never we are heard complaining, / because my gang is all made of people / who need to earn their money"),[199] but that lasted only one day because they realized the boss was paying them unfairly.

Being a foreigner, a dago, and having seven children to feed ("I have more than one bowl to fill"),[200] Andreoni must accept his life with the philosophy of the humble immigrant. Resignation and a contentedness are his suffered choice, and the bread of the poor. When not receiving a letter from home, Andreoni explains his preoccupation and refers to destiny's will with an ironical snarl: "It seems that destiny does it on purpose, / making me suffer until I die."[201] Nonetheless, he accepts everything with the immigrant's resignation: "I always let the good God do what he wants, / He always makes things right, and puts them at his will, / with patience I bear my sufferance / because bearing them is my duty."[202]

These last two autobiographies are remarkable for the musical form of their verse that transforms them into a light testimony of the familiar themes of immigration. They are almost playful, almost carefree in spite of their authors' labors. They are in the high tradition of epic adventure, of something to be sung to future generations.

3 Immigrant Artists

These Italian immigrants came to America to pursue an artistic dream; but they remain "immigrant workers" at heart. They strongly maintain the ethos of the artisan, with its mixture of manual labor and creativity, more than pretenses of artistic genius. They tell their stories in the quiet mode that links our autobiographies. One of them, especially, who does not find success, Luigi Olari, strikes a very human note in his description of failures. Even the quite known Alfred Crimi, a painter; Pietro Montana, a sculptor; and Luigi Lombardi, an orchestra director, never put on airs about the position they acquired but always highlight their struggles, being men of survival. Two of them, the actors Rocco De Russo and Emanuel Gatti, directly experience the decline of theater due to television, and their autobiographies become narratives of the end of an era more than tales of personal triumph. All of these artists started at the bottom, and they unabashedly admit that.

GIOVANNI ZAVATTI ∾ The tenor Giovanni Zavatti came to America as a water boy for woodcutters. The inauspicious beginning of his career started in the harbor of Naples, where he was almost defrauded of his belongings and his money.[1] At first he used to sing serenades for his friends' girlfriends in the dark, as he was too shy to sing in the daylight. When he sang on the day of his departure for America, only a horse recognizes his talent: "The driver begged me to sing something and I timidly started to sing 'Silenzio cantatore,' a song I used to sing with my brother Antonio. Slowly my shyness disappeared, my voice was pleasant and suddenly something strange happened. The horse that pulled the carriage stopped without a reason. The driver started to laugh and complimented me by saying that his horse stopped only when he heard a voice he liked."[2]

Zavatti was born in 1911 in Cansano, a small mountain in Maiella, in the province of L'Aquila. He was the son of an immigrant father, a miner, absent physically and also financially after the failure of his bank. Giovanni was the only hope for his mother and four brothers and sisters, "one of the merriest families of the village."[3] He was forced to migrate to the United States to reach his father and older brother when he was only fourteen: "unfortunately my father did not have my artistic passion so he imposed his will and made me leave."[4] His mother sewed double pockets on his pants and a double sole in his shoe to hide his money. The sadness of his departure is an important image in his story, as it is in most of these autobiographies.

He mingled with "the big crowd of immigrants" in the harbor of Naples. Piazzetta Maculatella, where the American consulate was located, was called also "the square of desirers, because all those people longed for an immigrant visa and not all were so lucky to get it."[5] Only seeing the great ship "Cristoforo Colombo" that has to take him to America, and hearing some immigrant singing "Santa Lucia luntana," Giovanni succumbed to emotion: "Suddenly I became sad and a thousand thoughts came crowding my mind: why was I leaving my native town? Why was I leaving my family? Why was I going so far? Where was I going? Why was I going? Would it really be better my life far from my beautiful Italy? Was it worth starting all over again? These were the questions I posed myself and did not know how to answer; some of these I still have to answer after so many years of life."[6]

Twenty-eight days later, Zavatti arrived in New York, and was not impressed with its unadorned buildings and its chain-gang labor. He took many different manual labor jobs through his travels for work in the West, and even tried boxing, but finally found various jobs with theater companies until his debut in Los Angeles with *Carmen*. Especially poignant is his explanation of how his crude beginnings had to remain a secret from the public as his new biography was created to go along with his rising artistic recognition. According to the producers, "the lie is necessary: your publicity has to be that of a tenor scriptured from Italy who sang for the pope and the church when he was a child."[7] If this is his public image, by the time he wrote his autobiography he had reclaimed his real life, his truth, his persona, and he cherished all the hard aspects of his life as an immigrant and as a miner.

Zavatti attained success in Phoenix, Hollywood, Oklahoma. His recognition finally brought his family together—mother, brothers, and sisters—in California. Writing at the age of sixty, Zavatti described all his performances and his successes as a tenor. He never forgot to paint himself as a proud Italian, and never stopped feeling love for his homeland: "I lived my life in America and with pride I serve my adoptive Motherland, but my blood is Italian and so it will remain until my last breath."[8] His Italian pride also pervaded his professional life: in Hollywood in the 1950s, he refused to dub the movies where the Italian plays a negative role. Here is his recollection of his big refusal to dub a military film where he had to be the mayor of a little Italian town who pulls his donkey to meet an American commander and "kneeled on his feet crying like a fool of an asylum":[9]

"Refusing it, I commented: You producers, give your soul to the devil for love of money, and step on anything, without thinking to the degradation of a proud people that gave civility, law, and order to your ancestors. It is true that Italy lost a war it did not wish, but it never lost its honor in thousands years of history. For me it would have been a real shame had I accepted to degrade the greatness and pride of my people."[10]

LUIGI OLARI ∾ A vastly different story is that of another singer, Luigi Olari. His autobiography has many weak and confused points, but also numerous striking images of a stubborn immigrant dreamer.[11] He had only a third-grade education, and claimed he studied voice with the worst maestri, who ruined his voice. Olari had a desperate need for an audience, and his bitter autobiography, exceptionally written in third person, is another attempt to find one, like when he sings to the birds of Central Park after a long day as a janitor.

Born "in Pegazzano, a small village on the Parmesan Apennine on February 16, 1894,"[12] he was called a "miracle baby" when a paralysis was healed. At seventeen he went to France for road work; in 1914 he traveled to San Francisco, for similar work. As soon as he could afford to, he bought a pair of suits, a watch with a golden chain, and found a voice coach.[13] His American artistic adventure started in difficult circumstances. He traveled to New York in 1923 and found odd jobs as a waiter and a dishwasher; he got a part in the operetta *Mikado,* but to work in it he has to quit washing floors, and he started going into debt for food. He slept in train stations and was in considerable debt: "He was a little ashamed because he owed money to everyone, 500 dollars more or less."[14] In the Depression, he could find no music jobs and he started cleaning floors again.

At fifty-seven, Olari made a last effort to find an audience and used a good cause, a fundraising for the kindergarten in his hometown, to organize a debut in Carnegie Hall. He earned just a little more than what he spent for the production and was able to send one hundred dollars to his town. This was the biggest attempt to make himself with his own strength, and he enrolled the services of his entire family to take care of every last detail: "he wrote the invitation letters to newspapers and music magazines. He prepared the posters, wrote his biography. The night of the concert his wife stayed at the cashier, his daughter helped the people to their seats and he himself stood at the door to collect the tickets."[15] He prepared a performance of twenty-four *romanze,* and had to bear the humiliation of making fun of himself for the sake of the audience, singing two songs dressed as a janitor with a broom in his hands. At the end of the show, he was broken. The dream of becoming a millionaire—to buy himself a new set of false teeth—was quickly forgotten.

Failure embittered Olari even further, and he took to singing to the birds in the park after work. His biggest triumph was that he sent a musical prayer to Berceto, and learned that they were singing it in church and teaching it to the children. When he visited Italy for a short time he had other small triumphs, such as a few concerts and the privilege of singing for the captain of the ship *Achille Lauro,* who upgraded him to first class. Olari thus inverted the myth, and saw Italy as his new promised land: "he had found more satisfaction in his brief visit to Italy than in the 41 years passed in America because in Italy there was still a little conscience and a little consideration for honest people."[16]

LUIGI LOMBARDI ∾ If luckier than Luigi Olari, the musician Luigi Lombardi was similarly imaginative in his autobiography.[17] Instead of writing his biography, he prepared his eulogy, half seriously half jokingly, depicting himself as somebody who is satisfied with his life, even if it hasn't been the most brilliant: "O promenader promenading / Along these silent premises / Of the underworld / Stop! / Bow your head (no more than you need to read these words) / Don't take off your hat (why should you) / And take home with you / An idea, oh, so mellow / Belonging to the fellow / On whose head you have your feet; / 'here rests / Lu-Lo in death / In life he did the same.' "[18]

Lu-Lo was the nickname of a musician with a big nose and a mane of white hair who spent only two pages on his real career, while dedicating the majority to his youth and his "golden dreams." For pages he described the orchestra he dreams of ("how clear and true that long dream appeared to me, the sweetest of all my professional dreams")[19] and the girl he fancied for a short time. The ideal in this book is stronger than the real. Luigi was born the last of seven children, in Lama, on the top of a rocky mountain of the Apennine.

When his family moved to Rome, Luigi was forced to study as a lawyer, but his real passion was music ("those who do not know me and persist following me through these pages, please take notice that music was my calling, and great music became my irresistible goal!").[20] He endured the opposition of his father, and secretly played the flute. At eighteen he finally started studying with a maestro and attended a conservatory while his parents conceded: "they decided to allow me to travel my own cherished path, for better or for worse, in happiness or misery, alone or in company, for a long life or a short one, as God willed."[21] His career was not as bright as he had hoped: his first piano compositions were unsuccessful, and at his final examination the professors humiliated him by talking and laughing during the performance. They eventually gave him his diploma on the condition that he goes to America and takes young Ettore with him, a promising but poor boy. On the night of his departure, his father hands him a lesson he will never forget: "my boy, you are now going to follow the career dearest to your heart. Doubtless you will be a fine gentleman and a fine musician, always. Should it happen that you find it hard to do justice to both, choose to be a gentleman."[22]

The day of departure, in 1904, he was full of hope: "For the first time in 23 years I found myself absolutely by myself . . . there I was: young, brilliant, happy and healthy; somewhat handsome to the eyes of those not so particular; well dressed, with 500 lire [that he spends before leaving] and a third-class steamer passage in my pockets . . . plenty of hair, a cute moustache, and an abundance of golden dreams."[23] His arrival in New York was triumphant: "on the deck of the big steamer, I felt like a king and poet, my soul absorbing all the spiritual sensations hitherto unknown to me."[24] His years in Philadelphia were not so easy while he struggled to pay the rent of a small room for his "Verdi Conservatory." He married an Italian girl, whom he met in northern Italy while visiting his brother, and shares his dreams with her: "to become American citizens became our cherished aim in the New World. Nearly all our young ideals were fulfilled."[25] In fact, he found jobs as a pianist in the hotels of Atlantic City, learned English, and finally became flautist and director of the Lombardi Quintet, though he still dreamed of an orchestra, so with the permission of the hotel owner he started conducting a twenty-piece orchestra. It was a success, and in 1912 the Lombardi Symphony Orchestra was born. He moved to Minnesota, where in 1921 he started conducting the Iron Range Symphony Orchestra. In 1939 he moved to Wisconsin and conducted there. These successes and fulfilled dreams lead him to conclude the book with this satisfied but unpretentious comment: "and so . . . the dreams that were born in a young man's heart, have been realized. I humbly thank my God for allowing me to so happily fulfill my mission."[26]

PIETRO MONTANA ∾ Another immigrant dreamer is Pietro Montana, a sculptor with white hair and deep dark eyes, who immigrated as a boy of fourteen, all alone, ready to start any kind of work.[27] He was born in Alcamo, Sicily, in 1892, from an imaginative father (*lu padre*) who made barrels and wine containers, crystal chandeliers for the churches, and even passenger balloons. Immigration was already familiar to the family, because his older brother left for America as a tailor, and, indirectly, because his family started a business knitting socks for those headed for America. It was his brother, Popo, who sowed the seeds of dreaming of America and who eventually sent him the money for the passage. He immigrated in 1906 and found himself all alone for the first time in his life. He started dreaming about his future and his American life on the ship. The week after his arrival he already found a good factory job, the first of many odd jobs that he was unable to keep due to his frail constitution.

Montana's real rebirth was not in immigration but in his encounter with art in the Metropolitan Museum of Art in New York: "It was a revelation to me, who had never been inside a museum, to see so many treasures and works of art. Here and there were artists sketching and copying pictures and paintings. There was an odor of turpentine that exhilarated my spirit, reaching my nostrils and seeming like a perfume to me. I felt at home there, as if I really belonged. That was a great day in my life, and I returned home feeling enriched with the idea that another horizon was opening up for my future."[28]

Art called him in a supernatural way as well: "It was a windy day when we were about walking. We had nearly reached our house, when a gust of wind blew a sheet of paper toward me. It stuck to my leg. I picked up and noticed a beautiful design of three roses in it. I liked it so much that I took it with me. The next day, I went to the art store and bought drawing paper, pencils, and charcoal and came home and began to draw the first drawing I had ever made. I copied the three roses, and that was the beginning of my artistic career."[29]

Even as he began to realize his dream, Montana remained a hardworking immigrant who did not avoid toil. Although keeping his day jobs, at night he would rush to the studio to study art. He opened a photography studio, and started winning art student prizes. For the subject of his first large bas-relief he chose the "tragedy of immigration," after being struck by the destiny of Italian refugees in World

War I: "when I read about the tragedy of the people of Friuli, who were obliged to leave their homes and all their possessions to flee to safety in a neutral and peaceful region, I was saddened. . . . I had that tragic picture clear in my mind."[30] Eventually, his career took off, and he was able to buy a house for his parents who have joined him in Brooklyn, "with a back yard where my father could cultivate a garden, something he loved to do. It was a wonderful feeling of independence for them to own their own home."[31] He married the blond Alfrida, not an Italian but a lover of Italy; they lived in Rome for nine years, all the while feeling nostalgic for New York. Italy remained his stepmother: "No income was derived from my stay in Italy, neither before or after returned there. I never earned money from Italian sources. Nevertheless I love Italy just the same."[32]

Montana's words show the satisfaction of a self-made man who rose from nothing to artistic glory, and he praised America as a land of opportunity. For him, writing his autobiography was like his art in that they offered immortality: "I am grateful that the name Montana will not die. It will still go on, engraved on my artworks in museums, universities, and public squares, in America and Europe."[33] Those works of art were his children, he asserted. Although his achievement showed great personal strength, he believed that was only one-third of the game, as he wrote: "a man's life is made up of three elements, chance, destiny, and character."[34]

ALFRED CRIMI ❧ The same credo is held by another artistic personality, Alfred Crimi, who in his old age wrote: "in reviewing my life I recognized that chance and circumstance played a major part in shaping my character as an individual and my career as an artist. Any success or failure is the result of the choices I made of the opportunities that presented themselves. There were times when I felt I had reached a nadir, but experience has taught me that adversity is often a challenge—a test of strength we must face with faith and fortitude, and from which we must draw renewed vitality. It is the price one must pay for the privilege of life."[35]

This is the credo of the quiet individual, for whom strength of character and will in life's choices are critical. The cost of life is always present in their minds, the price of certain choices and certain renunciations, or enduring the times of hardship and struggle that set every one of these immigrants back at one time or another. In these artists, too, we find an outlook on life that does not belong to the victorious hero, but, as Crimi puts it, to the shipwrecked who resurfaces from the abyss of history: "I consider myself very fortunate to have had the moral strength to bounce back and to retain my equilibrium and sense of humor. Mary has often said to me, 'You are like a cake of Lifebuoy—you always rise to the surface.'"[36]

Short, with a light moustache and smooth skin, Crimi was an oil painter and frescoist for American churches and public buildings. He was not an exuberant artist, but a quiet personality: even in telling the story of a lawsuit over his fresco in Rutgers Church that was painted over, he accepted the result. He told of the struggle not in epic terms, but as one of the many obstacles of life. Crimi was born the eighth of eleven children in 1900 in San Fratello (Messina), a town that survived two massive landslides, which he immortalized in his *After the Landslide of 1922*. He arrived to the United States as a boy of ten, following the tragedy of his brother's death in a work explosion that shocked his father. He remembered the simple life and idyllic memories of his childhood in Sicily, where he worked in a *bottega* to learn cabinetmaking. In front of him were stationed the shoemaker and the blacksmith, all craftsmen with immense love and ability for their work. This is the environment of tradesmen in which he grew up.

Crimi remembers his Americanization through school fights. He studied art and traveled to Rome to attend the academy. In 1933 he was employed by the government through the Federal Emergency Relief Act, part of a team of artists who worked on the walls of the Key West aquarium, where Crimi has to prove his ability as a frescoist by inventing a special process for working on sea-salted walls. This work has been erased by time and sea air, but Crimi's name is preserved on frescoes in other public places, such as in a hospital in Harlem and the main post office in Washington.

ROCCO DE RUSSO ❧ Rocco De Russo, an actor, was an important figure in the Italian American world at the beginning of the century.[37]

At eighty-six, he recorded a professional portrait full of Neapolitan spirit. His shaky memory did not hinder his vivaciousness. He chirped in Italian with effervescent Neapolitan inflections. Italian and Neapolitan are the languages of his career, since he performed for immigrant audiences. His portrait is in the style of a *macchietta,* without any preposterousness, and he heartily complimented all the actors he names, without a drop of bitterness.

Born in 1885 in Sant'Arsenio (Salerno), he lost his father and grew up with his mother and his little hand organ, a joy for the child but a trial for the neighbors. The boy's whole world revolved around that little old organ, which his hard-working mother gave away, and then rebought at the Fair of Saint Anna. When he was only six, he was invited to play at the gatherings of the *signori,* and started to earn money for his mother. His picaresque migrant life starts early, when a group of traveling musicians passing through Sant'Arsenio heard him and convinced his mother to let him go with them: he left in his Sunday suit, with his organ tied with a rope inside a cardboard box. He became the group's mascot, beloved by the audiences. One day, while the group was performing in Taranto, Rocco's sister went to pick him up and took him with her, despite his crying and begging. She was married to a theater actor, Salvatore Baccolini, who toured Italy. Living with them, soon he worked in his brother-in-law's acting company, where he learned *canzonette, macchiette, canzoni* and duets, dramas, and Pulcinella's farces. Still not able to read, he memorized his parts and earned billing as *"il piccolo grande artista."*

As he wrote, "And so among music and songs, *macchiette* and duets, and the study of school, I had no time left to have fun with my friends! At twelve I played the piano decently—music was my passion, like the stage to which I dedicated my entire life. To be what I was, I studied hard dramas, tragedies, comedies."[38]

As an adolescent he worked in the little theaters on the coast (Porto d'Anzio) where Roman ladies on vacation took him under their wing. They sewed his Pulcinella costume and paid for a leather mask because his cardboard one would fall into pieces under his sweat. "A stroke of luck," under the guise of a Roman lady and her husband, led to his debut at the theater Morfeo in Rome when he was sixteen. He also worked in Naples and Torre Annunziata, where he was flooded with compliments. There he fell in love with the daughter of his impresario. He found success, a salary, and love, but as fortune would have it, he had to join his sister again, and eventually went back to his mother and forgot theater for a while, becoming a volunteer soldier. But soon the idea of America started to lure him.

In 1905, after his marriage to a *paesana,* he left for New York, and immediately went to look for a job at the theater Villa Vittorio Emanuele III on Mulberry Street in New York's Little Italy, replacing no one less that Eduardo Migliaccio (known as Farfariello), "the best colonial *macchiettista,*"[39] who had to go back to Italy for health reasons. De Russo's first performance was welcomed with enthusiasm by the Italian American public. He generously remembered all the other immigrant actors, all of them coming "from the factory to the theater." When Migliaccio came back, they worked together, dividing the parts. However, De Russo's hot temper eventually got him fired and he was hired by New York's Lucania Hall and Grand Street's Villa Penza.

Family troubles with his jealous wife and disagreement with his singing partner Lina Baccicalupi brought him back to Italy where again, for the sake of his family, he tried to forget theater. He opened a hotel, where his wife and mother cooked for the guests. He wanted to settle down and forget theater, but songs still saddened him to tears: "I could have swum in triumphal peace, but there was no way of forgetting theater, I had it in my blood, in my heart and mind!! . . . like a worm that continuously eroded my brain!"[40] When a company of good actors stopped in town and lodged at his hotel, he helped them with an emergency substitution, and heard them say: "but what are you doing in this little town? . . . Take your uniform off and come back to art . . . the stage awaits for you."[41]

That was just too much for him, and he resigned from his job and once again threw himself into the theater. When his marriage fell apart, he left for New York and had a triumphal return in the city. He became head of a company and met an artist who became his second wife and partner in the duet called Fugero-De Russo in Chicago—just briefly, because she died young, at twenty-four. De Russo traveled around, eventually married another actress-stage partner, and moved around to Chicago, Boston, and New York, troubled by losses and his own actions (such as shooting one of his actors, buying false witnesses, and attempting to bribe lawyer and police). He ascribes his troubles to the force of destiny: "that act so little noble, that insane gesture that that man made me do, demoralized me so much that I decided to abandon everything . . . I did not have the courage to present myself in front of that public, those good families that adored me."[42] In 1931, with a twelve-artist company, he started a tour that lasted for twenty-six years through sixty-three locations in the United States: "what good time . . . what good money!"[43] The eventual decline of Russo's life paralleled the decline of theater, crushed by the power of television. Eventually, he dissolved the company and retired, moving to Providence, in 1956.

EMANUEL GATTI ∾ The same swansong for theater was sung in the autobiography of another actor, Guglielmo Emanuel Gatti, whose personal decline paralleled that of the age of theater and the rise of cinema.[44] A Fascist supporter of New York's Little Italy, Gatti prepared his book as a personal mausoleum, including letters and articles about himself.

Gatti remembered the humble beginnings of his career, when he fell in love with theater through a quirk of fate. Born in 1867 in Stupinigi Villa Reale (Turin), he left home at sixteen, rebellious and impatient, to find his own way in life. He went to Turin and spent many hungry days sleeping in the train station. It was there that destiny found him and his theater career began. He called it fate, which "used my precarious economic condition to put me on the way of my destiny. It would not otherwise be explainable, the huge passion for theater that I developed with its almost mystical charm."[45] He had never thought of becoming an actor, until one day, when "I was sitting, as I said, at my usual table (that of lunch and dinner too), half laying on the chair that sometimes was also my bed and my desk, when an elegant and distinguished boy almost my age came to me and asked me: 'Excuse me, are you an actor?' I did not have the time to say 'no' that the young boy went on: 'Even if you are a simple beginner, it doesn't matter. The great maestro Giovanni Toselli will make an artist out of you, and then . . . you will play in Piedmontese dialect. . . . I had played in boarding school and blatantly answered: 'yes, I can play.' Sometimes audacity is better than conscience!"[46]

Through other strokes of luck, such as meeting a count who took a liking to him and recommended him to the theater in Milan, Gatti started his own theater company that resisted the "inevitable tempests" for thirty years. In 1915, forced by his ruined relationship with family and colleagues that his rebellious spirit had caused, Gatti left for the United States to join his son. New York did not dazzle him, nor did its Italian theater: "I say theater tongue-in-cheek. The theaters in which Italian actors played were all in the low city, in the old New York and were all run by Russian and German Jews."[47] He nonetheless worked in the Italian American theater for the next twenty years, hardly hiding his contempt. His autobiography is darkened by dissatisfaction when he looks back at the failure of his projects, and registers his defeat: "With money I could have put a muzzle to the dogs that were barking at me, and going back to Italy, I could have opened a Theater in my native city. In fact I started well, but the Big War came . . . and then the restriction laws on immigration . . . and my dream fell like a cardboard building under a whirlpool."[48]

The decline of Gatti's career is quickened by the advent of cinema, his foremost enemy. Even physically, the Amsterdam Opera House, the theater where he worked with success for four years, shut down to become a film studio. He thus addressed his enraged curse to "the big photographic factory where the hot sun burns the wings to those Icaruses who imprudently try to get close to it."[49] He further predicted that cinema will prove to be a short-lived phenomenon, just a complement to theater and opera.

He eventually moved to California, ironically to Hollywood, where he wrote his memoirs. His autobiography seems to be the last attempt of an inconsequential man to give a value to his life—which he portrays as a battle. All he is left with are volumes of scrap paper: "Here I leave resting in peace my three volumes of scrapbooks in which all my artistic and patriotic patrimony is enclosed that, in a day not far, will be confined in an attic or sold to a ragpicker as recycling paper. Rest in peace."[50]

The autobiographies of these Italian immigrant artists show the images of artisans who are more conscious of their lowly backgrounds than they are of their greatest achievements. Their attitudes parallel many of the immigrant workers who value work with their hands. These workers do not flaunt their artistic theories and do not try to raise themselves on a pedestal. They are not showy, but quiet and modest. And they maintain the certainty that chance and destiny play a large part in man's life, while individual feats are limited.

4 The Spiritual Immigran

Of the next five autobiographies, three are of men for whom years of work gave birth to a new man—a man of God, a convert to spiritual faith. Luigi Turco, Constantine Panunzio, and Antonio Arrighi came to America as immigrant boys. They were not satisfied with the material enrichment the new land could bring; instead they looked to intertwine their immigration toward a better life with their continual search for a higher spiritual life. Immigration was not enough for them to change their existence, as Turco wrote to his son, Lewis Turco (a professor at Potsdam University, poet, and playwright): "I was never satisfied with the idea that life consisted in living three score and ten and then end into oblivion. I never was satisfied to see that life consisted in a terrific struggle to make a living."[1] Education and Americanization are parallel to religious conversion for these workers, who, though raised Catholic, became pastors of the Protestant church, the "American" religion par excellence. They Americanized so deeply that they came to resemble the first Pilgrims, choosing that adopted identity over the strong Catholic heritage of their native Italy. Their autobiographies sprang from their renewed life. Panunzio's and Arrighi's stories are the best known, both being first compelling romances of immigration, and only secondarily spiritual accounts. The autobiography of the shoemaker-pastor Luigi Turco is instead predominantly the spiritual autobiography of a man of God.

LUIGI TURCO ∾ Luigi Turco's autobiography is the first part of a bulky essay on his religious theology.[2] He wrote the book in old age, when almost blind—like Saint Francis. It portrays his life through the screen of conversion, making it a direct descendant of the "confessions," the spiritual autobiographies of conversion that from Saint Augustine pass through the New England Puritans. Turco was a shoemaker who thirsted for religious knowledge, but did not betray humility. He thus told his harshest experiences in a light style, because, as his son remembers him, he was not "some dour Calvinist or pompous Parson Goodbody."[3] As a typical first-generation immigrant, he was a man of many jobs: a miner, a mechanic, a chauffeur for the mayor of Rome, a shoemaker, a soldier in the U.S. Army, and a writer, though his English was never first-rate, according to his son who edited his autobiography.

"I was born in Riesi a little rural town in Sicily, the 18th of May 1890. It goes without saying, being an Italian, my faith was that of the Roman Catholic Church. . . . Until the age of 12, I never went to church, neither did any member of my family."[4] This ignorance of religion pushed him into an unholy life, as Saint Augustine before him. He lived in sin—even if living in Rome, the cradle of Christianity, while he was in the military service: "even there I did not learn much about the noble teaching of Jesus, the Christ; therefore my life was not ideal."[5]

Turco immigrated to the United States in 1913, following his sister, who was called to America by her husband. He settled in a poor Boston neighborhood and worked in a shoe factory with his sister. America did not show him her welcoming face, but instead presented him with the bottom of his sinful existence. He lived with his brother-in-law, a gambler and a drunkard, and in the deepest moment of sinfulness was touched by the hand of God: "The hunger in me for a better moral and spiritual life was very deep. It had created in me a melancholy attitude; the spirit of despair! I tried to satisfy this hunger in me like the rest of the young people of my time, by drinking, eating, smoking, gambling, and other pleasures of the flesh, but to no avail. The activity of the Spirit upon me, then not clearly known to me, was leading me to find a better way, the real way, to satisfy the thirst of my soul for a better living."[6]

The material betterment offered by immigration leaves him unsatisfied. "After a while I found a better job, one that gave me a better income to live a more comfortable life but that did not give me the satisfaction of soul for which I was longing. . . . I was very lonesome! There was a void in me and I did not know how to fill it in spite of the fact that I was young and had money to go to places of amusements."[7]

One day, he entered the Baptist Church of Boston, where Reverend Gaetano Lisi was preaching in Italian for the immigrants. His words were "like manna for my famished spirit; they were like the sweet and restful spirit coming from God to calm and lay my bitter and restless soul."[8] Turco thus converted, and changed his whole life, by quitting his smoking, drinking, and "illegal sexual relations." As a good believer, he suffered the criticisms of his own family, but he ended up converting his sister, who saw how much his life had improved.

But it was an accident on the job that made him become a minister. In the shoe factory he almost lost his right eye. A minister advised him to study for ministry, an idea he had previously refused, out of humility. He attended classes at the Colgate Theological Seminary in Brooklyn with five other Italian immigrants who had converted to Protestantism, men over twenty with little education. Having gone to grammar school, he was the best student, and he started his career in the Italian Baptist mission of Passaic, New Jersey, on the weekends. In his last school year he was sent to the Waldensian Seminary in Rome, and for the occasion he returned to Riesi, twelve years after his departure, not as a returned immigrant with a golden watch, but as a preacher at the Waldensian church, There, a congregation normally counted no more than fourteen people, but Turco eventually saw gatherings of almost 150 to his services: "even people of the neighborhood who knew me as a common young man going to America to make a fortune, and now back in Riesi after 12 years as a minister, came to see me preaching, just for the curiosity. The church was filled to its capacity . . . I preached the best I could."[9] He filled his parents' and his brother's eyes with tears, and after he spent the summer with them, he succeeded in converting the entire family. When he left, in 1925, he left a vigorous Waldensian church in the heart of Sicily.

Turco's religious career continued with his leading the second Italian Baptist church in Buffalo. He attended high school at thirty-seven, then continued on to college at Colgate and at Rochester Divinity School, but he never finished his bachelor's degree. At forty-three he married an American religious worker, May Putnam, and had two boys. In 1938 he was the pastor of the first Italian Baptist church in Meriden, Connecticut, where he stayed for seventeen years. His religious quest was not over yet, and at sixty-two he started to look for something more. He left his church two years later and, in a spiritual crisis, spent time in Riesi and in the Bronx, until in 1956 he encountered the Movement of the New Thought, which was based on a metaphysical interpretation of the Bible and physical and spiritual healing. He started studying again—religious science, theosophy, psychology, spiritualism, astrology, Hinduism—and he finally understood his next mission: starting a new church. "Gladly, I would have taken another Baptist Church if it had been given to me, but so far no such offer has been given me. Thus it is clear to me that the Spirit wants me to start a new church, based in the New Thought, here in Meriden where I have lived for 20 years, 17 of which as pastor of the First Italian Baptist Church. I am conscious of the great meaning of the words of Jesus which are also meant for me, namely, 'the Son can do nothing of himself, but what he sees the Father do . . . for the Father loveth the Son and showeth him all things that himself doeth; and he will show him greater works than these, that ye may marvel' [John, 2:20–21]."[10]

ANTONIO ARRIGHI ⌘ As the title of our next autobiography, *Story of Antonio, the Galley Slave; a Romance of Real Life,*[11] suggests, this 1895 book is in the style of a romance. It reads almost like a nineteenth-century educational novel, with a polished language redolent of adventure narratives of the age. It praises moral values, such as freedom, education, and love for the motherland, sometimes with high pitches of oratory. Arrighi echoes the style of the popular Italian novels or D. W. Griffith's movies in America: brimming with good sentiments, affectionate fathers who give help to others inspired by the love for their own children, heroic boys à la Edmondo De Amicis, rotten villains, evil men softened by the power of a song, and galley guards moved by speeches on filial love. It is hard to separate fact from fiction, but again we must trust the author when he says it is a "romance of real life." However, true or false, Arrighi's work nuances the portrait of the immigrant with a romantic touch that is all too rare.

Born in 1833, Arrighi started by describing his childhood in the town of Barga, Abruzzi, as the son of the *notaro* with a strong passion for drumming. At sixteen he was hired as a drummer boy for the Garibaldi army in the 1849 revolution, but he was taken prisoner in Rome by the allied forces of French, Spaniards, Austrians, and papacy, who all dominated over Italy in those times. He was jailed in the galleys—inhumane underground cells where prisoners lived as beasts—and he worked chained two by two in a treadmill of Civitavecchia for three and a half year. He escaped from the galleys tied to the bottom of a cart. In a rocambolesque way he was able to lose his chasers in the maze of Rome.[12] He was helped by a group of men fighting for national unity and found a job as a cabin boy in a ship directed to America. He arrived in New York in 1855 with a bitter welcome: he was taken directly to court because of resisting a policeman who hit him while he was sleeping in the park. He was saved by a doctor, an eyewitness, who told the true story. He also described a tragically funny moment from his greenhorn days when the only words he knows and uses are: "Hurry up. Get out. Fire," words he overheard in the street. He adds a note of criticism to his encounter with America: "My introduction to free America was peculiar, and entirely contrary to the expected spirit of freedom. I could not understand how a country that did not even allow men to sleep peacefully could be called Land of the Free. Not only that, but how can it be the Home of the Brave when a fellow-being is unjustly clubbed in a cowardly and brutal manner?"[13]

Antonio left the city and in the Midwest started working as a seller of ornaments made in plaster of paris, a job he appreciates for an Italian-sounding reason: "some had an idea that the work of selling plaster-of-Paris toys was degrading; but my experience tells me that it was both honorable and useful" because it helped beautify the homes of people who "had but a faint idea of ornamentation."[14] In Ohio, in 1858, he converted to Methodism. He explained that Catholicism was like an empty shell for Italian people who remained untouched in their life and even cursed God daily. He then undertook theological study at the Iowa Wesleyan University at Mount Pleasant; he became a pastor, married an American woman, and had three children. The day of his real Americanization, when he became a citizen, is described with epochal words. "I put on a new suit that I had bought on purpose, for I felt as though I was going to my own wedding. I did not rejoice because I was a son of Italy, or because I had been a drummer boy in Garibaldi's army or because I had been unjustly sent to the Galera and escaped; but because I had been declared by the laws of the land *an American citizen*. I have two documents that I regard as sacred. The first and the most important is the one that authorizes me to preach the Gospel, which certifies that as a Christian minister I belong to Christ's kingdom. The other document is my naturalization paper."[15]

Like Panunzio, Arrighi returned to the motherland, twelve years after his escape, without the immigrant's sack of gold, but with the gift of faith. He wanted to evangelize his land and see his parents again (who had already disinherited him at the news of his conversion). In 1881 he opened a church in Florence and widened its community, being able to count among the converted also his parents and relatives. Another moment of adventure awaited him there when he was saved by two young men from a lynching mob (spurred by an evil priest of San Marco). Upon his return to the United States he preached for fourteen years in Philadelphia, and at sixty-five, he wrote his autobiography.

Arrighi's story is surely one of survival: his own immigration is told as a miraculous salvation from the hell of the galleys. It is hard not to hear a soft screech in these words of apparent meekness. Antonio's individuality is stronger than the majority of our humble immigrants, and he is not afraid to assert it in one line: "This is not history of the city of New York, but the story of Tonio, Garibaldi's Drummer Boy, Tonio, the Galley-Slave, and Antonio the Preacher."[16] For Arrighi, individualism is more forced than natural, more reasoned than spontaneous.

CONSTANTINE PANUNZIO ∾ A similarly remarkable strength of individuality characterizes Constantine Panunzio's autobiography, *The Soul of an Immigrant;*[17] he even admits in his chapter "American Philosophy of Life" that the discovery of the individual is one of the most important American gifts.[18] However, Panunzio remains, as he puts it, an "average immigrant," an inconsequential man who did not reach the top layer of society.

One of the youngest autobiographers, the thirty-six-year-old Constantine Panunzio lists in his story of immigration a trail of adventures, much as the tale of Antonio Arrighi. Born in Molfetta (Bari) into an influential family of doctors and patriots (his grandfather was poisoned in a Bourbon prison), he had a happy childhood and left for America at the age of thirteen out of a thirst for novelty, irresistibly attracted to the sea and tired of strict Italian schools. Life on the boat is harder than he had expected, and Constantine immediately met the harshness of life. His arrival to Boston in 1902 was a struggle against the elements. Once in Boston, unromantic reality struck him in the face: unsavory fellow sailors, a nonpaying captain, a strange language. A litany of misadventures and close calls followed him until he was jailed under the name of Frank Nardi, the name a boss gave him replacing the difficult Constantine.

Then his hellish life changed, and he finally met the "real America" of good people. He was hired by a good Christian family with beautiful daughters and with them he discovered a new kind of life. He went to school to learn English; he read the Bible; he went to church with the family. According to his account, this was his luck, because his process of Americanization was passed through their good example— unlike many Italians who lived in isolation and never integrated. Americanization went together with education and, for Panunzio, with conversion: he was accepted in the Maine Wesleyan Seminary and started collecting literary prizes. Once naturalized, Panunzio worked with immigrant communities in the Protestant Mission of Boston, where people were resistant to any change, isolated in their enclaves, and never knew the "real America." He described the Italian community, the brave mothers and the strict fathers who worked with self-abnegation for their children. Panunzio never described his religious turning point, nor his ordination as a Methodist pastor. This is probably because his conversion to Protestantism was for him the natural outcome of Americanization, and this Americanization is what occupies the whole book. The unusual dimension of Panunzio's writing is the inward perspective of his description. While other autobiographies mainly speak of simple events and exterior facts, Panunzio turned introspective.[19] "This tale depicts the inner, the soul struggles of the immigrant more than his outward success or failure . . . it traces the liberation of a mind from the conceptions it brought from the Old World and pictures its development into the American consciousness. Not outward poverty, degradation, misery; but inner conflict, soul-struggles are here primarily depicted."[20]

Panunzio's perspective is often from the outside in, where he made the physical world a metaphor for the inner world. He lucidly delineated the immigrant's changes before and after America. He enumerated the losses he suffered from his immigration: the loss of his trustful simplicity, the loss of his manners and the respect for law and order, the loss of grip upon his health, and the loss of thoroughness and exactitude of work sacrificed to quick results. He listed some all-American characteristics such as mobility, America's freedom of changing the old ways for the new, optimism, and its practical idealism—all lessons that orbit around the discovery of the individual. He has learned the importance of the individual's opinion and disregard for others' expectations and to appreciate the worth of the individual character, and not the inherited worth of his ancestors.

FATHER SAMUEL MAZZUCHELLI ⁓ A Dominican priest, Father Samuel Charles Mazzuchelli was of an earlier generation of immigrant-missionaries; he published his autobiography in 1844 in Italy and it was eventually translated into English in 1915.[21] Mazzuchelli, a founder of the Sisters of Charity, sounds picturesque and gentlemanly. Born in Milan at the beginning of 1800 to a good family, Mazzuchelli asked to be sent to America after hearing a talk by Edward

Fenwick, a Dominican priest, about the New World missionary work. The speech fired young Mazzuchelli's imagination, and he was quickly transformed into the pioneer who evangelized the frontiers of the Wild West, through Michigan, Wisconsin, Illinois, and Iowa. He worked primarily with Native Americans, whom he came to love as the "poor in spirit." He learned their languages enough to translate a booklet of prayers and to alternate verses of the Latin mass with those in their language. He intelligently appealed to syncretism and allowed them to pray to the Great Spirit and maintain some of their customs within the ritual of the mass. He was a vociferous defender of Native Americans and denounced the injustices committed toward them. In the disordered society of those frontier towns, he also founded the Total Abstinence Society to discourage drinking, as well as the Order of the Sisters of Charity.

He wrote his autobiography at thirty-eight, shortly before dying of pneumonia in his mission. He used the third person, which does not transform him into the hero of an epic; rather it humbles him by becoming merely the detached recorder of events. This is his primary purpose, and in fact he often starts his chapters by speaking impersonally of the general historical conditions—the terrible life of Indians, the battles between Protestants and Catholics, the Mormons, freedom of speech in the United States. Only secondarily does he mention "our story" and "our priest." When he describes his immaculate behavior—"modest, unassuming, courteous," "among the virtues demanded of the priest in America disinterestedness is the most necessary,"[22]—he is not boastful; rather this is his way of evangelizing, since only irreproachable lives and preaching can give the good example.

Mazzuchelli's autobiography portrays the typical moments of the immigrant experience, but in a Roman Catholic religious light, always providing supernatural answers to the basic moments of immigration. His decision to leave is described as a mission: "Of all the duties of priesthood the most excellent and meritorious is the propagation of the faith among people who do not know it."[23] The fear of the long trip and the unknown is quickly consoled through faith: "Therefore do not be anxious saying 'What shall we eat?' 'What shall we drink?'"[24]

Even his most painful moments, the detachment from his family and his adoring father who begs him not to leave, is quieted with religious duty: "On such occasion one needs not to dwell in the physical separation from dear ones and native land. . . . To the flesh such a parting seems cruel and unjust, but to the spirit of the Christian it becomes sweet and gentle, for it is the yoke of Christ."[25] The blows of fortune that the immigrant must endure are also seen as gifts of God: "accidental events in our lives that seem unfortunate contribute to our welfare and prepare God's paths, of which we are ignorant."[26] These statements show how Mazzuchelli redefined his losses into gains for his mission and faith.

Mazzuchelli remained an Italian even in the American wilderness. He made an effort to bring not only religion, but also the Italian way of life to his missions. He explained away the lack of Italian artistry in his improvised churches ("There was no need for Italian marble for a pavement, which was found ready-made, the green grass in summer and hard frozen earth in winter");[27] yet he brought the sound of church bells to give a rhythm to the days: "in this happy place of primitive fervor, everyone rose at the sound of Ave Maria . . . at the noon Ave Maria the poor Indians did not fail to direct their minds and hearts again to the mystery of man's redemption by reciting the Angelus. They did so also at evening, when the bell called them to church for Vespers."[28]

FATHER GIACOMO GAMBERA ∾ More concrete is the autobiography of another missionary, Father Giacomo Gambera.[29] Written in a stern tone, this autobiography of the Scalabrinian priest is in a matter-of-fact style that sounds like neither a confession nor the story of a soul. It is instead almost a managerial, historical account that reminds us of the notes on a parson's register.

Born in 1856 in Lumezzane Pieve (Brescia), Gambera started his religious education at a young age, and was ordained in 1879. He joined the Scalabrinians in 1889 at the suggestion of their founder, Bishop Scalabrini, and he departed for what he had planned to be a five-year missionary period. Feeling guilty for leaving, he regarded his trip with anguish and expectation: "my American clothes were ready, but my spirit was at once beautiful and anxious."[30] Initially directed to

South America, at the last minute he was sent to New Orleans, a city with a bad reputation. Willingly or not, he stayed in New Orleans, where he worked in a parish of stingy parishioners for four years; there he witnessed the 1891 lynching of eleven Italian immigrants: "I felt my blood rush cold with shame and horror."[31]

Having served his five years, he was sent to Pittsburgh for sixteen months ("The Babel of our colonies had more embittered than satisfied me, and I wanted to leave that unpleasant environment")[32] and then on to Boston, where he became the pastor of Sacred Heart parish for six years. Long ready to return home, he was then asked to work for the Saint Raphael Society in Ellis Island for another four years, until 1905: "These orders were like a heavy weight falling on my shoulders and on my heart. A new parish and an assignment of grave responsibility! It frightened me!"[33] In Ellis Island, "Those halls echoed with complaints and bitter weeping, which pierced not only one's ears but the heart as well, because they were terrified by the thought of being sent back to where they had come from."[34]

Yet Gambera would not be sent back soon. At forty-eight, in 1905, he took over the parish of Addolorata in Chicago, where he stayed until 1921. There he distributed food to the unemployed and administered to them in time of influenza. During World War I his parish contributed 300,000 dollars in subscriptions to orphans and widows, and he never lost sight of the accounting aspects of his positions. Finally, in poor health, at sixty-four, he resigned from Addolorata to return to Italy, finishing a missionary period that lasted many times longer than he expected. He was a stranger now in his land: "The adults and the people that I knew had almost all disappeared."[35] Then in 1925 he was sent once more to the United States. He worked for various hospitals in New York and Connecticut. He died in his sleep in 1934, after a whole life in service of Italian immigrants.

To Father Gambera, the parish was the center of immigrant life: "I saw immediately that in the midst of our colonies the parish church was the focus of their most dear memories and most valuable comforts, of their closest union among our exiles, and that the missionary was the best and living representative of the most beautiful and sacred traditions of our fatherland, from the feast days to the songs, from the sacraments to the language, and that in the parish the migrant lived, breathed, and tasted the true *italianità*."[36] This "immigrant" priest was tossed from place to place not from destiny, but by his vow of obedience. He did not hide his difficulty being a priest; reading his story we can almost smell the heavy breath of a priest with liver problems caused by worries. He did not try to paint a hagiographic portrait of himself; he recorded his triumphs but also many of his miseries (he even described his alcoholic colleagues or the unfaithful nuns he met). He filled his memoir with the bitterness, solitude, and harsh law of obedience that exasperated him, and he praised his perseverance: "I worked, I suffered, I cried, and I also enjoyed myself."[37] He remained humble, though, because he turned down prestigious positions, including one from Rome.

With these autobiographies of the immigrant man of faith, familiar immigrant themes cross other thin boundaries. Humility becomes obedience, the theme of fate is intertwined with that of the will of God, searching a place in the world is also searching for a mission, and the immigrant dream of building a house is channeled instead into dedication to establish a parish and to serve others. Any newfound American individuality is blurred in these writers by their dedication to being humble servants.

5 Immigrant Women

It is rare to find women's voices among immigrant autobiographies. In the early years, there were fewer female than male immigrants, although the proportion increased steadily over the century, comprising a third of the total immigrants in the 1830s but more than half of the total after 1930s.[1] The sample of our women seems to follow that pattern. Only two of them, Rosa Cavalleri and Bruna Pieracci, belong to the earlier type of peasant immigrants. Anna Yona and Amalia Santacaterina were wives of political refugees, a Jew and a Socialist, who emigrated during Fascism. The majority of the women—Giuseppina Liarda Macaluso, Leonilde Frieri Ruberto, Elvezia Marcucci, Elisabeth Evans, and Maria Bottiglieri—belonged to the wave of U.S. immigration after the World War II. Evans and Bottiglieri were war wives, married to American soldiers. Even though they belonged to different times and recounted different stories, these immigrant women touch similar themes.

Women's autobiographies need to be explained by different kinds of critical instruments.[2] Scholar Estelle Jelinek has noted the many oppositions that characterize women's autobiography: men write "history" while women write "story"; men's autobiography usually centers on public lives while women privilege their private lives; men tell events, women write about people and family; the center of man's autobiography is the idealized life, while for women it is self-consciousness and self-analysis. These opposite approaches, a basis of one strand of the criticism, are useful but not completely true among our female authors.[3] Our Italian immigrant women complicate the notion of the ethos of work we have seen so far, because for almost all of them, having a job is their first taste of an independence they had never felt. Female immigrants are twice crushed under history, both by society and by their own families. These stories give a modern inflection to the concept of quiet individualism because women's individualism is generally a recent discovery.[4] Many of our women writers define themselves as being in the backgrounds of other people's stories, as mothers, sisters, or daughters with a limited scope of action, such as Anna Yona, who started writing as a way of completing her husband's task.

Some of these women are the prototype of the Italian American grandmother, a figure of mythic proportions in Italian American writing. This matriarchal figure is present as an origin myth that gives successive generations a sense of continuity with their ancestral past, and she provides a strong model of a powerful woman, even if it is one who is only in the background. These autobiographies are the voices of those mute grandmothers often depicted in film and novels.[5]

The prototype of women's autobiography in Italy is the novel *Una donna* by Sibilla Aleramo (1906), a work that celebrates autonomy and independence; some of our women authors reflect that tone of her work. Aleramo's book is considered to be one of the first Italian feminist books, with its deep cry for the liberty of a young woman, a fervidly vivacious spirit tied down by social conventions and the lack of comprehension. She decides to be a happy woman, rather than a tired, negative, hateful mother ("Why do we love sacrifice in maternity? . . . From mother to daughter we transmit this serfdom. It is a monstrous chain").[6] But the first woman to write an immigrant memoir was a nun, Sister Blandina Segale, whose diary *At the End of the Santa Fe Trail* reads more like an adventure tale.[7] Although their lives are not as full of Sister Blandina's excitement, some of our writers—Amalia Santacaterina, Elvezia Marcucci, Elisabeth Evans, even Maria Bottoglieri and Leonilde Ruberto—started new lives in America as autonomous women.

ROSA CAVALLERI ∾ In the story of Rosa Cavalleri we clearly see the imbalance between individualism and communalism in many works by Italian-American writers. *Rosa: The Life of an Italian Immigrant* is the as-told-to story of Rosa, a large Chicago cleaning lady,[8] but we should not forget the intervention of the secondary narrator.[9] Born in 1866 or 1867 in Lombardy, Rosa Cassettari (whose real name was Ines and whose last name was changed to Cavalleri in the narration) was raised in Bugiarno (the real town of Cuggiono, according to Ernesto Milani) by her foster mother, Mamma Lena, who adopted her.[10] She was educated by strict nuns in a repressive religious school, then worked in silk factories and in the *osteria* of Mamma Lena. When she was fourteen she was forced to marry an older abusive man, and they immigrated to the United States. Once there, her unhappiness took over when she followed her despised husband to the mine region of Missouri, where she worked as a cook for twelve men. Their relationship fell apart when she refused to run a brothel for him, and she eventually escaped his brutal violence. She divorced and married the sweet Gionin, a good Tuscan man who also worked in the mines. She worked as a cleaning woman in the Chicago Commons until her death in 1943. Her story spans almost her entire life.

In Cassettari's tale, as in many of these women's stories, we find the immigrant philosophy of survival. She was the last baby to be placed on the "torno" of Milan, where abandoned babies were put to preserve the mother's anonymity. Her entire life was a struggle to outsmart her destiny. She resisted her wedding with all her might ("it was not the beating or the starving that made me stop saying no. It was the fear of God").[11] When she saw that it is impossible to refuse it, she stuck to her conviction and did not pronounce her "yes" in front of the deaf priest.

As in male immigrants' autobiographies, the struggle for life is a continual process of starting over. In Cassettari's case this not only involved changing jobs many times, but also a psychological renewal that she found by recharging her inner life in prayer. Her tale of womanhood and immigration forms a zigzag through the obstacles of life. But her ally is the Madonna, and the many miraculous survivals she experienced were all motivated by her miraculous interventions. Cassettari's faith never withered: "The Madonna is the best friend I have!"[12]

It has been noted that Cassettari's main theme is the struggle over fear, possible only in America. Her liberation starts from the ocean voyage, where there was "no one there to scold me and tell me what to do."[13] Her individuation came from her learning English quickly and her courage in addressing Americans: "In America the poor can talk to anyone."[14] The final proof of her metamorphosis is visible when she went back to Italy to reclaim her son Francesco: "In America the poor people do get smart. We are not so stupid anymore."[15] She was able to insist she bring her second son, as she had not been able to do with her firstborn: "Mamma Lena didn't say anything—she didn't even scold. Before I went to America I would have been afraid to say no."[16] Even her love life was measured by the protection that men could give her against fear: she loved Gionin because "somehow I was not so afraid with Gionin beside me."[17] Rosa Cassettari not only tells her life, thus becoming a protagonist for once, she also uses writing to erase her history of oppression, to *write out* oppressive men. "The things he did to me are too bad to tell! I leave him out, that's all!"[18]

BRUNA PIERACCI ∾ Bruna Pieracci was the daughter of a miner from Frassinoro (Modena) who sacrificed her own presentation to tell her father's story.[19] She did not give her birth date, only hinted that "there was a baby daughter"[20] and "it was two years before he could send for his wife and daughter."[21] In her fifteen pages she described life in a coal mine camp, and often stressed the importance of earth—from her family, who "had their roots deep in the soil of a tiny Italian village, high in the northern Apennines" to their work, where they "managed to scratch only a part of their living from the unyielding soil,"[22] to her mother's burial: "she was laid to rest beside her husband and in her hand we placed a packet of soil from her native village."[23] Bruna explained her alienation in physical terms: "these immigrants had never seen wooden houses before, and they appeared flimsy indeed in comparison to the ancestral homes of stone with walls twenty inches thick."[24] The distance from home is given not only in miles but in feelings: "it was so far from Italy and all so strange and different. There was a great nostalgia for the "hills of home.""[25]

Pieracci's story highlights the tragedy of her parents' lives in Iowa: her father spent forty years in the mine "in which he saw little of either the seasons or his children";[26] her mother, a seamstress, became severely homesick: "it was soon evident that emotionally she was troubled. Within a few years, the mind of the good wife and loving mother shut out reality until she was no longer able to function as a mother, she grieved constantly for her native land. Her nostalgia knew no reason. . . . She remained all her life a stranger in a strange land."[27] Pieracci arrived in the camp when she was ten, but being the oldest child, she took part in the life of the mine and ran the house, looking after her brothers and the boarders, repairing their shoes, knitting their clothes. She studied, but she described herself as seen through her father's eyes: "he saw his children go to high school and graduate, some went to college and did not drop out."[28] Destiny is strong in this piece of writing, another example of the ethos of "person-in-history" typical of these writers. When describing disappointments, she twice conceded, "fate had decreed otherwise."[29]

ANNA YONA ∾ Almost forced to write, Anna Yona picked up the pen that her husband, David, left on the desk at the time of his death, after writing 223 pages of his life and covering only the first thirty years.[30] She continued his task in a subordinate way, as an imaginary dialogue to her grandchildren, and we soon discover that her wit was not secondary to her husband's, in spite of their different educations.[31]

While her husband's writing centered entirely on Italian history, Anna concentrated on family history, and adds the smaller details of daily life. David and Anna were Italian Jews, and, like many, less for religious convictions than for a sense of belonging.[32] David explained how he was first of all Italian: his father was called Gioberti and his mother, Itala. The Jewish identity of many Italian Jews was almost a Fascist discovery, as immigrant Carla Coen Pekelis asserted: "'What did it mean to be a Jewish girl in Italy at the beginning of the century?' What did it mean? Nothing, absolutely, nothing! There was no observance of rituals, nor celebration of festivities in my parents' house."[33]

Anna Yona described Italy under Fascism with the tone of a betrayed Italian woman: "some friends do not want to have their name implicated with us. Little by little, we came to recognize who was our friend and who was not."[34] Her husband refused to take the party's *tessera* and was cut out; some close Jewish friends turned to Fascism. There was a mock process for her father and brother, who was confined in isolation; the maids all turned informants; and the family was refused service at the Buitoni restaurant in Turin; her husband lost his job, and she learned how to weave in order to gain a livelihood. She would take the wool out of old mattresses, weave it, and make coats to sell: "it gave us some financial return and a great moral satisfaction to earn something because of our work."[35] Her father "was retired, read Shakespeare all day long and was brooding about the situation in the world."[36] In 1938, with the creation of racial laws, "we lived from day to day fearing for the next one": "the government took away our livelihood and the only thing was to emigrate."[37] When they decided to leave for the United States, at first only David could get his passport;[38] they all eventually left in 1939.

The impression of America was dreamy and harsh. In New York, in fact, the atmosphere is still one of fear. When her daughter risked a fall from the sixteenth floor, a Polish friend commented: "'what's the difference, falling now or being thrown down by the Nazis in three months?' . . . This was the atmosphere in July 1940 in Central Park."[39] David searched for a job "frantically"; they sold their embroidered lingerie and furniture to Americans; she worked making scarves and gloves for the Countess Mara boutique, but was fired for making a scarf for her friend. Nevertheless, Anna knows they are privileged: "We were all there without jobs and without money, with a continuous worry for our dear ones in Italy but we were alive."[40] When Italy declared war on the United States, she became an "enemy alien" and was fingerprinted: "I felt like a criminal." Suffering the double prejudice of being Jewish and Italian, they could not find a place to rent: "I was Jewish and Italian and I was proud of both."[41]

Yona started to find a new dimension through her hardship; in America she became alive as an intellectual and working woman who helped the economy of the house: "Our life really started to be really full of excitement and fulfillment"[42]: "We learned that one never airs the bedsheets outside the windows . . . and one throws [out] everything which is not of immediate use. I was accustomed in Italy to gather old newspapers and containers in the cellar while here nothing we saved at least at that time in 1943. I learned to shop once or twice a week, while in Italy I shopped twice a day . . . [and] to call by the first name people I barely knew, while in Italy I used to call people Mr. and Mrs. although I knew them for years and years. . . . to choose my friends according to my opinions and ideas, and not according to what was good to have as friends."[43]

David Yona found a job in Cambridge, Massachusetts, and they joined an anti-Fascist group of intellectuals who would meet regularly, interpreting Dante's *Paradisio* at night, and they picked up a strong attitude of social consciousness. They wrote articles for the review *Controcorrente*; she started working at the radio and learned to type; and she was responsible for the Italian program there. She spent hours discussing philosophy and politics in those heated days. These seem to have been the most exciting years of her life, because when the war ended, her narration also stopped, and she just hinted at her trip back home in 1947. "One thing I feel you should know, in all the turmoil of our emigration, of the search for work, of the anxiety and worry for our dear ones in Italy, and very scarce communication with them, of the lack of knowledge of the English language, of the pressure of the different groups to attract us to their side, I had always the great advantage to have David near me, morally supporting the hard period of life we were going through. . . . We always refused any recommendation in the Italian meaning and any association with groups whose tactics were based in nepotism open or hidden or compromised on issues we felt we should not compromise. . . . This also was different from today's philosophy: I was never in debt."[44]

GIUSEPPINA LIARDA MACALUSO ∾ Giuseppina Macaluso, a Sicilian woman, dreamed of getting a job as soon as she arrived in America: "When I arrived in Brooklyn, and I saw people coming and going from the local clothing factories, I felt a great desire and a strong hope that I too would be lucky enough to have, one day, a job as they did."[45] Told to her son, a college professor in New York, when she was ninety-three years old, Macaluso's story resembles Rosa Cavalleri's unorthodox autobiography. "My name is Giuseppina Liarda Macaluso. I am Sicilian. I was born in Polizzi Generosa, on the Madonie Mountains near Palermo, on April 11, 1906, in a small pretty house facing Piazza San Francesco. Growing up, I remember my mother always weaving. She was preparing the dowries for the future marriages of her three daughters."[46] Her marriage was not a happy story, though, especially because of the unloving family of her husband."

"I don't remember much about my trip to America, the first and only one I have ever taken by plane. . . . Coming from a small town, and being simple people, we knew little about restaurants. As we sat, for the first time, around a table for breakfast—compliments of TWA to compensate us for the late departure—I ordered three eggs for the family, I didn't want to take advantage of the airline. When the waiter came back, he placed three eggs in each of our plates. I showed my surprise and embarrassment."[47] Abundance is therefore the first gift of America. She had saved a piece of panettone from the airplane nicely wrapped in her luggage, but lost it once in the States because perhaps "somebody probably thought it was a piece of stale bread."[48] It was in America, through her job, that she discovered her independence, starting her life anew at the age of fifty-two. She became a factory seamstress, and that was the happiness of her life. She held that job for twelve years: "I never missed a day. That job was the greatest gift to me. It was my way of being independent, and thank God, I have been no burden to my children, or their families until this very day."[49]

For Macaluso, immigration was a late experience, the conclusion of a hard Sicilian life that started when Fascism ended. In 1958 she joined her two sons, who married Sicilian-American women, and her husband, who left in 1956. Macaluso's life was a harsh one, but her faith in God pulled her through. A supernatural help is always close to these immigrants, who are convinced they could never have succeeded without it.

LEONILDE FRIERI RUBERTO ∾ Leonilde Frieri Ruberto was also a seamstress, the seventy-year-old author of *Such Is Life* that her grandaughter, Laura Ruberto, translated and had published with a small press. Ruberto was an undereducated, poor girl, born in 1913 in the village of Cairano (Avellino). She reluctantly followed her husband to the United States in 1954, at forty-one. Her life was hard, and she had worked ever since she was a girl—washing the laundry of rich families, toiling in the fields, preparing her trousseau in a hurry because her mother was sick, and learning to embroider by machine in the midst of the envy of her friends who would not teach her. She married a man she barely knew through an arrangement, and became the servant of her new family: "I had to serve my in-laws because we lived with them. This is how it was done, the last son stayed with his parents."[50]

Immigration triggered women's individuality and solidarity. When Ruberto's husband went to war, was taken prisoner, and went away on other occasions, she raised her four children by herself for almost ten years: "we women were left alone, but we continued to always be together. We went to work in the fields together, one day on each piece."[51] When her husband eventually called her to Pittsburgh, "I had to do it, because in Italy with four children I couldn't give them a future."[52] Her years there were hardly a triumph: "I continued to do everything my mother had taught me, cook, make bread, make pasta by hand, and sew some things for myself. I have never bought myself a dress, I make them for myself, I crocheted, I knitted, worked in the yard, cut the grass, grew flowers, and had a vegetable garden."[53]

Leonilde Ruberto was psychologically given to resignation, as the last words of her piece show: "such is life" (questa è la vita!); Ruberto's autobiography is a sure example of quiet individualism: she is always subordinate to her family; she accepts what life offers her, and avoids any rhetoric of victory.

AMALIA SANTACATERINA ∾ Amalia Santacaterina wrote a beautiful and poetry-filled autobiography, *Il calicanto non cresce a Chicago* (The calicantus does not grow in Chicago).[54] The arbor of calycanthus, a sweet-smelling tree that blooms in winter in the Venetian region, is a metaphor for Santacaterina: "in all my trips between Italy and America, I always tried to bring to Chicago a branch of calicantus, but

I have never been able to make it grow. . . . perhaps I am like the calicantus that does not grow in Chicago."[55] Like Proust's madeleine, it is also what causes her autobiography to flow: "I have a branch of calicantus in my hand that smells sweet and awakens in me the beautiful memory of my youth."[56] A botanical expression is also used as a self-description by another immigrant woman, Lucia Bedarida, an Italian doctor, who followed her daughters to New York when she was eighty, after a broken skull and days in a coma: "I cannot say I am integrated in this environment. The trees, if transplanted old, grow with difficulty."[57]

Born in the village of Chiuppano (Vicenza) in 1905, Santacaterina was raised in Venice by an aunt because her mother died when she was three: "I was like a little bird taken from its nest and brought by a pool of water, always in danger of drowning."[58] When she emigrated from Italy during the Depression, she went by train to Chicago with her husband and son, and in Roseland, a suburb where many workers from Chiuppano had already settled, they immediately recognized the brick houses built by Italian immigrants ("The Venetians, with some help, all built their houses, often little villas built with their own hands").[59] There, life went on much as it had in the mountains of Veneto: "as in all Venetian families, they sold wine and hand-made *grappa*. In the basement there is a lot of alcohol to be sold and the distilling instruments."[60] The *paesani* shunned the area where black people settled, and prejudices against other Italians persisted as well. She could barely tolerate the proximity with Calabrese that she judged with her *campanilismo*: "We have to adapt to the uses of the people from Calabria, people that even lower themselves as to go to pick up coal with the buckets . . . they are proud to be among northern people that respect them."[61] The group of *paesani*, as she calls them with a bonding spirit, struggle together: "As in all misadventures, after a while resignation creeps in, the food is not missing, not even the wine that the government lets Italians produce, and the outlaw grappa. . . . Everyone has his own little piece of garden for the vegetables. . . . There are often dinners based on polenta and birds, wild hens, rabbits, mushrooms, and we compete for who finds more of them."[62]

Santacaterina was involved with an Italian radio program because she was one of the few who didn't speak only a regional dialect. During the war, she met with other women to make packages for soldiers; she became a "rich American" who helped the reconstruction of Italy by sending packages, raising money through her radio program, and helping a poor family to migrate. She also learned to be active and independent, and at fifty-six, she opened a gnocchi factory. It was her own idea: "There was the big problem of convincing my husband to let me go to Milan to buy the gnocchi machine. . . . I decided to leave with my ingredients and with the scarce consensus from my husband."[63] Her gnocchi, ravioli, and tortellini were a huge success, and her children worked for her. But in the end, she was the last to survive of her family, losing her husband and seven brothers.

ELVEZIA MARCUCCI ∾ Another woman who learned to recognize her independence in America was Elvezia Marcucci, a rocky and exceptional woman. Her "Le memorie di una novantenne smemorata (che sarei io)" (The memories of a forgetful ninety-year-old woman [that's me])[64] is written in a neat and trembling handwriting. She was born in 1910 in Grosseto, Tuscany, when "men were at the head of family situations."[65] She lost her father at sixteen: "If I think of everything that happened to me; with him close by I would have avoided it, perhaps."[66] Men were the first reasons for her suffering, starting with the violent Silio, whom she was forced to marry at seventeen. He tried to kill himself when she refused him, and then raped her: "With him I felt as if everything that surrounded me entered inside me, lacerating me. Then I saw him getting up, going toward the door and screaming: 'Now you'll have to marry me!' In my ignorance of sex, I immediately thought I was pregnant, then I should have married him!"[67]

All her pain was poured into the sonata she played on the piano when her mother came home—whose title she remembered ("Nel cor più non mi sento," "I do not feel in my heart") but not the composer. She gave up her dreams of becoming a pianist, and submitted to her husband.[68] In her marriage, resignation was her lot: "It was like swinging on a swing, up and down, always fearing to fall and be hurt, but I had to resign now that I had a daughter with him."[69]

Silio was a mean Fascist and went out with a stick every evening. Elvezia, who learned the ugly face of Fascism when her family's bar was burned down by the *squadracce* in 1922, hated him: "Inside me I detested him, knowing his innate violence."[70] One day he battered her with his stick and she ended up in the hospital with smashed kidneys. He then left as a volunteer for the war and died soon after, in 1944, burnt in his car, at age thirty-four. With the death of her husband, she returned to her happy life in Grosseto with her two children, and "found the pleasure to be still young and free to enjoy life."[71]

Her daughter Mirella married a scientist and left for America, and Elvezia Marcucci, at thirty-seven, followed her in 1947. On the ship from Naples to New York she saw some interracial couples, American soldiers with Italian wives. "I was surprised from that mixture of colors and I defined it as my first American experience."[72] She remembered her first walk in America: "I noticed that people did not talk aloud and gesturing like in Italy."[73] It was in America that Marcucci also savored the taste of independence; she found a job in a garment factory because she needed to be autonomous, and wanted her son to come to America. She even remarried and settled in Utica, New York. But this marriage was completely different; she was strong and she clarified from the beginning: "I am marrying him, but if we don't get along we shall divorce."[74] When he accepts they shake hands, as with a contract,[75] and even her walk through the church was different: "I was more sure of myself and I briskly walked toward the altar."[76]

After a few years of American life, Elvezia was a new woman. She left the factory jobs and worked in an office as a typist. She endured the boredom of her thirty-year marriage, but at least she remained independent: "I thought it was fine with Joe because he would have never had the courage to contrast what I wanted to do."[77] When she realized that her children (both twice married) did not need her anymore, she surprised everyone and returned to her roots: "I was 69 then and still in shape. Feeling still young [enough] to live alone in Grosseto and in my Maremma."[78]

Like Amalia Santacaterina, she lived her last thirty years split between America, where her family was, and Italy, where her soul was:

she visited the United States every year until she suffered paralysis in 1998. The return of the immigrant woman to her home town after thirty-two years is described in poetical sentences that are also a reflection on autobiography, the art of remembering: "in front of my country's sea I am back from another shore. I look at the waves and see my past come back, run on the sand leaving more or less deep traces. It stops, it moves, then with the sea waves it is again lost far away."[79]

ELISABETH EVANS ～ The spelling of Elisabeth Evans's name hints at the fact that her father was English and her mother was Italian. Her *Un attimo una vita* (1996) is a therapeutic confession of a suffering mind, following a model of the "uncertain self" that Diane Bjorklund identifies with the late nineteenth century, when the development of psychology offered autobiographers additional concepts and theories to explain their actions.[80] These characteristics are particularly evident in Evans's writing that focus on the decentering effect of emotions, and she especially treats the long-term struggle with her mother in Freudian terms rather than in common sentimental terms. Her manuscript, she informs us, is closed in a chest, and written by hand in pencil. Even this pencil seems to speak of a very quiet individual: "I feel like I have to apologize for my existence."[81]

Evans was a rebel, yet she suffered from severe depression and from her inability to find her place. Immigration was more a psychological dimension than a real one for her, since she lived in the United States only for a short while. She was not old when she wrote her story, but she did write after the many sorrows of her life had already taken place: "Love my children, nature, people, animals, but not myself. I do not exist. I died so many times that when I try to look for myself I realize I am not here anymore."[82] Born in Rome in 1947, she lived with her grandmother in an artificially well-to-do environment; she was shunned by her father, who never wanted to know her and always fought with her mother.

Her America was the America of Paul Anka and of the young soldier of Camp d'Arby (the NATO base), her first love and husband, Jim. He smelled of beer from the beginning, but she married him and followed him to the United States. Her immigration was full of pain. In New York she felt like an alien; she moved to Texas and then to Fresno, where her husband's parents were, and his drinking and violent behavior ultimately led to her first depression, followed by a miscarriage after more physical abuse, rape by her husband, and another pregnancy. She escaped from him, and lived in a homeless mission. When he left for Vietnam, she forgave him. They moved to Fort Sillis, Oklahoma, where "Jim and his father started to drink again. We have no money and I spend the nights glued to the TV watching the channel that gives tornado warnings."[83]

Elisabeth's America was mythless, naked, and almost surreal. It consisted of hospitals, homeless missions, pills, isolation, tornadoes, a gun that she kept for self-defense, and a drunken abusive husband. She remained there for three years out of stubbornness, almost betting on her own destiny. Her opinion of the United States in the 1970s was merciless: "I learned that here the incredible is normal, that there are no limits to violence. But the funny thing is that all is so covered up by such a well-to-do patina and by such a bigotry that exteriorly this country still succeeds as an example of ideals for the rest of the world."[84] Her American dream vanished in front of this hell, and she was finally free when she left. "There is a moment, when the Alitalia jumbo flies over New York and the vision of the Statue of Liberty lit in the night passes in front of my eyes, in which I feel almost a regret, a desperation, and while it disappears in the dark I cry. I feel I will not see this country anymore where I leave a piece of my life, good or bad. I am twenty-three but it is like being forty."[85]

Evans's autobiography continues with a second marriage, two more children, and an attempted suicide. It closed when she went to England by herself to meet her father's new family, and arrived there two months after his death. Elisabeth Evans's life story is noteworthy because it gives a modern dimension to the immigration of women in the United States.[86] She is not an immigrant worker, not a peasant, but a doomed immigrant wife.

MARIA BOTTIGLIERI ❧ A very different immigrant bride experience belongs to Maria Bottiglieri, author of *Sposa di guerra*,[87] a romantic short story of a young girl who met an American soldier in Naples, and was surprised that she could love an "enemy." "I hated all the allied, as I hated all those who had wanted this war."[88] "How could an American interest me? I hated the winners too much. In Naples I had suffered so much. It wasn't easy to forget the nights passed in the shelters, in the tunnels for the continuous bombing."[89] Like Elisabeth Evans, she was seduced by the America of a song played by the juke-box: *You Never Know.* She fell in love with a soldier and married him on her father's condition that he would not make her travel alone to the United States. Her departure was a moment of personal growth: "When dad hugged me I felt the wish of throwing it all away, of going back home with him, sitting on his knees, letting him cuddle me, but then I realized I had to finish a cycle of my life and start a new one. . . . It was my choice and I had to be brave. . . . Despite my good proposi-tions, when the ship left the harbor and I saw my family getting smaller, I felt evil, egotistical. When would I see them again? Would I have the strength to live without them? I cried for almost the whole trip."[90]

In America she found a job as an Italian teacher and was welcomed by her husband's family, conquered by her Neapolitan *pastiera.* She had two children, and overcame the initial problems with her hus-band: "I was always becoming more American. I ate their way, and sometimes I realized I was even thinking in English."[91] When they were ready to leave for a trip to Naples to celebrate her husband's retirement from flying, he was tragically killed in an airplane crash, on his very last trip. She left alone ("It was almost a pilgrimage I had to make"),[92] and her autobiography was a therapeutic act. The flow of her memories thus started when she was sixty, in Naples. The entire story is dedicated to her husband, written as if talking to him in the "tu" form. Her last words are: "Here I am, John. In Florence I bought a straw hat [as in their first trip together]. . . . And now I am in Naples on the bench in the park where we spoke for the first time. I am sitting with the straw hat on my knees while around me the tree leaves sing songs of love, of love, of love."[93]

The relationship between women and autobiography is a complex one because of women's special roles as storytellers and as memory keep-ers in the family. Our women writers are less concerned with their multiple natures; they feel them but they have no time and no interest to play with them. The writing style of even the more educated women keeps to the brisk manner of those housewives who are too busy around the house to lose time in contemplation. They are not detached enough from their life experience of immigration to allow themselves to play around. Edvige Giunta prefers to use the word *memoir* when discussing a separate genre: "the topic of memoir is not the recount of key events of life, but the exploration of the connections between moments that appear disconnected and that, through the reflection of the narrative voice, become part of a unified, if not homogenous, narrative text."[94] For our women authors, the emphasis is instead on the facts, the stories, and the people.[95] They cling to such ordinary bits and pieces, like the simple branch of calicantus, to tell the stories of their lives.

6 Toward Success

The writers of the autobiographies in this last chapter have achieved success as doctors, professors, or business people, so they belong to a different social class than the rest of our immigrant autobiographers. All share the work ethic that defined our earlier groups of Italian immigrants, but because of intelligence, luck, perseverance, or an indescribable mix of those and other qualities, they have gone on to varying degrees of what we would consider to be success—social, educational, and economic. They view the United States as a land of opportunity, but their standards and their achievements were on a different level from those of the average workers we have already seen.

The Graduate

The autobiographers in this group have studied and earned a college degree, either before leaving for the United States or immediately after. Their writing, naturally, is influenced by their education and their familiarity with words, and they express their thoughts easily. One of the merits of their writing is their ability to assess slices of immigrant life, describing the behavior of entire sections of population, such as sick immigrants or young immigrant students.[1] Even if their social positions do not really fit in the humble category, deep down, they remain the simple worker, aware of their roots. The writers

in this chapter are the ones who are most aware of the tensions between the Italian self and the American society that will become the
main topic for many Italian/American writers of second generation.

VINCENZO GROSSI ∾ A reluctant American doctor, Vincenzo
Grossi wrote his *Ricordi* when he was ninety-seven.[2] His memoirs are
sprinkled with the regret of never having been able to return to
Rome—which he had planned to do all his career. Born in Esperia
Inferiore (Frosinone), in 1891, son of the town's pharmacist, Vincenzo
belonged to an old family that traced its history and economic ven-
tures back two hundred years. His autobiography strongly echoes
those of the medieval merchants of Florence: on the very first page,
he annotates all the donations, inheritances, division of properties,
wedding endowments;[3] he lists the blankets, books, money, and es-
tates that passed through the family's hands. When he relates the story
of his early work as a doctor in Italy, he likewise notes all of his
earnings.

At nine, he entered the boarding school of Montecassino. He eventually studied medicine in Rome, where he worked as a tutor. His
brother Peppino became an engineer; the two became the pride of
their father, who felt "his destiny vindicated."[4] Grossi painted an affectionate portrait of this old world, complete with the feasts and dinners
of the well-to-do family, and he colored it with the regret of the immigrant who is aware of what he has given up: "when I remember our
little world, I ask myself whether it wasn't worth staying there to be a
doctor, like everyone advised me to do when doctor Calcagni died the
year of my graduation. It is true that when I vacation in a nice Italian
town with the nostalgia of the immigrant, after a few days I get bored,
but it is always beautiful to dream that perhaps I could have been
happy in Santupeto all my life."[5]

Grossi started his practice in little towns in central Italy, where he
was the respected doctor. When he failed the exam for assistant surgeon, he thought of America as an escape: "abandoned to myself, I
was so desperate I had the idea of escaping abroad."[6] He left for South
America first; he was back in Italy in 1922 with the hope of a fresh
start, but realizing he had to pay for his sisters' weddings, he thought

about going to North America.[7] He left with a letter of introduction from Mussolini in his pocket for the Italian consul, but to no avail, since the consul was not a Fascist. He passed his American examination in 1923, three months after landing in Boston. After his wedding, to Laura, whom he met in Rome in 1915, he practiced in Boston. He never fit in, and he suffered the company of the poor immigrants as well as the Americans who humiliated him, such as his friend's daughter: "secretly she asked me if a mouse had good flavor, because her school teacher had taught her that Italians eat mice."[8] In 1925 they move to New York, where he finds "gossip that damaged me."[9] Grossi has only dry descriptions of his life in America, and his narration is punctuated with sad events and losses: his wife and his sister lost three babies; his dying mother was "crying that she would not see me again."[10] His heart was clearly elsewhere, and with his wife he decided to leave America: "in 12 years of profession I had not changed my luck and the reasons why I had come were still valid: make a little capital to start a base in Rome."[11] When he saw that his son studied with "the sons of farmers," he sent him to study in Italy, and immediately justified himself: "I was not to be criticized if I sent my son to Italy to study because it was my deep conviction to go back to Rome for the rest of my life."[12] In 1937 his wife left America to stay in Rome with their son, while Grossi kept on working in America, though he wrote to her: "I will come to Rome to cry, we'll make sacrifices, we'll rent our rooms, but I'll die in Rome."[13] He tried to settle in Rome, but failed, and in 1939 he was back in New York: "America became an obsession for me, and in June 1939 I left from Rome, again won by my Destiny."[14] Here he bought a house and saw his son become a doctor in New York's Bellevue Hospital, then go to war in Korea. Beaten by destiny, Vincenzo Grossi was forced to give up his dream, and these are his last words of resignation: "the only vanished dream for me and Laura was that of living in Rome. Now that we could stay in the eternal city, every time that nostalgia lures us, we look at our four grandchildren that grow healthy and beautiful, and finally, we resign to our Destiny."[15] Here this theme of destiny is just as strong with a man we might think had more control of his life, because of privilege and education, as it had been with the poorest working immigrants.

MICHELE DANIELE ∾ A similar tale of loss is that of Michele Daniele, a physician who wrote his autobiography before dying in 1957,
and whose son published it two years later.[16] He was born in Agnone
in Molise in 1879, of an ancient family of sharecroppers who even had
a coat of arms and a motto: "Lavoro e Lealtà" (labor and loyalty), which
remained key words for Daniele. He started off his autobiography by
explaining his ethos as a doctor, a profession inspired by his uncle,
and that he had earned it with much study and great monetary sacrifice. In 1905, his medical degree in hand, he faced a dilemma shared
by many of our immigrants: "I had to balance the greater security of
staying at home, among my own people, against the opportunities
offered by boldly adventuring into a new land and attempting to build
a practice among strangers."[17] After his wedding to the mayor's
daughter, they decided to leave against the family's will ("only the
lowest, poorest, most illiterate element of Italy's population emigrated—what my father-in-law scornfully called la canaglia, the rub-
ble")[18] and went to live among barbarians. They arrived in New York
in 1905. He did not feel any thrill at the sight of the Statue of Liberty,
and even doubted that anyone else did: "it only served to remind me of
all that I had left behind—my family, my friends, my home. Perhaps if
my background had been somewhat humbler . . . I might have been
more excited by that symbol of freedom. Yet I honestly doubt that even
the poorest, lowliest paesano experienced any different sensation that
I did . . . This, I fully appreciate, shatters one of the dearest stereotypes
of romantic legend."[19]

The Danieles were examined in Ellis Island, and immediately set
off to the city, which they saw as a "frenzied maelstrom" of traffic,
noise, and rushing angered people: "where were they rushing to or
why was something I could not comprehend—and, for that matter, I
still cannot. And all of them seemed angry about something. Or if not
angry, at least worried."[20] They tried the elevated train, but feared for
their lives, and got lost outside the city. They finally discovered that
their mysterious destination, "la città dei giovani in Oeeo," was
Youngstown, Ohio, and there they settled, welcomed by their fellow
Agnonesi, who formed a large colony. Daniele described it: the houses

looked American except for Italian touches, such as the vegetable gardens, the religious statues in a corner, a painting over the door. "The interior of their houses remained stubbornly Italian"[21] with their large, gaudy furniture, but "for all its loudness and cheapness it had the breath of life in it; it was warm, alive and colorful."[22] These houses always displayed the hand-cranked phonograph with Italian music; votive candles around a religious image; large wall calendars with battle scenes from the Risorgimento; oil paintings of the Madonna, Saints, Venice or Naples; and portraits of the kings, Garibaldi, Verdi, and Mazzini. Daniele dissolved into this world and adopted the pronoun "we" to identify with these struggling peasants, even if belonging to a somewhat higher class: "we were political outcasts, we had to work extremely hard for whatever we got, our living conditions were not ideal, our health deteriorated. But then," he adds with immigrant philosophy, "where could one find any kind of existence that did not have its drawbacks and shortcomings?"[23]

His five and a half years in Youngstown were perhaps the best of his life, with a healthy wife and two children. He gathered a good practice, thanks to the help of Madame Caroline, a "fallen woman" who liked his honesty and spread his fame: "from a physician's point of view, Youngstown was an ideal place to practice . . . it was a natural breeding place of disease and accident."[24] His first experience was symbolic of the work immigrant doctors often had to do. He was presented with an incurable case of a dying man. In his impotence, he only gave a prescription for mountain air, but not that of Denver, that of Agnone: "he must go back to Italy to his wife and four *bambini*. At least he would die in peace among loved ones."[25] The prescription immediately lightened up the man's face, who eventually died in his hometown. Daniele, like other immigrant doctors, told of people's acute superstition, their fear of medicine and hospitals, and claims of dying children who were cured with magic potions. Daniele became an active crusader in the contraception movement, even though it clashed with his Catholic conscience; he started to sustain birth control after seeing women dying of consumption having had too many babies, or dying after trying to abort them.

Daniele's hard times started when he was forced to go back to Italy for his wife's mental illness and for his own restlessness. He moved back to Agnone, returning "not as an Italian, not even as an ex-Italian, but as an American. That to me was my proudest achievement."[26] They spent all their American savings on getting settled there and they built a magnificent house that was impossible to rent out. He found scattered jobs in various towns of central Italy, and when he was already deciding to return to Ohio, World War I broke out, and he was drafted in the army. He went back home only when his wife was afflicted by a nervous disorder that brought her to suicide. He was able to go back to Youngstown in 1919, and managed to bring his two sons to study in the United States, while his daughter married an Italian doctor. He moved to Cleveland, where he received the news of his daughter's death from typhoid, a tragedy that threw him into desperation and ultimately cost him the success of his practice. He moved about, among the rubber factories of Akron, to Los Angeles, where he could not find patients. At the outbreak of World War II he was called up again for military service. Daniele's conclusion to his autobiography is a negative litany of what his life had not been: I have not accumulated great wealth; in fact, I have never earned at any time in my existence anything that might be called 'great money.' I have not achieved fame. I have not a name. There are no great medical discoveries associated with me. I have not gained any position of power and importance in public affairs.[27]

His only satisfactions were his two sons, his honesty, and his "having lived through life:" "I too have lived through seventy-five years of wars, depressions, disasters, changes, upheavals, crisis, disappointments, triumphs. There are those who might reckon this, in and of itself, as a definite accomplishment."[28] The spirit of his autobiography is this sense of survival in history, the morale of the humble Italian immigrant across many trades and professions.

GIUSEPPE PREVITALI ∾ On the opposite side of Drs. Grossi and Daniele stands Giuseppe Previtali, who was the doctor for New York's East Harlem. He published his long autobiography, spurred on by his spunky American wife; it became a final gift to her after her death.[29] Born in 1879 in the village of Pontida on the Alps, Previtali remembered the first rumor of America as the land where you get rich. A childhood mentor inspired him to study medicine, but in medical school in Turin he wasted his father's money on games and drink, became acquainted with Socialist thought, and was inspired by the teachings of Lombroso, who theorized about the criminal brain. But he graduated with honors, and made his father very proud. The engrossing story of Previtali's graduation occupies the first half of his hefty book.

Shortly after graduation, he received a letter from a fellow student who had gone to America: "America," he wrote, "is a wonderful country. The people here really live a life of liberty and equality. Unlike in Italy, any man, however humble his origins, can make money according to his abilities and the measure of his hard work."[30] After seeing that jobs were not easily available in Italy, Previtali made the decision to leave. He did not praise his courage, for "it was as if a force greater than myself impelled me to go beyond the horizon."[31] His mother gave him a silver medal etched with the sentiment that many parents gave to their departing sons—and we have already seen forms of this wisdom in other autobiographies: "I don't mind if you return penniless or ill, but be sure your conscience is clear."[32]

Previtali arrived in the mining town of Pittson, Pennsylvania. "Everything looked black. Dark smoke rose slowly in the gray sky. A veil of coal dust filtered down from the clouds. A pall of sadness covered the whole town."[33] He was immediately shocked by the news that he had to practice illegally for one year at least until he could pass his boards, and that he had to learn English, and he was further dumbstruck by the ethnic prejudices toward different immigrant nationalities, including Italians: no bowing from the waist (only Germans do that), no kissing on the cheeks (like Frenchmen), no speaking too loudly (like Italians). His landlady apologized for having an Italian in her home. Nevertheless, he soon was able to exclaim: "Oh America! What sweet freedom I did not know in Italy."[34]

Previtali left for New York's Little Italy, where he substituted for an eccentric Italian charlatan: "If I must drown," he thinks, "I don't want to drown in a puddle. The big sea is for me."[35] He managed to pass his examination after only five months, and worked among the immigrants: "Most of the calls were within walking distance and practically all emergencies, to the callers anyway. We rushed, rushed, even if we had plenty of time. It looked better; a busy doctor, an important case."[36] Previtali's experience among the immigrants is captivating. He clashed against the ignorance of peasants, "worst of all is their passivity against illness. Their village priests taught them to accept death as the inexorable will of God."[37] He learned the tricks: never take down the medical history of the patient ("most people will question your reason for taking their names and addresses");[38] to show self-confidence, make a quick diagnosis on the spot without the help of the laboratory; "use a familiar name to them [the immigrants]. Better still, tell them a disease they would like to have. This always works well"; learn the regional Italian names for afflictions.[39] Previtali was shocked by his first experiences, gained the admiration of his patients, and came to love them: "They may be poor, ignorant in their way, but their hearts are pure gold."[40]

Previtali was mainly the doctor of immigrants and the poor, at least before he worked in the pediatrics ward of Bellevue Hospital. He was proud of his Italian origins, and he believed he could treat his patients better than American doctors. "They were incapable of comprehending the problems of their Italian patients. They had no feeling for their hardships. The Italian doctors, even if some of them had some questionable conception of ethics, had the gift of understanding the psychology of their people. Patients would pour out their hearts to them. They told them the story of their economic distress, family perturbations, emotional anguish, so often the factors in the vicious circle that surround illness. . . . [The Italian physician] was able to exert a beneficial influence upon his patients in the areas that bordered on their sickness. On this ground he had the advantage. He was able thus to accomplish the mission of the medical profession more fully."[41]

Previtali kept his immigrant ethos alive. When he described himself and the other young doctors he wrote: "we were young men who were going places. We had this in common: we had come to America to seek our fortune; none had found it."[42] In a theme that runs through many of our immigrant autobiographies, at Previtali's first trip back to Italy, he felt utterly divided between two lands: "I had the sensation of being two persons. I felt double. . . . I was two personalities, ambling along pleasantly together. One took part in the daily life of the ship in a sort of undertone, while the other lived a life that was more real, more beautiful, the life of which I was making my journey. My mind, in fact, had traveled ahead of me to my home in the Alps."[43]

DON PEPPINO ∾ A trimmed moustache, well-built and well-groomed, with good eyes: this is the doctor who worked after hours to fulfill his duty toward his patients and his family.[44] His real name was Giuseppe Tomasulo, but Don Peppino, his pen name, is more faithful to his own inner image. "It seems more indicated for my nature, which prefers the familiar language, that which gives a sweet sensation of intimacy, so dear to simple beings."[45] He thus identifies deeply with his job and with the way his patients address him. His entire autobiography is an apology of this straight man, spurred by a sense of duty toward his profession and his family. On his loyalty to these two values he measured his morality and his weight as a man.

Born 1877 in Sanfele (Lucania) and writing at about eighty years of age, Tomasulo adopted the mode of the American success story, based on individualism and a recipe for success à la Ben Franklin. Like immigrants Angelo Massari and Costantine Panunzio, Don Peppino dedicated the last part of his book to "the exposition of the principles that I followed from the day I started my career to the day that I gave it my farewell."[46] Here he described his principles as a doctor, the importance of even the poorest clients, his consideration for communicating in simple language, the equal weight given to curing the body and the mind, and to prevention.

"If, despite my innate reluctance, I decided to write not my biography but a modest chronicle of my life, I only did it to oblige the desire of my family, clients, and friends to whom I dedicated the few copies of this publication."[47] Notwithstanding all this, he stresses his own individual importance, even elevating his profession to the level of gods with a quote by Cicero: "in nothing man gets closer to the gods than in giving back health to other men."[48] His sense of individual self is shaped by Virgil's verse "audaces fortuna juvat" ("luck helps the brave") that he adopts as his own: "I have always been brave and I owe my modest successes to my audacity. No difficulty seemed insuperable to me. No contrariety made me desist from perseverance."[49]

He studied medicine in Naples, but being one of the poor students, he worked hard and never forgot that he belonged to the class of fighting people. America was the way out of his family's debts and building his own career. He arrived in New York and after only two months, at twenty-four, took the exam for his license. He became a family doctor for the Italian community. He dedicated a large part of his autobiography to his friends and colleagues, to the *pensione* Bosi, where he would eat his lunch, and to his patients: the one who cuts his cheek with a razor one night in the darkness, or the lady who makes him "confused and very mortified" by telling him, "we have to pray God to make us sick before seven at night!"[50]

At the end of his career, due to nervous stress after fifty years of work, "Doctor Peppino" made a balance of his life as a material man, a *homo economicus*: "my economical situation was the following: I had a house but I did not own my office anymore. I had bank titles but not enough to satisfy our needs."[51] He was a happy man with a rich wife and six children, and he immersed himself in the universal flux of life. This is how the "average" immigrant sees his life, as a shiny, interesting moment that sinks again under the waves and merges into the flux of universal destiny: "I enjoyed youth and maturity like I now enjoy old age . . . this philosophy of mine makes me consider old age as the survival of the individual spirit in the spirit of the universe."[52]

JOSEPH TUSIANI ∾ Just as the physician immigrants in our study formed a diverse but connected unit, a group of four college professors are the next group. The most accomplished of these writers is Joseph Tusiani, who reached fame not only as a professor and a literary critic, but also as a translator and a poet in English, Italian, and Latin. Tusiani's exceptional autobiography, which the critic Martino

Marazzi recently defined as "the great and true book" of Italian American literature,[53] covers his forty years in America. Written in Italian and published in Italy, it comprises three volumes, all centering around the word *la parola: La parola difficile, La parola nuova,* and *La parola antica.*[54] Each is a complete book built on a self-sufficient thematic knot: the first is about his birth to new life with his arrival, the meeting with his father, and the birth of his brother, his search for a job, his entry into Italian American and American literary circles, and his friendship with the writers Arturo Giovannitti and Frances Winwar. The second revolves around the inner conflict between his American brother and his Italian self—another version of the second-generation complex of split identity. The third is about the resolution of such conflicts and the conclusion of the parable of migration with the death of the first immigrants, his father and uncle. The internal conflict that drives the third book is threefold: the protagonists are the American son Michael (Maichino), the Italian son Giose, and the immigrant mother, Maria, who does not speak English. They represent three different degrees of Italian American identity: the first still rooted in Italy even if her body is in America, the mother; the second split between loyalty and love toward the motherland and the opportunities offered by America, Giose; and the third that completely refuses Italy in order to embrace the new land, Michael. The three levels are played out on the different language of choice, which is a game for a poet like Tusiani: Mike speaks only English, the mother sticks to Italian, and Giose translates between the two languages, speaking Italian—but not like his mother—and English—but not like his brother. As we can see, there is a strict correspondence among the dramatic conflicts of life in America: father-son in the first book, brother-brother in the second, mother-American family in the third.

The first is a book of dawn, reflecting the inner condition of starting life anew. Even though he was already a college graduate in Italy, he was still unable to call his father "papa." The second book is the conflict with his brother, and it is a work of high noon, completely immersed in the activity of American life, while the third is a twilight work, with its heartfelt homage to the old immigrants and its melancholic vocabulary. Tusiani's harmonious, elegant, and refined English prose has echoes of Latin and Italian, and his Italian prose is on the verge of pomposity, but always touching. He plays with words and with semantic antitheses, as when defining the "people from San Marco who came here to suffer more in order to suffer less" or Arturo Giovanitti, "punished by life for having won death."[55]

Born in 1924 in San Marco in Lamis on the Gargano, Tusiani arrived in the United States after his graduation, joining his father, whom he did not even remember. He defines himself as "two strange halves of one man" in his poem "Gente mia." He is the writer of Italian America: he avoids speaking about his physical birth and his Italian youth, but begins right at the time of his metaphorical birth to the American life, his arrival in the harbor of *Nuova York,* which are the first words of his autobiography. His first American period is dedicated entirely to the search for a job, because *la giobba* is what defines the immigrant: Tusiani's description of Italian touches in a foreign land reveals the profound love that the writer feels for both, the original Italy and the recreated one ("like all immigrants I ended up giving half of my heart to both of them").[56] When he arrived in the Bronx, his eye caressed the houses of his countrymen, all distinguished by "a horse shoe well visible in the center of the gate, a little statue of Saint Anthony in a grotto or colored stones, a statue of a black servant with a lantern that the wind made swing, and some meters of garden with its last fiery red tomatoes."[57] He captured the pleasurable pain of how the immigrant's dual situation could trigger an almost unbearable nostalgia: "those who never stepped outside Italy do not know what it means to hear a sudden song from the native village in a foreign land. Your eyes get wet, all the faces of old friends pass in front of you as if on a magical screen, you see each grassy slope, each steep alley, you clearly hear the bells of the churches, and you pass your finger on your eye to dry a tear without shame."[58]

Tusiani is attracted to his immigrant group and at the same time, he feels the sting of prejudice for belonging to it, as when a teacher asked him about his knife in school, or when he was ashamed of his people who ate squirrel and stole public flowers. The double soul of the immigrant was clear to him when he returned to Italy after an absence of seven years: "my roots were there, but my branches were elsewhere. In sum, I was in an incredible limbo, between ecstasy and anguish, between pleasure and duty. I was and I was not myself: I was between two worlds, two dreams, two concrete civilizations still not wholly comprehensible."[59]

As Paolo Giordano noted, Tusiani "is the only Italian/American author who looks at the language question as a spiritual dilemma more than a sociological problem."[60] Tusiani sees the tragedy of those who remain entrenched in the old language of Italy: his old friend Coco, who learned too late, when he was eighty; his mother, who is heard saying English "is a language as ugly as a debt;[61] and the old architect who refused English tout-court in his house, *la lingua maledetta,* and died alone and silent, forever rejecting the America at his threshold and forever rejected by it.

The same loving portrait of the old immigrants is present in *La parola antica,* the third part of his autobiography. Tusiani's tragedy of miscommunication reached its apex in the heartbreaking scene of Nonna and her grandchildren, who go on for many lines speaking two different languages, misunderstood, brushing each other and never meeting. "What are you saying?" "sei? Non siamo sei [six]; siamo tre [three]: Maico, Polina e Nenì . . . Tre." "Tray? Nanny wants to see the tray" . . . "I love you, nanny," "ai l'ova [eggs] iu"—"Well, those 'eggs' that wanted to mean affection and love, she could not digest still."[62] As a middleman, Tusiani is able to speak both to the America of his brother and the Italy of his parents, and to describe the drama that has generated many of our autobiographies.

FRANCESCO VENTRESCA ∾ The next three writers deeply differ from Tusiani. They can be considered almost second-generation, and their ethos is less lacerated than Tusiani's. Left as a humble working man, Francesco Ventresca, born in 1872, graduated from college in the United States and wrote his autobiography, a Horatio Alger story in which "very little about the author's inner life is revealed. Instead, Ventresca concentrated on recording his actions and the people he meets on his rise to prosperity."[63] Ventresca wrote his story in 1936, when he was sixty-four and at the apex of his teaching career.[64] He was thus completely absorbed in his success story, dissected for his readers in all its stages. It is a didactic story whose implied readership is not his close family, but the wider public, starting with his classroom, as he was chairman of the department of foreign languages at Manley High School of Chicago.

Ventresca's education is the protagonist of this life story and the metaphor of his life. He left Italy ignorant of English (he studied until third grade), and this vexed his first American years, during which he made little money with humble jobs. When he was nineteen he discovered that he hungered for knowledge more than anything else, and this marked his growth into an American citizen. Education is his "way" to America, as it appears from this image: "I bought an Italian-English grammar not later than the second day in New York. I still have and prize that grammar which I bound, myself, with a railroad map of the United States."[64]

Ventresca's dependency on his group of fellow immigrant laborers ended when his distinction in education began. His detachment from the mass, the group, the material men, began with a book: "from now on I was living with my countrymen in body, but not in heart and mind. While they chattered and played and sometimes cursed, I was busy reading my lessons as loud as I dared and looking up definitions in the dictionary."[65] He went on to attend primary school at twenty-one and eventually earned a master's degree from the University of Chicago: "Wonders for me! The atmosphere of the campus and the beautiful dignified buildings . . . were uplifting to the man with the right kind of mind and soul!"[66] The schoolhouse and the campus are two concrete locations that make it possible for him to mark his success on a map.

Success stories like this one buy into the individualistic American mode of narration, breaking with the communal tradition that is still strong in our humble autobiographies. Benjamin Franklin was Ventresca's model, in its reflections on his healthy habits such as not drinking and his daily prayers. There is no halfway here, as in the humbler autobiographies: the old gods have been discarded completely and a new American identity is born: "I am not a bit superstitious," Ventresca writes, "I have lost entirely what little superstition was taught me by neighbors, who thoroughly believed in ghosts and in witches and in the wizards to whom the witches had to report at midnight on certain days of week."[67] With this autobiography we find a shift in the themes that have linked our immigrants' stories so far, because here the hero is not merely surviving, he is not simply accepting destiny that is handed to him. He is instead making his own way, following Franklin's more independent-minded prototype of American success. When Ventresca recounted two episodes of seemingly miraculous situations (a boulder rolls down from an open car and stops an inch from his foot; he jumps away from a train passing at incredible speed) he took all the merit for himself, refusing—even if tempted—to think of a higher fate.

LEONARD COVELLO ∿ Leonard Covello wrote his autobiographies in the 1950s, after having become established in the world of academics.[68] He remained humble and down to earth, even refusing a university career to remain faithful to his vocation as a high-school teacher and principal in underprivileged schools of New York. According to James Holte, Covello's book was "intended as a lesson. . . . [It] reaches out from personal experience of one man to address universal concerns. And in so doing becomes part of the great traditions of American personal writing."[69] Covello's immigrant self became inseparable from his teaching self: he designed a new method to teach Italian immigrant students and appreciated his students' heritage and made them comfortable with it.

His ethos as a teacher is established from the first page, where he counts the forty-five years spent as a teacher in public schools and twenty-two as a principal of Benjamin Franklin High School in East Harlem. Born in Avigliano (Potenza) in the 1880s, Covello devoted much of his book to his difficult childhood and the attitudes of his authority figures toward the position of children. In 1896 his family left to join his father, an immigrant in America. In New York he started his American life divided between being Italian at home and American at school, as is the pattern of a second-generation immigrant. Education was for him a gift of his new land, together with the hope of something better: "The very essential difference between working hard in Italy and working hard in America became apparent to us who were young. In Italy it was work and work hard with no hope of any future."[70] Never shying away from difficult jobs (since he was twelve he worked three hours before school delivering bread), he made his way with scholarships and graduated from Columbia University.

Covello's highest accomplishment was spreading the teaching of Italian in New York high schools. His own experience of shame and alienation made him discover that the best way to the students' Americanization was not to forsake their native language, but to use it. He also knew that knowing their culture would only enhance their self-confidence: "the idea was to acquaint these young men with their Mediterranean culture and give them an appreciation of and a pride in the country of their parents."[71] It is only after a long path teaching English and French that Covello became reconciled with his own language. It took him a while to go back to his own roots and start spreading the Italian language. As in Joseph Tusiani's work, language has a strong presence in this autobiography. In 1920, he entered a classroom of twenty-five boys "who formed my first class in Italian at De Witt Clinton High School, perhaps the only Italian class in any public school in the country at that time."[72] Against the accusation of segregating his students and keeping them out of America (especially in a time of postwar conformity), his program succeeded, and he saw the enrollment grow from twenty-five students in 1920 to over five hundred students in 1925. He published a textbook, *First Book in Italian*, in 1923.

ANGELO PELLEGRINI ❧ With Angelo Pellegrini in particular, we find an example of clear and simple Americanization through education.[73] A university professor, Angelo Pellegrini wrote *Immigrant's Return* by starting with the poetical dilemma of whether to be buried in Italy or America. His entire book is a mild success story, but most of all it is a reflection on what America has given to him.[74] Like Covello, Pellegrini can be considered a second-generation immigrant: he arrived in America when he was only nine years old. He remembered his childhood in the little town of Casabianca (Florence), but his trip to America in 1913 was for him a new birth. America appeared with its "Great American Breakfast," a buffet where one only has to *"just ask for it!* So that was America! Just ask for it! Or, *just reach for it!"*[75] He settled in the wilderness of the state of Washington in the mill town of McCleary. He offers interesting reflections on what it meant to be an Italian peasant—accustomed to fences and landscape "endings," to elbowing people, to fighting a sterile land—now suddenly lost in the wide American spaces, where nature is wasted and man just takes from it and moves on. An example of this for him is wood, chopped badly in the forest, with stumps left in the ground, and burned unendingly with a conveyer belt that throws it into the fire. The conveyer belt becomes the metaphor of the incommunicable distance between Italy and America: he never succeeded in describing the conveyor to his Italian relatives, because "in the language of an Italian peasant there were no words adequate to describe such good fortune as we had found. The New World simply could not be communicated in the idiom of the Old. The conveyor and the perpetual fire, out of their context, would have seemed to my friends in Italy the vision of an irresponsible mind. And at that time I could not have supplied the context necessary to give the phenomenon meaning."[76] Language also measured his distance from his parents. He could not explain to them the ways of his American world: "When I tried to explain to them in Italian why it was important that I should play in the baseball team and participate in school programs, the language not only proved inadequate to my needs; it made my preoccupations sound silly. The glory of a home run was simply not transmissible in Italian."[77]

Pellegrini stuck to his origins and remained proud of his double language. He never traded his culture for America. He was conquered by America as only an almost second-generation immigrant can be, relinquishing completely the double identity that some of our earlier autobiographers had shown, when he emphasized: *"I am not an Italian; I am an American. I issued from my Mother's womb in Italy; but I was born in America."*[78] This autobiography, as Francesco Ventresca's, begins to show a blurring border between autobiographies of immigration and autobiographies of Americans. Pellegrini and the other doctors and college graduates in this section enlarge the scope of immigrant life, giving new perspectives to the idea of quiet individualism, as it is seen from the standpoint of someone who has attained success but still has a modesty and an awareness of their humble past.

The Sweet "Self" of Success

This last section of autobiographies is devoted to the stories of immigrants who have been particularly successful. They constitute a small percentage of our autobiographies; however, they also represent what until now has been the most typical idea of an immigrant autobiography as a mere success story. They belong to that category that critics of immigrant autobiographies have read as stories of Americanization and American individualism. The first signal that points to the fact that these lives have a strong American inclination is the very fact that they are all written in English. The language connotes a clear choice in the ethos of these immigrants.

ANGELO MASSARI ∾ The very title betrays Angelo Massari's autobiography as a success story: *The Wonderful Life of Angelo Massari*.[79] This is the story of a self-taught man who rose from the streets to become the head of the International Bank of Tampa, a bank that survived the 1929 crash. His autobiography was written for the family, he says, but it is geared to exalt the figure of the successful banker.

Born in 1886 in Sicily, at sixteen Massari immigrated to Tampa, where a community of Sicilians were settling, and he started working in the cigar factories. He had received only eight months of formal education, but he avidly read books. He immediately embraced "the practical side of life,"[80] and first opened a fruit stand, then a fruit shop, and finally, in 1925, a bank "that could protect and abet the interest of our countrymen, serve without any selfish motive our community, and show the local ethnic groups and also the natives that the Italians of Tampa were capable of accomplishing big things in the financial world."[81]

When he returned to Sicily twenty years after his departure, at thirty-seven, he portrayed himself as an exception among returned immigrants: "I was only thirty-seven years old and financially I had been quite successful. I had returned to my homeland in a much better position than the others."[82] "I am a positivist. I am a modest thinker. I am a good executive, I have initiative and plenty of imagination, but above all I am a hard worker."[83] "I have always used to live my own way without any outside help. I was never taken ill. . . . This seems hard to believe, but it is true."[84]

He boasted of being the individual who detached himself from the herd: "The common herd annoys me and I detest it. Dealing with intellectuals I gain, with the others I lose."[85] Individuality and freedom were his American values: "The main reason why I have never sought association with others is due to the fact that I have always wanted to be and remain free, and to act freely in accordance with my free will." The last chapter of his autobiography is dedicated to his "word of advice" for future generations, six pages with the list of his principles in the tradition of Benjamin Franklin. Among this advice are rules: keep to oneself, do not show off, be sincere, never humiliate people, never create revulsion against yourself, say nothing if you cannot speak well of a person, look at people straight in the eye, and never offend or neglect anyone.

GUIDO ORLANDO ∾ Another individualist is the publicity agent Guido Orlando who wrote *Confessions of a Scoundrel* in 1954, a book that seems his ultimate act of self-publicity.[86] Born in 1909 in Barisciano, in the south of Italy, Orlando emigrated from his home when, at a young age, he was lured by the promises of America. Orlando's ethos is that of a working-man, but most of all that of a "scoundrel" who is not ashamed to use any trick and lie to move people to do what he wants. He started young, when he pretended to be playing in a band, without knowing music at all, in order to sell guitars: "playing to an audience and making a profit out of it. This was the first successful bluff I ever threw."[87] His entire life was a rhetorical bluff: he was a public relations man who built movie stars out of nothing (these included Greta Garbo, with her image of shyness, Zsa Zsa Gabor, and Rudolf Valentino), who could sell the desert (Desert Palm Spring in California), and help politicians win (Roosevelt and La Guardia, who both forgot him afterward, and De Gasperi, in Italy, in 1948). Power fed his ego. His autobiography hypes his public image, which naturally shakes our faith in the storyteller, though he has a colorful character and a gripping story. The book gives another side of Italian immigration—the immigrant as a trickster.

His persona is built through the episodes of his life, and at one point he encountered one of the most famous Italian poets, Gabriele D'Annunzio, during a visit to his elementary school. Young Orlando asked him: "Sir, how can I do what I want to do when I grow up?" D'Annunzio replied: "You have asked a very good question, young man. First, you decide what you want to do—then, don't let anyone stop you."[88] When he won a scholarship offered by two wealthy Americans, he arrived in Boston only to find that they were dead. When he instead started to work with his father, Orlando started selling newspapers and even used his own immigration as a persuasive means. When he finds clients hard to convince, he tells them: "Look, mister, I am a poor boy from Italia, trying to help my family buy food," or "I'm just an immigrant kid, trying to work my way through school."[89]

His self-creation was the great gift of immigration, and through that self-promotion he learned to promote other peoples' images as well. At forty-four, he was still selling newspapers on the street, as a well-thought publicity stunt that stresses the success of his story as an individual who made it: "On July 29, 1953, I went out on the streets of Paris for the 5th year and sold newspapers. What began as a simple piece of self-promotion had turned into an annual event. The original purpose of the trick was to remind caste-conscious Europeans of the fact that I was something of a Horatio Alger American. The idea that a man of any stature was ever a newsboy remains unbelievable to most citizens of France, Germany, and Italy. And it was worth business and money to me to pose as an alien eccentric—within limits. It fitted their idea of what an American should be. And therefore, it was always good for free newspaper space."[90]

FORTUNE GALLO ᔆ Very similar to Guido Orlando is Fortune Gallo, who also worked as an impresario in the shadow of famous stars. His autobiography, written at the age of seventy, tells the story of a man whose very name is luck: Fortunato.[91] Born in 1878 in Torre Maggiore (Foggia) at his birth his father explained to the priest: "Upon this baby I bestow the name of Fortunato, combined with the family name of Gallo, it will be a perfect description of him, I hope—Lucky Rooster."[92] Fortunato played the harmonica and became a young musician, he organized a little band, and thus started his job as impresario at a young age. He was immediately lucky in starting his own business, adapting quickly to American life: "I missed the slower tempo of life back in Italy. It took a determined effort on my part to get back into the swing of things, to attune myself to the quicker pace."[93] He married an American girl from San Francisco, and spent thirty-seven years bringing Italian opera and operettas to America.

VINCENT SARDI ⌘ Another immigrant whose name identifies with his business is the restaurateur Vincent Sardi, whose autobiography tells the story of his restaurant.[94] Even if this is a success story Sardi's work ethic is clear from the start, where he outlines the story of his humble beginning and then of his life through the restaurant, with the description of his clients. Sardi basked in the reflected light of his patrons, and also gave the example of Tony Curtis, who shined shoes in front of the restaurant until he became a famous actor and a client. But Sardi also remembered the drama of the fellow immigrant, Mr. Frank Cavaluzzi, the ice man, who day in and day out, never missed a day, until one morning collapsed and died in the restaurant without even seeing one of his many children return from the army.

Born in 1885, in the village of San Marzano Oliveto (Alessandria) in Piemont of a well-to-do family, Sardi attended boarding school. He was a mischievous boy and was sent to work on a ship as a punishment: "That's what families did to incorrigible boys in those days. I decided not to run away after all. The prospect of going aboard a real ship was fascinating." Like Panunzio, he learned the hard life of the schooners when he was only eleven and a half years old. He went to London with his uncle and worked as a waiter in an Italian restaurant. He learned good manners as a servant for a surgeon, and thus was able to find work in elegant restaurants and hotels. At twenty-one he knew his job well, but had experienced a hard life: "I was telling some of my boyhood experiences in London to my son. 'Why, Dad' he said, 'that sounds like something out of Dickens.' 'I don't know about that,' I said. 'But I do know that in those early days, I certainly had a dickens of a time.'"[95] This idea of living the novelistic life without knowing it is common among immigrants: their life was adventurous and interesting even if they didn't realize it.

In 1907 Sardi left with his brother for America. His first image of New York was shocking: "I thought I had never seen anything so ugly. The streets . . . were drab and dark, and the storefronts were covered with soot and grime. . . . Sometimes the noise really got on my nerves. Everything was shaking. Now after 50 years it is truly my home."[96] Sardi worked in fine restaurants, and met his wife, who was from Castel Afero, near Canelli. He bought the restaurant from his friend Mario Cremona, also from Canelli, and struggled to pay the bills with a second job at a nightclub. Sardi eventually became completely Americanized, and when he returned home for his mother's burial, he was surprised to realize he was no longer an Italian. He even started eating only American brands of pasta: "It was hard for me . . . to get used to the way of speaking with the hands. And of all things, I missed the drinking water!"[97]

FRANK CAPRA ∾ The autobiography of the movie director Frank Capra actually has relatively little on his experiences as an immigrant.[98] As he said to Vito Zagarrio, that one is an identity he wishes to forget because his life started anew in America: "I was only six years old. What roots could I have had? . . . Before the big ship I don't remember anything."[99] Capra brushed over his humble beginning in America, in the Sicilian ghetto of Los Angeles, only explaining in the book's preface how he hated being poor. "I wanted out. A quick out. I looked for a device, a handle, a pole to catapult myself across the tracks from my scurvy habitat of nobodies to the affluent world of somebodies."[100] His hard work saw him through: "conquering adversities was so simple I began to think of myself as another Horatio Alger, the success kid, my own rags-to-riches hero."[101]

Capra's autobiography is less about being an Italian immigrant, which he downplayed, and more about his success. After many years he went back to see the shack he grew up in, and manipulated the episode into a sentimental cinematic narrative: "How could they know that their run-down house had been built by courage; the courage of two middle-aged, penniless, illiterate peasants who had dared travel halfway around the world to meet the unknown fearful challenge of a strange land, a strange people, a strange language? and who slaved like oxen and fought like tigers to feed and clothe their children. And who fed them. And clothed them. And one of them became a film director."[102]

It is only in these last stories that we encounter a few autobiographies of immigrant authors who are so successful and self-confident that they begin to be exceptions to some of our critical characterizations of these writings as a whole. In fact, their optimistic, self-assured, and self-satisfied attitudes provide the counterpoint that actually defines and clarifies my conclusions about immigrant autobiographies in general. This last section—which we might say has a few "loud" individuals—provides what we now recognize as the exception, not the rule of immigrant success. A few of these last writers tell of their lives as a machine of achievement, not as a battered cog in history. These exceptions to Italian immigrant life are far from the stony ground of the humble working immigrants who picked rags, trash, stones, and mine walls in an effort to eke a subsistence from the earth. For this last group, Italian life is memory that is deliberately sublimated to the background in favor of American ways.

Conclusion

We have now witnessed in these pages proof of the reversal of Giuseppe Prezzolini's 1963 conclusions about Italian immigrant autobiography—his claim, which we read earlier, that the immigrants didn't want to remember their past, how they left no written word, how "Immigration was a great mute tragedy. . . . The survivors do not want to remember."[1] This book is full of evidence of how ardently these people wanted their memories preserved. Italian American autobiographical material has existed all along, but its study was hampered by the fact that it didn't match the heroic claims of greatness that fit with the mid-twentieth-century view of what was worthy material for an autobiography, what could be deemed a literary work, what could bear analysis and scrutiny as a historical document, or what might be an ideal achievement of an immigrant in America.

That earlier generation of readers and critics were not prepared to acknowledge anything other than stories that followed idealistic templates of Americanization, of great transformations, of fabulous rags-to-riches tales. But when we read over the many autobiographies sampled here, we can see the overwhelming evidence of what really took place: the preponderance of descriptions of good, solid, working-class lives are in stark contrast to the isolated but often-cited "autobiographies of success." And even the "success" for most of the men whose lives we just reviewed in the last chapter was not

155

equated with fame among movie stars; it meant higher education, an advanced degree, a professional career—but still, a simple life.

In the large center of the bell curve of our Italian immigrant autobiographies are numerous accounts of humble achievements of simple, hard-working people. Each had a modest but satisfied sense of his or her accomplishments after the earthquake of immigration, a sense that they had lived their lives not perfectly, but not dishonorably, and in a way that justified the small indulgence, at their age, of writing their story.[2] Likewise, my characterization of "quiet individualism" fits all but the extreme stories at the lip of the bell: the vast majority of our writers didn't win life's big prizes, but they made it through, they lived their lives well, weighing modest successes with life's letdowns. Hear how quiet individualism drove even Dr. Michele Daniele: "Judged simply and solely by the worldly measure of things, mine I am afraid could not be called a 'success story.' I have not accumulated great wealth; in fact, I have never earned at any time in my existence anything that might be called 'great money.' I have not achieved fame. I have not a name. There are no great medical discoveries associated with me. I have not gained any position of power and importance in public affairs. Thus from a purely mundane standpoint my life has been anything but a resounding, resplendent triumph."[3]

This group of some sixty Italian Americans who tell their stories here experienced universal struggles shared by all of us, and suffered immigration traumas comparable to those that many ethnic immigrant groups have faced; in this way we can see many universal truths in these examples. But these stories of Italian American lives offer local color and cultural detail that isn't provided by immigration statistics, something even more vivid and illustrative than photographs of immigrants. For we have here the voices of these men and women, inflected with their various regional dialects, telling their stories that are shaped by their own Italian ethnic customs, values, oral traditions, and domestic styles. Their voices, their Italian English words, speak to us simply but vividly to fill in the otherwise empty silhouettes of the survivor, the quiet individual.

Notes

Introduction

1. This short portrait, of Pietro Riccobaldi's father-in-law, is taken from Riccobaldi's autobiography: Pietro Riccobaldi, *Straniero indesiderabile* (Milan: Rosellina Archinto, 1988).
2. Giuseppe Prezzolini, *I trapiantati* (Milan: Longanesi, 1963), 409, 242. All translations of autobiographical and scholarly material in this book are my own unless otherwise indicated.
3. Ibid., 403.
4. The only work similar to mine is Camilla Cattarulla, *Di Proprio pugno: Autobiografie di emigranti italiani in Argentina e Brasile* (Reggio Emilia: Diabasis, 2003) where she gathered eighteen autobiographies by Italian immigrants from the cities of Argentina and the Brazilian countryside. Cattarulla's work presents several stylistic and sociological comments that find confirmation in my research. She started her research by regretting the absence of interest for these "submerged" writers that are catalogued as ignorant (11) and she saw autobiography as a vital way of "reuniting the different pieces of the mosaic of the I" (13). She claimed it to be a democratic right belonging to every living person, regardless of the life's exemplary value. If there is one involuntary flow to her work it is that all texts are translated in a correct standard Italian that overly purifies them and does not reveal the truer broken voices of immigration that are evident in their original Italian.
5. Francesco Durante, *Italoamericana: Storia e Letteratura degli italiani negli Stati Uniti* (Milan: Mondadori, 2005), 2 vols.
6. These include excerpts by the bootblack Rocco Corresca, the pick-and-shovel poet Pascal D'Angelo, the anarchist Carlo Tresca, the preacher Constantine Panunzio, and the teacher Francesco Ventresca.

7. Piero Bevilacqua, Andreina De Clementi, Emilio Franzina, ed., *Storia dell'emigrazione italiana: Partenze* (Rome: Donzelli Editore, 2001), and *Storia dell'emigrazione italiana: Arrivi* (Rome: Donzelli Editore, 2002).

8. "È certo che l'autobiografia ha un grande valore storico, in quanto mostra la vita in atto e non solo come dovrebbe essere secondo le leggi scritte o i principii morali dominanti." Antonio Gramsci, *Quaderni del Carcere*, ed. Valentino Gerratana (Turin: Einaudi, 1977), 1718.

9. The two largest waves came ashore in the period of the Great Migration (1880–1924) and after World War II (1947–1969). According to the Bureau of Census, 1880 is the first year to see more than ten thousand immigrants (12,354); in 1903 there were 230,622 immigrants, nearly twenty times as many. The peak year of the Great Migration was 1907, with 285,731 entries. The numbers decreased in the years generally around World War I (1915–1920), but saw another peak in 1921 with 222,260 immigrants. After the Quota Act of 1924 the numbers never raised to more than 22,327 (1930). After World War II, the highest number of immigrants entered in 1956 (40,430). U.S. Department of Commerce, Bureau of Census' Statistical Abstracts and Reports, gathered in Luciano Iorizzo and Salvatore Mondello, *The Italian Americans*, rev. ed. (Boston: Twayne, 1980), 285.

10. Jerry Mangione and Ben Morreale, *La Storia: Five Centuries of the Italian American Experience* (New York: Harper Collins, 1992), 364.

11. This expression "autobiographies from unexpected places" is from Martha Ward, *A Sounding of Women: Autobiographies from Unexpected Places* (Boston: Allyn and Bacon, 1998), devoted to autobiographies of women.

12. Ibid., xvii.

13. Holt was the editor of New York's *The Independent* between 1892 and 1921. His collection was my source for the autobiography of the bootblack Rocco Corresca, discussed in this volume. See Hamilton Holt, ed., *The Life Stories of Undistinguished Americans, As Told by Themselves* (New York: Routledge, 1990).

14. Scott Sandage, *Born Losers: A History of Failure in America* (Cambridge: Harvard University Press, 2005), 9.

15. "My mother-in-law could wield a spade and thread a needle with undisputed authority, but the one thing I rarely saw in her hand was a pen," wrote Bea Tusiani in her autobiography dedicated to the powerful figure of her mother-in-law, Maria, from whom she was always divided by the language barrier.

16. The original Italian of the quotations from autobiographies is included in the endnotes as a reference.

17. As Werner Sollors explains, "our own age of multiculturalism has tended to ignore language as a factor in American literary and cultural diversity"; see Marc Shell and Werner Sollors, eds., *The Multilingual Anthology of American Literature: A Reader of Original Texts with English Translations* (New York: New York University Press, 2000), 2.

18. In Shell and Sollors, *Multilingual Anthology*, two Italian texts appear, one in Italian, "Poet's Lament" by the librettist Lorenzo Da Ponte, and the other in French, Luigi Donato Ventura's *Peppino*, which Alide Cagidemetrio has shown to be an intricate case because it shows different connotations, depending on the language it is written: it was written in French by an Italian author, then cleaned up when translated into English, as if readapted for a different audience.

19. Werner Sollors, *Beyond Ethnicity: Consent and Descent in American Culture* (New York: Oxford University Press, 1986). He stresses the evils of a limitation based on descent that favors a kind of "biological insiderism." The struggle between descent and consent has been described in other terms, by Rose Basile Green in *The Italian-American Novel: A Document of the Interaction of Two Cultures* (Madison: Fairleigh Dickinson University Press, 1974). She is perhaps the first one to consider immigrant writers according to a fourfold model of assimilation–revulsion–counterrevulsion–rooting. Her distinctions have been used by several other critics, but few openly refer to her book. Related to this is the more general quarrel between the local and the universal. Aijad Ahmad questions a simplistic worldview that divides the globe into first, second and third worlds, and underlines a more complicated and rich landscape. He challenges a simple definition of the critic (Jameson, in this case) departing from his ethnic origin: "Where do *I*, who do not believe in the Three Worlds Theory, in which *world* should I place his [Jameson's] text: the first world of his origin, the second world of his ideology and politics, or the third world of his filiation and sympathy?" Aijad Ahmad, "Jameson's Rhetoric of Otherness and the 'National Allegory,'" *Social Text* 17 (1987): 24.

20. Sollors, *Beyond Ethnicity*, 6.

21. As Steven Hunsaker emphasizes, all autobiography is a way of negotiating the concept of one's nation; see his *Autobiography and National Identity in the Americas* (Charlottesville: University of Virginia Press, 1999).

22. Samuel Baily stresses positive personal responses to the experience of migration in his two books: *One Family, Two Worlds: An Italian Family's Correspondence across the Atlantic, 1901–1922* (New Brunswick, NJ: Rutgers University Press, 1988); Samuel Baily, *Immigrants in the Lands of Promise: Italians in Buenos Aires and New York City, 1870–1914* (Ithaca, NY: Cornell University Press, 1999). The immigrant should not be seen as "a helpless victim of large impersonal structural forces such as economic cycles and labor markets." Baily, *One Family*, 2.

Chapter 1
Autobiography: The Literary Genre of Immigration

1. Gramsci thus criticized the intellectual class: "the importance of details is much greater the more actual reality in a country differs from appearances, deeds from words, the people who act from the intellectuals who interpret these actions" Antonio Gramsci, *Quaderni del Carcere,* ed. Valentino Gerratana (Turin: Einaudi, 1977), 1723.

2. Roy Pascal, *Design and Truth in Autobiography* (Cambridge: Harvard University Press, 1960), 1.

3. One of the latest contributions that try to give some order to the field is Linda Anderson's 2001 *Autobiography: New Critical Idiom*, which opens with the statement that any writing may be judged to be autobiographical.

4. Georg Misch, *A History of Autobiography in Antiquity* (Cambridge: Harvard University Press, 1951), 5.

5. Roy Pascal, *Design and Truth in Autobiography* (Cambridge: Harvard University Press, 1960), 182.

6. Ibid., 10, 19.

7. Ibid., 180.

8. V. S. Pritchett, "All About Ourselves." *The New Statesman* (May 26, 1956): 601–2, 601.

9. James Olney, *Metaphors of Self: The Meaning of Autobiography* (Princeton: Princeton University Press, 1972), 24. The expression's use as a verb is from a poem by G. M. Hopkins.

10. Ibid., 30.

11. Ibid., 31.

12. There is not only a transitive sense in this "*fare*": America is not only the object "made," literally "built" by the Italian immigrant. There is also an intransitive sense of the verb, where "*fare*" refers back to the subject. It

defines the successful immigrant who has been able to own part of America, and has in turn become part of its prosperity. The Italian American writer Robert Viscusi notes that *"fare l'America"* has always had two meanings: "make Italy in America" (in the Little Italies) and "make oneself": "'fare l'America' also means to endow oneself with the status that only comes from making oneself through this particular route, which passes through America. To make America means to construct oneself." Robert Viscusi, "Making Italy Little" in *Social Pluralism and Literary History: The Literature of The Italian Emigration*, ed. Francesco Loriggio (Toronto: Guernica, 1996), 61–90, 61.

13. Pietro Toffolo, *Alla ricerca del nido: Pensieri e testimonianze di un emigrante* (Pordenone: Ente Autonomo Fiera di Pordenone, 1990), 38.

14. Philippe Lejeune, *On Autobiography* (Minneapolis: University of Minnesota Press, 1989), 11. In fact, autobiographies are generally not interested in playing Pirandellian games of ambiguity. And, for certain, I must add, our immigrant autobiographies speak of the real, as the banker Angelo Massari admits: "I do not know if calling it a history, a biography, or a confession, but in all truth it is my life" (Angelo Massari, *The Wonderful Life of Angelo Massari* [New York: Exposition Press, 1965], 1). Later, even more clearly, he names the "truth": "I can however assure the reader that I have written the truth, and the truth only" (ibid., 24).

15. Lejeune, *On Autobiography*, 4.

16. Trust in the accuracy of autobiography was undermined in 1979, when Paul de Man published his "Autobiography as De-Facement," in which he questioned the truth of its linguistic medium. See Georg Misch, *A History of Autobiography in Antiquity* (Cambridge: Harvard University Press, 1951), 5; Paul de Man, "Autobiography as De-Facement." *Modern Language Notes* 94, 5 (December 1979): 919–30.

17. Paul John Eakin, ed., *American Autobiography: Retrospect and Prospect* (Madison: University of Wisconsin Press, 1991), 5.

18. James Olney, *Metaphors of Self: The Meaning of Autobiography* (Princeton: Princeton University Press, 1972), 12–13.

19. Robert Elbaz, *The Changing Nature of the Self: A Critical Study of the Autobiographic Discourse* (Iowa City: University of Iowa Press, 1987), 8–9.

20. Carlo Ginzburg, *The Cheese and the Worms* (Baltimore: Johns Hopkins University Press, 1980), xvii.

21. David Vincent, *Bread, Knowledge and Freedom: A Study of Nineteenth-Century Working Class Autobiography* (London: Europa, 1981), 6.

22. James Olney, *Metaphors of Self: The Meaning of Autobiography* (Princeton: Princeton University Press, 1972), 37.

23. Ilaria Serra, *Immagini di un immaginario: L'emigrazione italiana negli Stati Uniti tra i due secoli (1890–1924)* (Verona: Cierre, 1997). What I call *imaginaria* translates the Italian concept of *"immaginario,"* which means the production of mental images about a subject that often find concrete representation.

24. For an effective anthology of stereotypes and beastly figurations of Italian-Americans, see Salvatore LaGumina, *Wop! A Documentary History of Anti-Italian Discrimination in the United States* (San Francisco: Straight Arrow Books, 1973). A recent book that has greatly stirred public opinion in Italy by reminding Italians the inhumane way they have been treated in different countries of immigration is Gian Antonio Stella, *L'Orda: Quando gli albanesi eravamo noi* (Milan: Rizzoli, 2003).

25. Diane Bjorklund, *Interpreting the Self: Two Hundred Years of American Autobiography* (Chicago: University of Chicago Press, 1998), x.

26. Emile Benveniste, *Problemes de linguistique generale* (Paris: Gallimard, 1966), 259.

27. Among the former, Roy Pascal, James Olney, and Georges Gusdorf analyzed autobiography in an existential light, through its ties with philosophy and the study of mankind. Among the latter, Diane Bjorklund, Robert Elbaz, and William Spengeman adopted a historicist point of view, basing each autobiography on its own time and place. In *The Forms of Autobiography: Episodes in the History of the Literary Genre* (New Haven: Yale University Press, 1980), William Spengeman looks at the history of autobiography from a Marxist point of view in order to establish the historical root of the discourse on the self, and to "understand the conditions that have led different autobiographers at different times to write about themselves in different ways" (xiii). The same historical perspective is chosen by Robert Elbaz in *The Changing Nature of Self* (Iowa City: University of Iowa Press, 1987), where he inserts autobiographies in the continuous fight between freedom and determinism, human agency and transcendental power. In her *Interpreting the Self* Diane Bjorklund sketches out a chronology of the thinkers of the self through the fluctuating concepts of will, reason, passion, and grace.

28. Both the French historian Georges Gusdorf and the German Georg Misch insert autobiography in the history of the West, in its correlation with the discovery of individuality typical of the Renaissance. Georges Gusdorf, "Conditions and Limits of Autobiography," (1956) in *Studies in*

Autobiography, ed. James Olney (Oxford: Oxford University Press, 1988); Georg Misch, *A History of Autobiography in Antiquity* (1907); trans. E. W. Dickes (Cambridge: Harvard University Press, 1951). Their works signal a rediscovery of autobiography in the 1950s.

29. Gusdorf, "Conditions and Limits of Autobiography," 28–48, 39.

30. Leigh Gilmore, *The Limits of Autobiography: Trauma and Testimony* (Ithaca: Cornell University Press, 2001), 6.

31. Ibid., 7.

32. The critic William Boelhower summoned this concept first formulated by Philippe Lejeune and tied it with a discourse on ethnic identity: "According to ethnic semiotics, in the beginning was the name. In order to discover who he is, in order to begin, the subject must interrogate the beginning of his name. Ethnic discourse is a discourse of foundations." William Boelhower, *Through a Glass Darkly: Ethnic Semiosis in American Literature* (Oxford: Oxford University Press, 1984), 81.

33. "Il cambio all'attuale Fabrizi è avvenuto, non richiesto, quando nel 1932 mi fu concessa la cittadinanza americana. Per uno sbaglio di trascrizione nel certificato di cittadinanza il mio nome risultò amputato della vocale 'o.'" Fabrizi did not really care too much about this change, but he was instead incredibly attached to his past in the town of Sandonato; his typewritten booklet is a description of how it was then, from the priest to the last midwife. His memory is amazing, and the time freezes in his words. The typescript is in the Immigration History Research Center (Ettore Fabrizi, "Papers," Immigration History Research Center, St. Paul), 125.

34. Michael Lamont, "Michael Lamont" in Maria Parrino, ed., *Italian American Autobiographies* (Providence: Italian Americana Publications, University of Rhode Island, 1993), 41–54, 54. Born in West Virginia, Lamont was a simple man who worked as a shoemaker and forty-one years as a postal worker.

35. "Avevamo paura di tutto. Non avevamo alcun documento . . . gli uomini in divisa ci spaventavano; magari erano soltanto postini, pompieri o spazzini; per noi erano sempre tutti poliziotti in caccia di 'stranieri indesiderabili'" (Piero Riccobaldi, *Straniero indesiderabile* [Milan: Rosellina Archinto, 1988], 117–18).

36. Emilio, Franzina, *L'immaginario degli emigranti* (Treviso: Pagus, 1992), xi.

37. Joseph Tusiani, *Envoy from Heaven* (New York: Obolensky, 1965), 174.

38. "Si siede affianco mio e midice voi siete uno americano, io sono nato in questi paesi in America mi chiamano Italiano qui michiamano Americano." Antonio Margariti, *America! America!* (Salerno: Galzerano, 1983), 129.

39. "Tutto quello che innanzi è scritto e una cosa sommaria dei miei ricordi, lo fatto come ricordo ai miei figli perché alloro interessa di sapere quale e la loro discendenza" (Lorenzo Musci, "Storia di famiglia," 1956, manuscript, Archivio Diaristico Nazionale, Pieve Santo Stefano, 21). This ninety-three-year-old man who lived in the Bronx wrote his life story in a telegraphic style on an American school composition notebook. It is his spiritual testament to his children and grandchildren. He was a returned immigrant who portrayed himself as a victim of the events, while his son tells us in an afterword that he was an active Communist and escaped Italy because of Fascism, after he was beaten up by the Ovra police that left him an invalid all his life. Born in 1862 in Santeramo (Bari), he just recounted the financial difficulties of his family after the death of his father and his marriage with Rosa Tangora, with whom he had sixteen children. She made him leave for Ohio in 1911 to reach his five older sons, and she made him come back after a few years because she missed Italy. They returned and in 1939 during a trip back, he is mistaken for an American spy and kept under control until he decides to return to America.

40. Tosi was an upper-class immigrant who leaves for a sense of adventure, not because he needed money: "I decided to go to America. Again, I must say I was fortunate. Unlike many poverty-stricken Italians of the south who were going to America at the time, I was going because I wanted to and had the means to travel, rather than because I had to in order to earn bread for a family. . . . I wanted to strike out immediately, so . . . I started out alone" (Humbert Federico Tosi, "My Memoir. Le mie memorie," 1968, typescript, Staten Island Center for Immigration Studies, 11).

41. Ibid., 1.

42. Michele Daniele, *Signor Dottore: The Autobiography of F. Michele Daniele, Italian Immigrant Doctor (1879–1957)* (New York: Exposition Press: 1959), 136.

43. Michael La Sorte, *La Merica: Images of Italian Greenhorn Experience* (Philadelphia: Temple University Press, 1985), 138.

44. "Il primo a sinistra è un giovane serio serio di cui io solo conosco i pensieri." Tusiani, *La parola difficile: Autobiografia di un italo-americano* (Brindisi: Schena Editore, 1988), 290.

45. Lamont, "Michael Lamont," 54.

46. "Così il lettore se avesse letto il libro del Cherry Mine Disaster scritto del F. P. Buck che alla pagina 124 Fater Hanney, St. Mary Chiesa, dice che il prete cattolico di Mondota fu lui che camino ben 3,000 piedi dal pozzo all'usita per venire in nostro soccorso e che invece questo non è vero siamo stati noi che siamo venuti fino a 50 metri da questo benedetto pozzo e che nussuni d'altri si e sacrificati per noi." Antenore Quartaroli, "Grande Disastro della Mina di Cherry, Ills. 13 Novembre 1909 scritto da Quartaroli Antenore, Uno dei Superstiti, Otto giorni Sepolto vivo nella Mina," Archivio Diaristico Nazionale, Pieve Santo Stefano, 29. Quartaroli wrote "Grande Disastro della Mina di Cherry" (privately printed, no date, Pieve Santo Stefano, Archivio Diaristico Nazionale). This little thirty-six-page booklet, printed on crumbling paper, takes our breath away as we follow the eight days during which Quartaroli was buried in the mine, fighting against death. He tells of his friends dying, writing to their wives, waiting for death hugging each other, searching for water and for food and for air. The rhythm becomes exhausting while we suffer along with him: "My pen is not strong enough to write the hardship I had to live to pass the 7 North. I was so weak, hungry, thirsty, tired that I hardly could lift my legs and I would tell to myself, 'how can a man my age be reduced to this state, I could not believe in myself'" ("La mia penna non è abbastanza forte per descrivere la fatica che feci per passare il 7 Nord. Ero così debole, fame sete, stanco che a stento poteva alzare le gambe e diceva tra me. 'Ma come mai un uomo della mia età essere ridotto in questo stato; no non potevo credere a mé stesso" [6]). He doesn't tell his entire autobiography, only this separating event, the most important episode of his life that causes his rebirth.

47. Costantine Panunzio, *The Soul of an Immigrant* (New York: Arno Press, 1969), 118.

48. Giuseppe Prezzolini, *I trapiantati* (Milan: Longanesi, 1963), 392.

49. See Steven Hunsaker, *Autobiography and National Identity in the Americas* (Charlottesville: University of Virginia Press, 1999); James Holte, "The Representative Voice: Autobiography and the Ethnic Experience" (*Melus* 9, no. 2, [1982]: 25–46); and two collections of essays: Paul John Eakin, ed., *American Autobiography: Retrospect and Prospect* (Madison: University of Wisconsin Press, 1991) and James Payne, ed., *Multicultural Autobiography: American Lives* (Memphis: University of Tennessee Press, 1992). Payne's volume contains Fred Gardaphé's essay, "My House is Not Your House: Jerre Mangione and Italian-American Autobiography."

"Other's" autobiography springs from historicism, since, as Julia Swindells says, ahistoricism is an advantage of Western educated men who can speak of their ideological environment and be seen to represent it. But for women, blacks, and working-class, there can be no claims of universal or representative status. See Julia Swindells, *The Uses of Autobiography* (London: Taylor & Francis, 1995). In the same way, Judy Long, *Telling Women's Lives: Subject/ Narrator/ Reader /Text* (New York: New York University Press, 1999) attacks the canon that includes only great lives by great men, accusing Olney and Pascal of their "claim to universality by suppressing difference" (21): they function as gatekeepers, filters for inclusion and exclusion. Books such as Becky Thompson and Sangeeta Tyagi, *Names We Call Home: Autobiography on Racial Identity* (New York: Routledge, 1996) begin to satisfy the need for this perspective.

50. William Boelhower, "The Making of Ethnic Autobiography in the United States" in Eakin, ed., *American Autobiography*, 123–41.

51. In particular Italian American autobiography has been studied in Holte, "The Representative Voice," and "The Newcomer in America: A Study of Italian and Puerto Rican Personal Narrations" (PhD diss. University of Cincinnati, 1978); Michael La Sorte, who concentrates only in the "greenhorn years" of immigrants (Sorte, *La Merica*); Fred Gardaphé, *Italian Signs, American Streets: The Evolution of Italian-American Narrative* (Durham: Duke University Press, 1996) and Gardaphé, "The Evolution of Italian American Autobiography" in *The Italian American Heritage: A Companion to Literature and Arts*, ed. D'Acierno Pellegrino (New York: Garland Publishing, 1999), 289–321; and William Boelhower, *Autobiographical Transactions in Modernist America: The Immigrant, the Architect, the Artist, the Citizen* (Udine: Del Bianco, 1992), who uses structuralist tools to undertake a literary criticism of ethnic autobiographies.

52. Prezzolini, *I trapiantati*, 255.

53. William Boelhower, "The Making of Ethnic Autobiography" in Eakin, ed., *American Autobiography*, 123–41, 132.

54. William Boelhower, *Immigrant Autobiographies in the United States* (Verona: Essedue Edizioni, 1982), 17. Boelhower is also the first to establish the immigrant autobiography as a genre, by stapling the two rules of the genre: there must be an organization of a double self or "*two* cultural systems, a culture of the memory and future and a culture of memory, into a single model" (ibid., 29); and there must be a reflection of "the three fabula moments of anticipation, contact, and contrast" (ibid., 40),

that is Old-World reality vs New-World ideal (utopia), New-World Ideal vs New-World reality (antithesis or unification), and New-World Reality vs Old-World Reality (comparison).

55. The texts are by Constantine Panunzio, Pascal D'Angelo, Emanuel Carnevali, and Jerre Mangione. The model resonates with Rose Basile Green's four stages. In the first, the narration is a confirmation of the codes of the dominant culture; in the second, it is a variation of these codes; in the third, it is a negation of the dominant codes; and in the fourth, it is a substitution of the dominant culture with a counter-cultural alternative. Rose Basile Green, *The Italian-American Novel: A Document of the Interaction of Two Cultures* (Madison: Fairleigh Dickinson University Press, 1974).

56. Second-generation or immigrant children, for example, have three, not two, systems of reference: they are confronted with the Real Old World as they can see it when they sometimes visit Italy; they deal with the Real New World that comes from their first-hand experience; but they are also presented with an Ideal Old World given to them by their parents (that often does not correspond to the old-world reality).

57. Gardaphé's explanation of the Heroic Age in fact better describes these autobiographers: "During this stage an aristocracy would develop against which the common people would revolt as they attempted to gain greater control of their lives. Out of this struggle would rise heroic figures who, as culture heroes, replaced the divinity of the poetic age as models for human behavior during the mythic age." Fred Gardaphé, *Italian Signs, American Streets*, 55. Besides, our writers also live a geographical shift between two eras: from Italy, a predominantly agricultural society, feudally organized, to the urban centers of America where they mostly settled, and where they learned to fight for their rights (the anarchist and socialist writers are more aware of this passage). This also fits Vico's interpretation of the age of Heroes: "Vico," writes Gardaphé, "notes that this shift occurred along with the shift away from agrarian culture and into urban culture, away from a theology based on fear of the gods to one in which men and women began to struggle with the gods" (Ibid., 55–56).

58. In the United States, Edward Stuart Bates, *Inside Out: An Introduction to Autobiography* (New York: Sheridan House, 1937) is a rare case of a study that provided Depression-era autobiographies of various everyday types and classes.

59. *Quarterly Review*, 1826, as quoted by Bjorklund, *Interpreting the Self*, 10.

60. Ann Fabian, *The Unvarnished Truth: Personal Narratives In Nineteenth-Century America* (Berkeley: University of California Press, 2000). These writers grow out of the American oral culture of unfortunates who peddled their stories, even inviting questions. Fabian's authors range from beggars to soldiers, and their eccentric stories become chapters of a larger story, "for the cooper, the minister, and the sailor, this had been the story of the nation; for convicts, it had been the story of sin and evil; for slaves and soldiers, it had been the story of freedom" (ibid., 172).

61. Vincent, *Bread, Knowledge and Freedom.*

62. John Burnett, David Vincent and David Mayall, *The Autobiography of the Working Class: An Annotated, Critical Bibliography, Vol. I, 1790–1900* (New York: New York University Press, 1984). An important difference between British autobiographers and our immigrants is that ours are very aware of the novelty of their work while British "authors were secure in the knowledge that in different ways and in different contexts the common people had always been historians of their own lives." Ibid., xiii.

63. Ibid., xiv.

64. Philippe Lejeune, *On Autobiography*, 167. In the chapter "Autobiography and Social History in the Nineteenth Century" he gives a census of twenty-three French autobiographies of craftsmen and workers that he discovered lying under years of dust in a forgotten room of the Bibliothèque Nationale de France.

65. Ibid., 165.

66. "These texts must therefore be considered not as causes, but as signs. We should not be misled by their small number or their meager distribution; what appears here in autobiographical form is an omnipresent discourse on the social life of the nineteenth century." Ibid., 171.

67. Anna Yona and David Yona, "Memoires," transcript, 1971. Immigration History Research Center, St. Paul, 1.

68. See Emily Hicks, *Border Writing: The Multidimensional Text* (Minneapolis: University of Minnesota Press, 1991), xxiii.

69. I am thinking of the production by Martin Scorsese (the grandfather's portrait or the lost first generation of *Italianamerican*), Nancy Savoca (the legendary first generation of *Household Saints*), Francis Ford Coppola (the generational gaps of *The Godfathers*), Helen De Michel (the puppets or the recovered first generation of *Tarantella*). For the written production I am thinking of the overwhelming presence of *nonni* (grandparents) in Italian-American fiction and non-fiction.

70. Constantine Panunzio, *The Soul of an Immigrant* (New York: Arno Press, 1969), 254.

71. Helen Barolini, *Chiaroscuro: Essays of Identity* (West Lafayette: Bordighera, 1997), 5. The poet Joseph Tusiani described a similar scene between his mother and her American grandchildren. When they asked, "Tell us a story about Italy!" she told them a story of misery from another planet that—even with translation—they do not understand: "I translated, but it was useless. Between grandmother and grandchildren there was an abyss. More than the language, a different civilization separated them" ("tradussi, ma inutilmente. Fra nonna e nipoti c'era un abisso. Più che la lingua, li separava una civiltà diversa.") Joseph Tusiani, *La parola antica: Autobiografia di un italo-americano* (Brindisi: Schena Editore, 1992), 98. Poet Lawrence Ferlinghetti saluted this generation in his poem "The Old Italians Dying" (in *From the Margin: Writings in Italian Americana*, ed. Anthony Tamburri, Paolo Giordano, Fred Gardaphé [West Lafayette: Purdue University Press, 2000], 135–38) "waiting . . . for their glorious sentence on earth / to be finished").

72. Sau-Ling Cynthia Wong referred to this confusion when she criticized Boelhower's schematization in *Immigrant Autobiography in the United States*. She sensibly remarked, "It would seem reasonable to expect immigrant autobiography to be written by immigrants"; Sau-Ling Cynthia Wong, "Immigrant Autobiography: Some Questions of Definition and Approach" in Eakin, ed., *American Autobiography*, 142–70, 147. Likewise, Boelhower groups first-generation Italian writers Panunzio and D'Angelo together with the second-generation Mangione. Their different experiences spawn different narratives. This is why Rose Basile Green divides her Italian American authors into two different categories: on one side the first generation characterized by a narrative of "explanatory reports or autobiographies" (31) or sometimes by the "revulsion" caused by the desire to assimilate, and on the other side the younger generation characterized by an act of "counter-revulsion," "a return to the old sources, reiterating the Italian American theme from a more highly developed integration with the native culture" Basile Green (*The Italian-American Novel*, 91).

73. Roy Pascal, *Design and Truth in Autobiography*, 12, 9.

74. Pierre Bourdieu, *Distinction: A Social Critique of the Judgment of Taste* (Cambridge: Harvard University Press, 1984), 7.

75. Paulo Freire developed this idea in his political concept of "selective democracy," a tricky democratic system shunned, first of all, by those who

refuse what they are refused. In this system the impoverished ones who are not supposed to vote also refuse to get involved and interested in politics. Paulo Freire, *Education to Critical Consciousness* (New York: Seabury Press, 1973).

76. Ibid., 44.

77. William Covino, *Magic, Rhetoric, and Literacy: An Eccentric History of the Composing Imagination* (Albany: State University of New York Press, 1994), 92. Inspired by rhetorician Kenneth Burke, Covino asserts that "true-correct magic is *generative*, practiced as constitutive inquiry or the coercive expansion of the possibilities of human action" (93).

78. William Boelhower, *Autobiographical Transactions in Modernist America: The Immigrant, the Architect, the Artist, the Citizen* (Udine: Del Bianco, 1992), 57. For Boelhower, the writer only has to take the "blueprint" of the official version, and make it his own, by adapting himself to the American model of self-made man, which in "the United States is already framed, being already inscribed by a master-plot: the immigrant autobiographical narrator must simply position himself/herself in it as citizen" (Boelhower, "Autobiographical Transactions," 99). Boelhower is fond of models, and in his article "Immigrant Novel as a Genre" he compiles another model for the immigrant novel: "an immigrant protagonist(s) representing an ethnic world view, comes to America with great expectations, and through a series of trials is led to reconsider them in terms of his final status" (William Boelhower, "Immigrant Novel as a Genre," *Melus* 8, no. 1 [Spring 1981]: 3–13, 4).

79. James Holte, "The Representative Voice: Autobiography and the Ethnic Experience," *Melus* 9, no. 2 (1982): 25–46. The subjects are African American Malcolm X, the Italian Constantine Panunzio, and the Puerto Rican Piri Thomas, who write their conversions from immigrant to ethnic, from the old to new world, and from atheism to religion.

80. The problem with this kind of reading is denounced by some critics by saying that it is mainly a Western ideal created by white male critics who have the luxury of forgetting about sex and race. But what about women? (as Susan Friedman asks in her essay "Women's Autobiographical Selves: Theory and Practice, in *The Private Self*, ed. Shari Benstock [London: Routledge, 1988]). And, we might ask, what about oppressed minorities, or *wops?*

81. "Tornavo dopo vent'anni. Non avevo fatto grandi fortune, ma sentivo di essermi comportato bene, di aver tenuto fede alle origini e agli insegnamenti della mia famiglia. C'era in me un senso d'orgoglio." Pietro Riccobaldi, *Straniero indesiderabile* (Milan: Rosellina Archinto, 1988), 132.

82. Edward Banfield, *The Moral Basis of a Backward Society* (Glencoe: Free Press, 1958), 83. Far from being a surpassed concept, "amoral familism" is used by the historian Allen Ginsborg to explain the roots of the Mafia and the failing of the Italian state (Allen Ginsborg, *A History of Contemporary Italy: Society and Politics, 1943–1988* [London, New York: Penguin Books, 1990]).

83. Joseph Lopreato, *Italian Americans* (New York: Random House, 1970), 59.

84. Patrick Gallo, *Ethnic Alienation: The Italian-Americans* (Rutherford: Farleigh Dickinson University Press, 1974), 78, 114.

85. Fred Gardaphé, "The Evolution of Italian American Autobiography" in *The Italian American Heritage: A Companion to Literature and Arts*, ed. Pellegrino D'Acierno (New York: Garland Publishing, 1999), 289–321.

86. "La mia gente non era cambiata, lottava e lavorava soltanto per essere povera. Il mondo allora era povero e triste, ma la mia gente non era triste; ci voleva così poco per renderla felice! Aveva la capacità di accettare." Pietro Toffolo, *Alla ricerca del nido: Pensieri e testimonianze di un emigrant* (Pordenone: Ente Autonomo Fiera di Pordenone, 1990), 18.

87. Giuseppe Previtali, *Doctor Beppo: An Italian Doctor in America* (privately published, 1984), 217.

88. Toffolo, *Alla ricerca del nido*, 48.

89. See Virginia Yans-McLaughlin and Victor Gioscia, "Metaphors of Self in History: Subjectivity, Oral Narrative, and Immigration Studies," in *Immigration Reconsidered: History, Sociology, and Politics*, ed. Virginia Yans-McLaughlin (New York: Oxford University Press, 1990), 254–90.

90. Ibid., 274.

91. Guido Orlando, *Confessions of a Scoundrel* (Philadelphia: John Winston, 1954), 132.

92. Gallo notices this persistence of powerlessness and alienation from the outer political world in Italian Americans, that is greatest in the second generation, and declines, but it is not eliminated, in the third. "Moreover, the individual feels that he cannot influence the government in any meaningful way" (Gallo, *Ethnic Alienation*, 135).

93. Angelo Pellegrini, a successful immigrant, notices this shift in mode between Italy and America: "Had I remained in Italy, my childhood experience would have prepared me to accept frustration with patience and humility; in America they have matured as habits of work, thrift, and self-reliance as are necessary in the achievement of a certain measure of self-realization" (Pellegrini, *Immigrant's Return*, 28).

94. Luigi Barzini, *The Italians* (New York: Atheneum, 1965), 157.

95. Beppe Severgnini, *Un italiano in America* (Milan: Rizzoli, 2001), 221.

96. An interesting description of the different spaces was drawn by the immigrant journalist Adolfo Rossi when he returned to Italy: "l'Italia pare un bel cimitero. Con le scarse vetture, rari tram, con la mancanza di ferrovie all'interno, le nostre maggiori città mi sembravano silenziose e come addormentate. Le strade poi apparivano strette in modo straordinario. . . . Il Po, l'Adige, il Tevere erano diventati per me fiumiciattoli. Trovavo tutto piccolo, gretto, meschino." ("Italy looks like a nice cemetery. With a few cars, rare tramways, lack of railways inland, our major cities seemed silent and almost sleeping. The streets appeared extraordinarily narrow. . . . The Po, Adige, and Tiber rivers had become small brooks for me. I found all small, petty and belittled" 167). Rossi is an interesting figure. He was born in 1857 in Lendinara, a provincial town in the Po estuary (Rovigo), but he was a rebel. He became a post office clerk but was lured by the idea of emigrating to the United States. In 1879 he arrived in New York. His wallet was stolen on the ship and he arrived as a poor man who adapted himself to any job. He moved to Colorado, then returned to New York, where he worked in *L'Eco d'Italia* in 1880 for a few weeks, and in the daily *Il Progresso Italo-americano* until 1884. He found his way as a journalist and after his three years in America, went back to Italy, where he worked as a skilled journalist for *La Tribuna* of Rome and for *Corriere della Sera* (after 1894). In 1901 he researched a big scoop on the Italian immigrants swindled in Brazil, he covered up as one of them and saw the exploitation and the cheating in the *fazendas*. His work had a concrete result, and it brought the 1902 law that forbids workers to leave with tickets already paid or anticipated from Brazil (because then the debt reduced them to slaves). In 1903 he was in Capetown and Mozambique to check on the living conditions of Italian workers in the mines. In 1904 he was made inspector of immigration for the United States and traveled to New York and San Francisco. His two books on the United States, *Un Italiano in America* (1891; Treviso: Buffetti, 1907) and *Nel paese dei dollari: Tre anni a New York* (Milan: Max Kantorowics Editore, 1893) are not real autobiographies, but interesting and lively journalistic sketches of immigrant life, including some character descriptions and an interesting piece on "Itanglish."

97. Pellegrini, *Immigrant's Return*, 39–40. He later observed that man does not have to bend the American landscape, like the Italian: "Nowhere we

could see evidence that human hands had worked to subdue the environment to human needs" (45).

98. William Boelhower attempts a similar reading of American versus Indian allegory by saying that the space of the American is that of the town or the road, while the space of the Indian is the forest. This difference in places of *habitare* creates a larger difference in modes of understanding, which brings the destruction of the Indian as a body and as a discourse (Boelhower, *Through a Glass Darkly*).

99. Giovanni Veltri, *The Memories of Giovanni Veltri* (Ontario: The Multicultural History Society Ontario Heritage Foundation, 1987), 17.

100. "Ma eppure bisognava lottare fino all'ultimo momento anche sicuri di morire." Quartaroli, *Grande Disastro*, 16.

101. Michele Daniele, *Signor Dottore: The Autobiography of F. Michele Daniele, Italian Immigrant Doctor (1879–1957)* (New York: Exposition Press, 1959), 237.

102. David Yona, "Memoires," 1971, transcript, Immigration History Research Center, St. Paul, 1.

103. Ibid., 2–3.

104. Visually, we could see these seeds of individualism as represented in the landscape of the Florentine "society of towers," with those stone towers looking like architectonic individuals sticking out in the landscape of the city, connected with bridges made of wood, ready to be burned in self-defense.

105. Christian Bec, "Mercanti e autobiografia a Firenze tra '300 e '400." Paper read at the XXXVI Corso di aggiornamento e perfezionamento per italianisti "Verità e finzioni dell'io autobiografico." Venice, Fondazione Giorgio Cini, July 9–26, 2002.

106. Medieval autobiographies rely on facts more than on the inner life, because they see facts as models for teaching or finding a moral, according to the motto "multorum disce exemplo, quae facta sequeris, quae fugies; vita est nobis aliena magistra": "the Middle Ages looked in Life something that could look like a behavioral model," Walter Berschin writes ("Biografie ed autobiografie nel Medioevo" in *L'Autobiografia nel Medioevo. Atti del XXXIV Convegno storico nazionale, Todi, 1997* (Spoleto: Centro Italiano di Studi sull'Alto Medioevo, 1998), 3.

107. "Intendente, virtuoso e d'assai era, ma troppo grande gittatore del suo e dell'altrui, ché poco si curava di nulla se non seguire i suoi apetiti e volontà, e a me diede assai fatiche, mentre visse in questo misero

mondo." (Lapo Niccolini, *Libro degli affari proprii di casa*, 569, as cited by Christian Bec, "Mercanti e autobiografia.")

108. "E di poi la detta monna Antonia mi mosse lite e quistione sopra d'una casa ch'io avevo comperata dal detto ser Francesco." (Lapo Niccolini, *Libro degli affari proprii di casa*, 568, quoted by Christian Bec, "Mercanti e autobiografia.")

109. "Mi misi a lavorare da un fabbricante di macaroni a 9 scudi alla settimana e tavola e alloggia." Gioanni Viarengo, "Memoriale di Gioanni Viarengo. Partenza d'Europa ed arrivo in S.U. d'America," manuscript, no date, Archivio Diaristico Nazionale, Pieve Santo Stefano, 3.

110. "Mi misi a lavorare da falegname per conto mio." Ibid., 4.

111. Giovanni Giannini, *Teatro popolare lucchese* (Turin: Carlo Clausen, 1895) as quoted in Maria Berdinelli Predelli, *Piccone e poesia: La cultura dell'ottava nel poema d'emigrazione di un contadino lucchese* (Lucca: Accademia lucchese di Scienze, Lettere ed Arti, San Marco Litotipo Editore, 1997).

112. Maria Berdinelli Predelli, *Piccone e poesia*, ix.

113. Ibid.,61.

114. See, for example, Gardaphé, "The Evolution of Italian American Autobiography."

115. Francesco Ventresca, *Personal Reminiscences of a Naturalized American* (New York: Daniel Ryerson, 1937), 37–38.

116. "Novelle? . . . ma che dici o biscarina? Le novelle 'en quelle che racconta tu ma' sulla befana. Le mi' novelle 'en fatti veri?" In Divo Stagi, "Quaderno di Divo Stagi," in Archivio Diaristico of Pieve Santo Stefano, 5. Divo Stagi remembers his father (1883–1966), who lived in San Francisco as a farmer for nine years and never stopped telling his stories.

117. Walter Ong, *Orality and Literacy* (London: Metheun, 1981).

118. "La vita dei grandi viene scritta dai grandi storici e remane nella Storia, ma per me che sono come un granello cascato nello spazzio e fuore del mio vicinato nessuno sa che io Esisto." Antonio Margariti, *America! America!* (Salerno: Galzerano, 1983), 87. The linguistic akwardness is in the text.

119. Ong, *Orality and Literacy*, 174–75.

120. David Vincent, *The Autobiography of the Working Class*, xiv.

121. Ibid.

122. Pietro Montana, *Memories: An Autobiography* (Hicksville, New York: Exposition Press, 1977), 54, 104.

123. "Ecco, uditori, un giorno di allegrezza / ecco, uditori, un giorno di conforto, / ecco, uditori, la più contentezza / che un uomo può provar

pria che sia morto." Antonio Andreoni, *Passaggio di Andreoni Antonio nell'America del Nord*. Berdinelli Predelli, Maria. *Piccone e poesia: La cultura dell'ottava nel poema d'emigrazione di un contadino lucchese* (Lucca: Accademia lucchese di Scienze, Lettere ed Arti, San Marco Litotipo Editore, 1997), 222–23.

124. "Grazie per aver ascoltato la mia storia." Tommaso Bordonaro, *La spartenza* (Milan: Einaudi, 1991), 134.

125. Anna Yona and David Yona, "Memoirs," transcript, 1971, Immigration History Research Center, St. Paul, 164.

126. Ong, *Orality and Literacy*, 102.

127. "Io cosi la penso. Gli altre la pensano come vogliono." Emanuele Triarsi, "La solitudine mi spinge a scrivere," typescript, 1986, 73.

128. Carlo Dondero, *Go West! An Autobiography of Carlo Andrea Dondero, 1842–1939* (Eugene, OR: Garlic Press, 1992), 18–19.

129. "Il sonno non vuole venire, tante cose mi si accavalavano una sopra l'altra nel cervello e chiusi gli occhi per vederle meglio, la prima inanzi l'amara partenza; il treno che doveva portarmi a Parigi il Bastimento, il mare, l'America del Nord coi suoi tesori, la gran baia di New York grande metropoli, La colosale statua della libertà che con il suo braccio destro in alto stringe con la mano una gran torccia acesa, simbolo di protenzione e di libertà a tutti i popoli; e troneggia maestosa in mezzo al mare sull'entrata del porto. D'irimpeto la collosale cità col suo incesante trafico a migliaia gli automobili gli autocarri un strepito indiavolato, coi suoi titanici palazzi detti gratanuvole data l'imensa altezza, vedo ancora le numerose Fabriche Stabilimenti Fattorie coi suoi poderosi camini tutti fumanti tutti lavorano, tutti vivono, e bene, quì si muore dal'inedia." Antonio De Piero, *L'isola della quarantina: Le avventure di un manovale friulano nei primi decenni delle grandi emigrazioni* (Florence: Giunti, 1994), 63–64. The linguistic awkwardness is in the manuscript.

130. Ong, *Orality and Literacy*, 42.

131. James Bowd, "The Life of a Farm Worker," *The Countrymen* 51, no. 2, 1955 (manuscript, 1889), 297.

132. "Self-analysis requires a certain demolition of situational thinking. It calls for isolation of the self, around which the entire lived world swirls for each individual person, removal of the center of every situation from that situation enough to allow the center, the self, to be examined and described" (Ong, *Orality and Literacy*, 54).

133. Camilletti, Giuseppe, *Autobiography of Giuseppe Camilletti*, trans. by Robert Scott, typescript, 1982, Immigration History Research Center, St. Paul.

134. "Lavorai molto forte che alla sera mi faceva male laschiena anche le coste . . . con la stanchezza di poter morire." Ibid., 1.

135. Adolfo Rossi, *Un italiano in America* (Treviso: Buffetti, 1907).

136. "L'Italiano non buono e il Siciliano perfetto e venti parole inglese." Calogero Di Leo, "Mai Biuriful Laif," typescript, 2001. Archivio Diaristico Nazionale of Pieve Santo Stefano, 118, 137.

137. "Una sera che giocavamo a carte io tiro un arso lei a sentire arso si e messa a ridere che non si poteva fermare, mamma mia che o detto che questa signora si ride tanto puoi mi a fatto capire che la parola arso in inglese vuoldire CULO io non lo sapeva, arso si scrive ACE e si pronuncia eis, e la signora e chiaro che doveva ridere quanto io o buttato un culo sopra il tavolo fatti veri." Ibid., 123.

138. "Dolorosa e straziande è stata la spartenza, ma trovando tutto al contrario di ciò che io credevo. Non potevo immaginare ciò che ho trovato." Riccobaldi, *Straniero indesiderabile*, 46.

Chapter 2
The Working-Class Writer

1. "La giobba, cioè l'impiego, io non l'avevo e non ero, dunque, nessuno in questa terra ove si è qualcuno solo se si lavora." Joseph Tusiani, *La parola difficile: Autobiografia di un italo-americano* (Brindisi: Schena Editore, 1988), 38.

2. "Se finisce il lavoro, finisce l'America; e che cosa rimane? Rimane l'illusione di parlottare una lingua straniera, il ricordo, cioè, di tutti quei suoni, più o meno corretti che sono serviti a rendere possibile la "giobba" e il suo prolungamento per anni, fino al giorno della pensione; rimane l'acquisizione di usi e abitudini, meccanicamente ripetuti di anno in anno ma senza alcuna radice di fede nell'anima. . . . e resta, infine, la dolorosa sensazione che, ora che l'America non ha più bisogno di te, non ti vuole più neppure la tua Italia, dove, se ti decidi a tornare dopo tanti anni, non ti riconosce più nessuno: e che ci vai a fare dopo una vita? soltanto a morire?" Joseph Tusiani, *La parola antica: Autobiografia di un italo-americano* (Brindisi: Schena Editore, 1992), 54.

3. Mattia's autobiography is on loose sheets, collected by his son-in-law. Peter Mattia, "The Recollections of Peter B. Mattia," typescript, no date, Immigration History Research Center, St. Paul, 11. Named Petrino, from "a small mountain town of Calabritto, province of Avellino, on April 22, 1869, of humble parents," Mattia immigrated to Newark in 1874 with

his family to reach his father, a woodcutter. After the episode of the pick and shovel, Petrino worked as a bootblack, a barber, and for thirty years as an inspector of tenement houses, a job he loved and found socially useful: "the law must be obeyed by both the tenant and the owner, but an inspector can show the cheapest way as the good way to do it." He died in 1953. He never gave up his artistic penchant though and, while keeping his jobs, also worked as a photographer, a painter for theaters, and a local community-theater producer.

4. Ibid., 5.

5. "Tutti coloro che emigrano col baldo ardire degli antichi avventurieri spagnoli—degni figli di Cristoforo Colombo—sognando attraverso l'oceano l'Eldorado non devono vergognarsi di dire che—pur di sbattacchiarsi onoratamente la vitaccia—hanno fatto di tutto." Giuseppe Gaja, *Ricordi di un giornalista errante* (Turin: Editore Bosio & Accame, no date), 460.

6. See Adria Bernardi's oral history of immigration, *These Hands Have Done a Lot* (Highwood, IL: privately published, no date). She gathered photographs of sculptures of hands and eight oral portraits of immigrants.

7. "Ma la mano non poteva essere pronta a scrivere quando per dieci ore al giorno s'erano attaccate etichette e mossi barili." Camillo Cianfarra, *Diario di un immigrato* (New York: Tipografia dell'Araldo Italiano, 1904), 113, preserved in the Immigration History Research Center, St. Paul.

8. "Fra una settimana le mie mani riprenderanno la vecchia gloria del mio artigianato." "L'arte tramandata di padre in figlio per tre generazioni." Michele Pantatello, *Diario-biografico, l'ultimo immigrante della Quota, 25 nov. 1922* (privately published, 1967). The copy I used, in the Immigration History Research Center, St. Paul, is dedicated to a friend who clearly did not think much of its prose—he commented on the cover that the book was not worth the paper consumed to publish it with its "bad grammar and puerile stories," and donated it to the archive.

9. "La tentazione è una brutta cosa e chi vuol far fortuna, sappia che la migliore via è quella del lavoro; l'ozio è il padre di tutti i vizi." Ibid., 84.

10. "Guardavo le mie mani e pensavo, quale metamorfosi a causa della guerra. Per tre generazioni, provetti artigiani da padre in figlio ed io con le mani pulite. 'Non va.' Il giorno dopo davo le mie dimissioni." Ibid., 65.

11. "Incominciavo a perdere la pazienza, ero disgustato dall'America, bisognava lavorare come cavalli per guadagnarsi da vivere. Ma il destino

voleva cosi. In [sic] fascismo si era consolidato ed io non potevo tornare in patria, ammeno [sic] che piegare la testa, la qualcosa non l'avrei mai fatto." Ibid., 81–82.

12. "Il 13 Novembre 1894 è la data della mia nascita. Per alcuni il numero 13 è considerato porta fortuna e contro il mal'occhio, altri lo considerano catastrofico. Per me che a distanza di tre giorni, il 16 novembre 1894, quando un forte terremoto si abbatte sulla nostra Città e paesi vicini, con danni incalcolabili, se ho potuto sopravvivere, posso chiamarmi fortunato. . . . Ho raggiunto l'età di 72 anni ed ho scongiurato il mal'occhio. 'Stupidaggine, superstizione,' diceva Benedetto Croce, 'ma è sempre bene guardarsi.' " Ibid., 5.

13. "Un vecchio detto dice: 'Dio affligge ma non abbandona.' " Ibid., 57.

14. "Nei momenti di tristezza e di angoscia causati da parenti ed amici, una mano suprema mi è sempre giunta a propizio, incredibile!" Ibid., 59.

15. "In questo paese, chi non sa farsi strada a forza di gomiti, rimane sempre indietro." Ibid., 86.

16. "L'America è la terra delle opportunita,' oggi sei povero, domani è tutt'altro, per una strana combinazione si può diventare ricco, senza andare in cerca, si è verificato migliaia di volte." Ibid., 119.

17. "Per rinnovare una lapide al Cimitero del mio paese dove riposano le ossa del mio Genitore, che era sbiadita e, questa volta venne fatta in marmo con lettere di bronzo per ricordare ai posteri, per sempre il nome di una famiglia scomparsa dal Paese, per le circostanze della vita." Ibid., 124.

18. Giovanni Veltri, *The Memories of Giovanni Veltri*, trans. John Potestio (Ontario: The Multicultural History Society Ontario Heritage Foundation, 1987), 76.

19. I am using here the translation by John Potestio, who published it including family pictures in a Canadian press. Giovanni Veltri, *The Memories of Giovanni Veltri*. Ed. John Potestio (Ontario: The Multicultural History Society Ontario Heritage Foundation, 1987) (Immigration History Research Center, St. Paul).

20. Ibid., 21.

21. Ibid., 35.

22. Ibid., 58.

23. Ibid., 59.

24. Ibid., 73.

25. "Io, Nino e Antonietta siamo andati a comprarti l'ultimo regalo, cioè la casa eterna. Dove andammo non rimasi soddisfatto; andammo in un

altro posto e trovammo quello che volevo per te, e così comprai l'ultimo palazzo per te e per me." Emanuele Triarsi, "La solitudine mi spinge a scrivere," privately published, 1986, Triarsi family collection, 102.

26. "Io avrei voluto darci un castello ma non avevo altro che questo nido di cacarocciole. E guardando questa situazione, in silenzio o promesso a me stesso che se Iddio mi aiuta io fabrichero la casa del suo sogno. Col tempo cosi o fatto. O fabricato con l'aiuto di Dio, la nostra abitazione (la casa del sogno)." Ibid., 60.

27. Ibid.

28. "Non vi posso dire che sporcizia, ma intanto si lavorava e si stava bene anche in mezzo alla 'merda.'" Ibid., 75.

29. "L'america e buona se si lavora. Ma se non si lavora sono guai e anche brutte." [sic] Ibid., 57. Later, he said "as you see, life in America is full of roses, but there are also thorns." ("Come vedete, la vita in America non e coronata solo di rose, ma ci sono pure le spine.") Ibid., 61.

30. "A—se fossi uno scrittore!" Ibid., 102. And "Non ho istruzione e di conseguenza non penso di scrivere un romanzo, ma solo una piccola storia, il meglio che posso." Ibid., 1.

31. "Fame e anche nera." Ibid., 31.

32. "In Italia a dire il vero non mi potevo lamentare." Ibid., 55.

33. "Passando tutti questi episodi sempre uscendo a galla di ogni difficolta, mi sono convinto che cè Iddio dietro a me che mi aiuta." Ibid., 81.

34. "Ma io anche con quello scoraggiamento che ho ricevuto o continuato" [sic]. Ibid., 77.

35. "Ma vedendo che non potevo andare in Italia tanto presto pensai di portare l'Italia ad Highwood. . . . informa Piccola piccole edeficai la Chiesa ed il Campanile del mio Paese di Sant'Anna di più afianco gli eressi Casa a Capanna di Casa del Colle. Feci fotografare cartoline delle quali che ne vendevo a migliaia che ancora ne vendo sempre." Aldobrando Piacenza, "Memories," typescript, 1956, Immigration History Research Center, St. Paul, 35.

36. "Avicinandosi pero la partenza dopo di aver provato il piacere di sentirni apagato per Emigrare che gli era stato il mio più grande desiderio, e poi di ritornare un giorno col bel vestito e l'Orologio d'oro, pure non potevo pensare allo strazio di distacarmi dalle persone da me amate e del mio Paesello che benche povero pure vi erano le mie più sacre memorie, Non dovevo più sentire il melodioso suono delle sua Campane e le sacre funzioni, il mormorio dei suoi Rii ed il Gaieggiare gli Augelli, mi sentivo

turbare da una profonda amarezza. . . . [His parents'] sacrifizi che avevano fatto per me . . . crearono una determinazione che avrebbi fatto ogni possibile per rendere alla mia cara mamma e mio caro Padre quella consolazione che tanto si meritavano. . . . Partivo con la sidetta Compagnia, col più amaro strazio che io possi ricordare da mio caro Padre e mamma e sorelle alla volta del America. . . . Tante e ben tante volte anche nella lontana America quando pensavo al distacco di questa mia prima partenza piangevo amaramente, e delle volte quando venivo sorpreso nel mio pianto, dicevo non e niente." Ibid., 8.

37. "Misto fra i Vapori scorgevo i Grattacieli ed il Grandioso Ponte di Brooklyn, con le enormi costruzzioni di ferro, non posso negare che mi empirono di Stupore." Ibid., 10.

38. "Interminabili Praterie Boschi ed immensa incoltivata terra Riviere immensi Laghi che sembravano Oceani. Si viaggiava per ore senza traccia di Abitazione. . . . Tutto ben diverso che di quello che avevo veduto in Italia." Ibid., 10.

39. "Con onesto lavoro mi sono edeficato un discreto ricovero qui in America." Ibid., 55.

40. "Senza lingua poca scuole e senza nessuno innizio di un mestiere." Ibid.

41. "Senza tanto romanzare"; "senza un minimo mormoro." Ibid., 32.

42. "Se tutti questi anni d'America che o speso per liberare Casa del Colle e per riedificarla, e poi ultimamente non posso godere, e sentirmi oltragiato era pure meglio che non fossi io stato il Padrone." Ibid., 55.

43. "Tutta la gente tanto sia Italiani che Americani dicevano quanti soldi a Aldo Piacenza. Ma il vero fatto e che se io adesso dovessi fare un Viaggio in Italia bisognerebbe che io andassi di nuovo imprestito dalla Banca." Ibid., 56.

44. Pio Federico, *An Autobiography*, privately published, 1960; a copy is in the Staten Island Center for Immigration Studies. This booklet is in Italian with an English translation by his niece, Helen Federico.

45. "In questa storia, cercherò di descrivere, nel miglio [sic] modo possibile, tutto ciò che ricordo del mio passato, dall'infanzia fino ad oggi. È una semplice storia, scritto da un'uomo [sic] all'età di sessantanove anni, di professione sarto, con la minima istruzione [sic] della quinta classe elementare, percio.' Ve ne sono grato, se non sbeffegiato." Ibid., 2. The translation is by Helen Federico.

46. "Visto che non poteva andare avanti come lui desiderava, pensò di emigrare in America, e' [sic] così fu. Prima di partire mi promise che appena sarebbe in condizione, mi avrebbe richiamato. In pochi mesi la moglie

e figlio lo raggiunsero. Nel 1909 mantenne la promessa; mandandomi il biglietto l'imbarco [*sic*]." Ibid., 18.

47. "Per cento lire, non potevo andare in America." The "cento lire" were made famous by a song of those years. Ibid., 24.

48. "Uscito, non sapevo dove andare con quella valigia e quel sacco, che pensavano [*sic*, probably *pesavano*] quasi più di me." Ibid., 26.

49. "Facemmo un giro in detta carrozza, sotto l'arco di Washington. E a casa, dove passammo l'undici e il dodici, giorno dedicato a Colombo. Il giorno dopo a lavoro." 40.

50. "Presi una macchina da cucire da Tranquillo, che aveva a casa, andai ad un posto dove vendevano macchine di seconda mano, acquistai una macchina per pressare, tavole, sedie, e ferri per stirare, c'erano nel posto. Così preparai, la mia prima fattoria, di sei persone." Ibid., 34.

51. "Vendemmo la merce la fattoria, con una perdita di seimila dollari, tutto il lavoro e tempo speso senza percepire un soldo." Ibid., 84.

52. "Abbiamo cominciato in tre e così rimarremo." Ibid., 62.

53. "$80,000 che sarebbe stati nelle mie tasche, se fossi stato solo. E questo è quello che mi costò per mantenere la promessa fatta." Ibid., 82.

54. "Lei [Lillian's mother] aveva perso la prima figlia della mia età, e con il mio nome, si chiamava Pia, e diceva che il Signore le aveva mandato un'altro per rimbiazzare [*sic*] la perdita. Mi voleva proprio bene come un proprio figlio." Ibid., 38.

55. "Ringrazio il buon Dio che mi ha dato forza e volontà, nel cammino della mia vita, che quantunque un po' turbolente, non mi dispiacerebbe affatto percorlerla di nuovo, cominciando dall'undici marzo 1891. Ho sempre fatto da me con le mie braccia e il mio cervello, senza aiuto di nessuno, soltanto una persona sono grato: Tranquillo Placido, questo era il suo nome." Ibid., 94.

56. "A che vale pretendere di essere vivi, quando si è già morti da lungo tempo? Quando si è più in condizioni di creare una famiglia, di iniziare una nuova azienda, di speculare nell'acquistare e vendere, nel recarsi al mare o in montagna, e nel godersi i piaceri della vita, come si può dire di essere vivi? A che vale vivere a lungo se tutto questo è nel passato? . . . quel che rimane e un bamboccio rivestito." Ibid., 118.

57. Giovanni Arru, "Ricordo della mia infanzia," manuscript, Pieve Santo Stefano, Archivio Diaristico Nazionale."

58. "Per chiarire l'agiatezza della mia famiglia di allora, il paese era diviso in tre categorie: Signori, Messeri e plebei. La mia famiglia quindi considerata Messeri, era una delle famiglie considerate ben estante." Ibid., 1.

59. "Visto che in Sardegna non vien niente da fare solo che scavare pietre, pensai di ritornare in America anche perché avevo diritto a viaggio gratuito. Arrivato in America era d'inverno e non vi era niente altro da fare che andare a spalare la neve per pulire le strade." Ibid., 11.

60. "Senza darmi una parola di vanto, devo dire che il mio arriva d'America a Pozzomaggiore ha portato un po' di civiltà, non solo perché ho fatto il caffè e il trattamento su detto . . . anche la prima vetturetta, la prima radio e la prima TV." Ibid., 12.

61. Rocco Corresca, "The Biography of a Bootblack," *Independent* 54 (December 4, 1902): 2863–67, reprinted in Holt Hamilton, *The Life Stories of (Undistinguished) Americans: As Told by Themselves* (New York: Routledge, 1990); 29–38.

62. Seeing the bootblack's stress on learning and education, we can assume he wrote the story himself.

63. Corresca, "The Biography of a Bootblack," 33.

64. Ibid., 34.

65. Ibid., 37.

66. Ibid., 38.

67. George Guida, *The Peasant and the Pen: Men, Enterprise, and the Recovery of Culture in Italian American Narrative* (New York: Peter Lang, 2003), 33.

68. Tommaso Bordonaro, *La spartenza* (Milan: Einaudi, 1991).

69. "La mia origine è proveniente dalla Grecia di famiglia nobile dei primi tempi della venuta di Cristo che si sono stabiliti in Sicilia nei tempi di Dionisie che governava la Sicilia. Ma nei tempi che io son nato la mia famiglia erava di bassa contizione povera quasi nella miseria." Ibid., 5.

70. "La mia mamma dal pianto le lagrime le regavano le guance, i miei fratelli più piccoli di me non avevano nessun coraggio. . . . Io per la mia mamma ero disposto a dare la vita." Ibid., 11.

71. "Il mio corpo e mio sangue mi sono concelato"; "ho preferito più all'amore propio e al rispetto, e alla sincerità più che ai bene stare." Ibid., 9.

72. "Mi faceva impressione dei miei defunti famigliari, mentre il mio primo lavoro in America ho dovuto fare il becchino per guadagnare un tozzo di pane duro e notrire la mia famiglia, scavare fosse e seppellire morte." Ibid., 54.

73. "Fino a spendere tutti i diecimila dollare che mi aspettavano per mio figlio e per far conoscere al popolo ignoto che non avevo bisogno di perdere un figlio per vivere." Ibid., 73.

74. "Io ho provato tanto piacere arraccogliere tutta qualità di frutta speciale, arraccogliere dei mandorli degli alberi che io avevo piantato 30 anni prima, che adesso eravano mandorli vecchi." Ibid., 130.

75. "Io sono stato in tutta la mia vita sempre sfortunato nei miei affare, nel mio lavoro, fino ad essere anche nell'amore." Ibid., 100–101.

76. Calogero Di Leo, "Vita di un emigrante turista milionario," typescript, 2000, Pieve Santo Stefano, Archivio Diaristico Nazionale. I came across this by chance when the author himself was looking for someone to type his manuscript in a computer, and found me. His three hundred pages of large handwriting, incoherent syntax, and surprising concatenation of thoughts have now become familiar to me. He died in 2006 in Florida.

77. "Come di solito tutti attorno al pacco per aprirlo, come se si dovesse aprire un tesoro, si apre il pacco si va uscento piano piano, un paio di lenzuola mamà esclama o che sono belli nuovi di zecca, Quattro camicie o che sono belli perte Giuseppe, tre pacchetti di spagnoletti: filo laghi e spille, o che sono belli, Quattro abiti per donna questi perme e perte a mia sorella, un coppo di zucchero in quatretti questo per il caffe,' un vestito piccolo che dice in un pezzetto di carta attaccato al vestito questo per mio nipote Calogero salto in'aria e grido grazie S Antonino, un bel vestito di lana colore latte e caffe chiaro, nuovo di zecca la taglia era perfetta come se Don fifi mi avrebbe perso la misura quanto me lo metteva somigliavo a un figurino mai avevo avuto un vestito intero, sempre spezzato camicia e pantalone di fanella e più crescevo più corto si faceva il pantalone. E proprio un Santo quell'uomo viva America viva zio Antonino viva li spaghetti e viva le porpetti, io incomincio come poter antare in America." Ibid., 77.

78. "Quello che va per il mezzo e il povero emigrande." "Lemigrante passa tante ingiustizie e umiliazione e delle volte non si può difendere." Ibid., 117, 148.

79. "A tutti le altre negozi che sono grande catene come tacco viva Sbarro pizza, Japponese, Cinese ecc . . . noncera problema che sono pesci grande, io che sono una sardina e con una famiglia da mantenere e malato e paganto da sempre in tempo laffitto e responsabile in tutto." Ibid., 167.

80. "O ritornare intietro diretto in Italia anche mi tocca morire di fame. Dico no Calogero coraggio che chi la dura la vince."

81. "Con quella che rimane alla vite si possono caricare camion e camion di uva se non si vede non si crede. Ricordo quando facevamo la grande

vedemmia dei duecento vite che aveva nonno Calogero Bacino nella vite non rimaneva nemmeno un chicco di uva che differenza." Ibid., 163.

82. Donna Gabaccia uses this phrase by Robert Paris in her *Italian Workers of the World: Labor Migration and the Formation of Multiethnic States*, ed. Donna Gabaccia and Fraser Ottanelli (Chicago: University of Illinois Press, 2001), 3.

83. A monumental autobiography that becomes more a philosophical and political treaty is written by Carlo Marzani, *The Education of a Reluctant Radical* (New York: Topical Books, 1992).

84. Antonio Margariti, *America! America!* (Salerno: Galzerano, 1983). The editor wisely maintained the poor spelling of this writer that retains all its magical power.

85. For a study of the relationship between immigrants and workers, see Donna Gabaccia, *Militants and Migrants: Rural Sicilians Become American Workers* (London: Rutgers University Press, 1988).

86. "La patria E' dei padroni, La patria dei poveri sideve fare ancora"; Margariti, *America!*, 12.

87. "PEPPINO si sperse nella America e non solo nona mandate monete ma sià dementecato della mamma e tutti e neppure i soldi del suo viaggio amandato." Ibid., 92.

88. "Io son venuto in questa lontana terra nel 1914 all'età di 22 anni e quiho trovata lavita tutta diversa e anche qui e siste l'INGIUSTIZIA anche qui chi lavora e non cia tanto oniente e chi non fa niente e cianno tutto e sono i padroni." Ibid., 1.

89. "Io no scrivo per L'arti O' per La gloria / scrivo per quello che bolle nel mio ciriviello / scrivo e miribello al vecchio mondo . . . ricordo la mia lunga esistenza poca felice ò vita se vita sipuo chiamare cioe il mio duro passato, la vita dei grandi viene scritta dai grandi storici e remane nella Storia, ma per me che sono come un granello cascato nello spazzio e fuore del mio vicinato nessuno sa che io Esisto e forse sipuo anche pensare che io scrivo per Imbizione senza Imbizione non si fa niente." Ibid., 87.

90. Gregorio Scaia, "Diario," 1953, manuscript, Archivio Storico del Castello di Trento. The page numbers refer to the original in the Archive of Trento, but the diary has been published in G. Poletti, ed., "Un pezo di pane dale sete cruste. Diario di Gregorio Scaia (1881–1971)," *Judicaria* (May–August, 1991), 1–71.

91. "Nato nel tempo del estate quando si tagliava il furmento, la sera di sant Giacomo il giorno 25 luglio 1881, nel comune di Prezzo val Giudicaria Tirolo." Scaia, "Diario," 1.

92. "Mi e somamente grato d'incominciare questa mia storia col volgere un saluto et un auguro a voi tuti letori e letrice, e spero che aceterete con benevolenza questo mio scrito, e saprete conpatire se troverete in eso qualche erori e cosa da sbiasemare, in questo libro si scrive la storia e la vita, viagi e aventure di Gregorio Scaia, e l'origine dele vechie colonie e nuove colonie dei nostri paesani Trentini dela vale Giudicarie che hano stabilito in Australia e nele Americhe, Alaska e sula costa del pacifico, verso la meta del secolo pasato. Credo che questo sia l'unico libro che sia mai stato scrito al giorno d'ogi in riguardo ale nostre colonie cominci-ate al estero, l'unico e sol motivo di scrivere questo mio libro, e di narare et informare e conservare nel cuore e nela mente, dei nostri popoli e dele nostre future generazioni, i lavori ostacoli e lote che hano dovuto combatere nei viagi di mare e di tera, e sacrefici che hano dovuto afront-are e soportare i nostri Trentini, in qualunque parte del mondo, in paesi sconosciuti cosi lontani dai paesi nativi, tuto per guadagnare un pezo di pane dale sete cruste, cosi dicevano i nostri poveri avi da una volta." Ibid., 1–2.

93. For this information, see Erik Amfitheatrof, *The Children of Columbus: An Informal History of the Italians in the New World* (Boston: Little, Brown, 1973).

94. Ibid., 233.

95. Wallace Sillanpoa, and Mary Capello, "Compagno/Compagna," in *Hey Paesan! Writings by Lesbians and Gay Men of Italian/Sicilian Descent,* ed. Giovanna (Janet) Capone, Denise Nico Leto, and Tommi Avicolli Mecca (Oakland: Three Guineas Press, 1999), 290–302, 298.

96. Bartolomeo Vanzetti, *Una vita proletaria* (Salerno: Galzerano, 1987); *The Story of a Proletarian Life,* trans. Eugene Lyon, was published in 1923 and recently reprinted (London, Kate Sharpley Library, 2001).

97. "Un giorno lesse su *La Gazzetta del Popolo* che a Torino quarantadue avvocati avevano concorso per un impiego da 45 lire al mese." Vanzetti, *Una vita,* 21.

98. "Quel periodo di tempo fu uno dei più felici della mia vita. Contavo vent'anni: l'età delle speranze e dei sogni, anche per chi, come me, sfo-gliò precocemente il libro della vita." Ibid., 22.

99. Ibid., 24.

100. As part of the prize, the book has been published in Italy: Pietro Ricco-baldi, *Straniero indesiderabile* (Milan: Rosellina Archinto, 1988).

101. "Vedevo i monti della mia Liguria allontanarsi; mi venne in mente il brano dei *Promessi Sposi* e mentalmente lo recitavo: 'Addio monti sor-genti dalle acque ed elevati al cielo." Ibid., 71.

102. "Emigrare, cercare lavoro fuori era considerato una dichiarazione di resa. Perciò quasi tutti rimanevano aggrappati ai loro vigneti, orgogliosi di esser proprietari, di lavorare in proprio." Ibid., 1.

103. "Mi sforzavo quasi a procurarmi un senso di indigestione; ingoiavo senza masticare così da poter dire una buona volta:—Basta, sono sazio, ne ho abbastanza—; non vi riuscii mai. Ingoiavo tutto e digerivo tutto, avrei digerito anche i sassi, come le galline." Ibid., 14.

104. "Se l'inferno esiste, la 'tubiera' lo è!" Ibid., 75.

105. "Avevo sempre sete, una sete infernale; ero sempre attaccato al bidone dell'acqua: bere, bere, bere e più bevevo e più sete mi veniva. Sudavo e bevevo e mi sentivo sempre più debole . . . Tutta quella craccia incandescente che era stata attaccata dalle griglie con la pinza mi cadeva ai piedi." Ibid., 72–73.

106. "Divenni così allegro che non sapevo più quello che facevo. Mi lavai, mi feci la barba e mi preparai anche nell'animo per il salto nella nuova vita." Ibid., 114.

107. "Quelli furono i giorni più felici della mia vita. . . . Non ero più 'indesiderabile,' ma soltanto straniero." Ibid., 102.

108. "Sono passati altri anni ancora, molti e in America non ci sono più tornato. Alcuni anni fa, ne avevo ormai 73, mi venne il gusto di un viaggio come turista. A New York avevo lasciato tanti compagni e un po' della mia vita; speravo che le leggi fossero cambiate e ora la mia età potesse essere vista come una garanzia, ma i moduli per ottenere il visto, così pieni di domande. . . . Troppe inquisizioni, troppe vessazioni morali; avrei dovuto dire troppe bugie, mi scoraggiai, lasciai perdere; E da qualche anno ero tornato ad essere cittadino italiano e dunque più che mai 'straniero indesiderabile.'" Ibid., 160.

109. Carlo Tresca, "Tresca Memorial Committee Records, 1938–1962," carbon copy of typescript, microfilm, New York Public Library, Special Collection, Manuscripts and Archives Division, Room 328. It has also been recently published: Nunzio Pernicone, ed., *The Autobiography of Carlo Tresca* (New York: John D. Calandra Italian American Institute, 2003). The version I studied is the original typescript in the New York Public Library. Pernicone claims this was ghostwritten by Max Nomad, since the original English version by Tresca has been lost.

110. Ibid., 7–8.

111. Ibid., 14.

112. Ibid., 56–57.

113. Ibid., 81–82.

114. Ibid., 98.

115. Ibid., 140.

116. Nunzio Pernicone, *The Autobiography of Carlo Tresca* (New York: John D. Calandra Italian American Institute, 2003), 5.

117. "E meritavi quindi un'altra sorte / cioè d'una vecchiaia veneranda / il placido tramonto e non la morte / violenta ed esecranda" (Efrem Bartoletti, *Emozioni e ricordi* (Bergamo: La Nuova Italia Letteraria, 1959), 67.

118. Pascal D'Angelo, *Son of Italy* (New York: Macmillan, 1924), 63. There is also an Italian translation with the same title: Pascal D'Angelo, *Son of Italy*, trans. Sonia Pendola (Salerno: Il Grappolo, 1999).

119. Ibid., 9.

120. Ibid., 169.

121. Ibid., 185.

122. Ibid., 74–75.

123. Antonio De Piero wrote his autobiography, "Le mie memorie scritte nell'isola della quarantina," in 1922. A photocopy of the typescript is in the Pieve Santo Stefano, Archivio Diaristico Nazionale (MP/93). In 1993 it won the IX Edition of the Prize Pieve-Banca Toscana, and was published as Antonio De Piero, *L'isola della quarantina: Le avventure di un manovale friulano nei primi decenni delle grandi emigrazioni* (Florence: Giunti, 1994).

124. "Entro in casa mia moglie mi domandò la mia preocupazione, che gli risposi subito. Senti Catina gli dissi; i nostri risparmi si sciolono come la neve al sole i nostri sogni svaniscono, nò casa, nò campi, e stando così ancora un poco anche la poca moneta se ne và, ed in breve resteremo nella più nera miseria." Ibid., 62–63.

125. "Presi il sacco nelle spalle, sperdendomi nell'oscurità, le strade a quell'ora erano deserte solo quà e là si sentivano i latrati dei cani svegliati al rumore dei poveri viandanti. Rasegnato con passo cadenzato, a capo chino sotto il peso del fardello, Principiando a lottare col destino e la via principiava a spalancarsi verso. . . . L'ignoto." Ibid., 25. This is the graphics used by De Piero in his manuscript. Ibid., 25.

126. "Infette tifo, vaiolo, scarlattina febbre giala, tutti quà gli mandano questi e da paura che la malatia si slarghi in cità e si propaghi la epidemia. Dunque voleva del coraggio che ne dite? Ma i cento dolari netti al mese mi fecero venire il coraggio." Ibid., 68.

127. Carmine Iannace, *La Scoperta dell'America: Un'autobiografia*, trans. William Boelhower (West Lafayette, IN: Bordighera Press, 2000), 162. The

autobiography was first published in Italian: *La scoperta dell'America* (Cittadella: Rebellato Editore, 1971).

128. Ibid., 178.

129. Ibid., 190.

130. "Bevemmo nella giara di cristallo che avevo portato dall'America. . . . e si rispecchiò nelle mille faccette di vetro, il calore moltiplicato dei loro occhi. E il vino faceva ridere il vetro. . . . 'Questa è l'America,' dicevano, passandosi la giara e fermandola appena all'altezza degli occhi." Ibid., 177.

131. "Mi torturavo notte e giorno. Una via d'uscita ci doveva essere. Non poteva finir così. Zappare come tutti gli altri, fino all'esaurimento. Annullare nel lavoro tutti i desideri. Dormire esausto fino all'alba, per ricominciare di nuovo? No! Il solo pensiero mi faceva venire i brividi e le gambe mi incominciavano a tremare. Mi sentivo accasciato, debole, ammalato. . . . La partenza fu fissata per il 15 ottobre. Come la prima volta ch'ero partito né mio padre né mio fratello mi accompagnarono alla stazione. Questa volta però, ne fui contento, quasi che l'America già cominciasse lì, da quel distacco violento dai miei." Ibid., 192.

132. Pietro Greco, "Ricordi d'un immigrato, Brooklyn, 3 Maggio 1965," 1965, microfilm, Immigration History Research Center, St. Paul.

133. "Mio fratello mi giudicava dalla timidezza! Non li saltò mai in mente che la mia timidezza era frutto d'eccessiva sensibilità, che nulla aveva in comune con l'imbecillità." Ibid., 23.

134. "Io e l'amico Procopio ci sdraiavamo, dato che ciò era permesso, sopra enormi mucchi di giubbe e pastrani, gettati sul pavimento, come se si trattasse di cenci, senza alcun riguardo ai soldati che dovevano indossarli, e leggevamo ad alta voce, le poesie dello Stecchetti, allora in voga, attorniati da una schiera d'allegre e bellissime ragazze, nel fiore degli anni, fresche e fragranti come le rose di maggio, che amavano la poesia, e il modo come io e Procopio la leggevamo." Ibid., 93.

135. "In nessuna fabbrica occupava un numero così rilevante di italiani dove si parlava esclusivamente l'italiano. Mi trovavo bene! Forse fu questo il motivo che non mi fece ritornare in patria! . . . era come se mi fossi trovato in Italia." Ibid., 94.

136. "Era ne l'ufficio con un ometto che litigava, voleva che pubblicasse il suo sonetto. Non sa chi sono io, sono il professor Alberico Torquato!—Un plagiario, dice Cordiferro e tira fuori il poemetto del Foscolo da cui aveva copiato." "Ci siamo incontrati col Foscolo . . . non lo feci di proposito. Ci siamo incontrati, ecco tutto." Ibid., 136.

137. "E' d'uopo che l'uomo colpito si rassegni, se non vuole perire. Mantenga accesa la fiaccola della speranza e sorrida alla vita! Si crei una nuova esistenza! Raccolga i rottami. . . . Reagisca al dolore. . . . Vivere, anche se costretto ad adattarsi entro limiti modesti, ma vivere!" Ibid., 36.

138. "La poesia di Mastro Gaspare non veniva posta sulla carta per essere conservata; aveva la durata di certe combinazioni panoramiche di nuvole che, nell'immensità azzurra della spazio, appaiono belle e suggestive, ma che subito il vento scompagina e dissolve, e possono rimanere solo nella memoria di chi le vede." Ibid., 141.

139. "Nella bottega di mastro Gaspare ogni cosa pareva avesse un legame con la poesia e fosse governata dal suo ritmo, tutto armonizzava: dal lento stillicidio della piccola fontana con la bacinetta, a un angolo del salone, fino al monotono e lento battito dell'orologio, sospeso alla parte sinistra di chi entrava." Ibid., 142.

140. "Tu mi vedi in modo diverso dagli altri, loro mi guardano meccanicamente come si può guardare un povero asino vecchio e spelacchiato. . . . Che cosa vede in me chi mi guarda con li occhi e l'intelligenza che non sono tuoi? Niente più che un uomo alto 6 piedi!" (143).

141. Gabriel Iamurri, *The True Story of an Immigrant* (Boston, Christopher Publishing House, 1951).

142. Ibid., 84.

143. Ibid., 35.

144. Ibid., 37.

145. Ibid., 21.

146. Ibid., 37.

147. Ibid., 47.

148. Ibid., 48.

149. Ibid., 49.

150. Ibid., 90.

151. Pietro Toffolo, *Alla ricerca del nido: Pensieri e testimonianze di un emigrante* (Pordenone: Ente Autonomo Fiera di Pordenone, 1990).

152. "New York non era come è oggi nel 1927, ma a me sembrava così nuova, così grande, dalla metropolitana ai grattacieli simili alle Alpi, però questi fatti dall'uomo. Quei palazzi tante volte più alti del campanile della mia chiesa mi spaventavano e mi facevano sognare; sogni di ricchezze: tornare e portare il nonno attraverso l'Oceano e mostrargli tutta la meraviglia di questo nuovo mondo, come egli mi aveva mostrato il nostro piccolo mondo." Ibid., 18.

153. "Ricordo bene che dopo le cene non mi stancai mai di guardare le scintillanti luci di New York; la fiamma tra le mani della statua della libertà, i riflessi argentei dell'acqua del porto, le luci del ferry-boat che scivolavano da e per Staten Island e tutto questo non era un sogno!" Ibid., 35.

154. "Nell'ottobre del '69 ero di nuovo a casa. Doveva essere per sempre quasta volta, ma il mio cuore era diviso in due, non soltanto segnato. Lasciare gli Stati Uniti per sempre sarebbe stato peggio che morire. Quarantadue dei miei 58 anni di vita li avevo vissuti laggiù, dov'ero arrivato quando avevo 16 anni, là avevo imparato a vivere, un modo di vivere che vorrei per la mia gente e per tutta la gente di questo mondo. Perché nonostante le sue deficienze e i suoi errori, e a considerare bene le cose, negli Stati Uniti qualunque uomo può vivere in libertà e dignità umana, purché lo voglia. La sua identità consiste nella sua individualità, non in un numero, e non deve far scintille mentre cammina per essere notato." Ibid., 48.

155. Carlo Dondero, *Go West! An Autobiography of Carlo Andrea Dondero, 1842–1939* (Eugene OR: Garlic Press, 1992).

156. Ibid., 179.

157. Ibid., Introduction.

158. Ibid., 105.

159. Ibid., 181.

160. Ibid., 2.

161. Ibid., 63.

162. Emanuel Carnevali, *The Autobiography of Emanuel Carnevali,* ed. Kay Boyle (New York: Horizon Press, 1967), 24.

163. Ibid., 73.

164. Ibid., 76.

165. Ibid., 76.

166. Ibid., 149.

167. Ibid., 197.

168. Maria Berdinelli Predelli, *Piccone e poesia: La cultura dell'ottava nel poema d'emigrazione di un contadino lucchese* (Lucca: Accademia lucchese di Scienze, Lettere ed Arti, San Marco Litotipo Editore, 1997), 61.

169. Ibid., 62.

170. Ibid.

171. Raffaello Lugnani, *Sulle orme di un pioniere,* ed. Aquilio Lugnani (Massarosa: Tipografia Offset, 1988).

172. The source for this information is the immigrant's son, Aquilio Lugnani, whom I met him in his house in Massarosa (Lucca) in summer 2002.

He showed me his father's leather notebook and the record player that his father sent on a ship: "sa odor d'America."

173. "Sarà un divertimento pei lettori, / che nella salza metteran gli odori." Lugnani, *Sulle orme*, 17.

174. "Quello è vero, vi do la mia parola, / ché le lische ci ho ancora qui alla gola." Ibid., 274.

175. "Di cambiare il destin abbiam tentato / soddisfatti sarem d'aver provato." Ibid., 25.

176. "L'America mi ha preso i miglior anni, / pochi soldi m'ha dato, assai malanni." Ibid., 17.

177. "Quel monte strano." Ibid., 26.

178. "Pareva un demonio / di quelli nati prima del Messia." Ibid., 108.

179. "Vid'io tutte le stelle e il paradiso." Ibid., 132.

180. "Fra gente strana in paesi lontani." Ibid., 196.

181. "Non si deve turbare il mio cammino: / uomini siamo e dobbiamo affrontare, / niente al mondo ci deve sgomentare." Ibid., 24.

182. "Fa sognar quella donna a contemplarla: / sembra ti voglia toglier la paura, / la libertà lei insegna a trovarla / ai miseri che vanno alla ventura, / ma s'illude chi tiene quel pensiero: / qui un libero diventa schiavo vero." Ibid., 27.

183. "Il sole quel terren, che mai vedeva, / ora potea baciarlo pien d'amore; / anche l'erba, che l'ombra nascondeva, / riprendea la rugiada alle prim'ore / parte nasceva e l'altra si rialzava, / pieno d'ardore il sole la baciava." Ibid., 39.

184. "L'inglese è una bella lingua da ascoltare, / ma si può intender salacca per aringa." Ibid., 42.

185. "Potete immaginare che età fiorita / passai, così lontan dai genitori; / così presto sacrificar la vita, / come l'autunno il bel colore dei fiori, / ma era il mio destin quel da affrontare; / non potevo ormai indietro ritornare." Ibid., 51.

186. "Tranquillo poi a letto riposavo / sapendomi in paese in mezzo a cento." Ibid., 82.

187. "Io sempre con coraggio andavo avanti, / trenta miglia di laghi sul ghiacciato, / in compagnia sol di tutti i Santi, / sempre attento a guardarmi da ogni lato. / Non si ricorda là chi siamo stati: / la vita là si fa da disperati." Ibid., 138.

188. "Sembra un sogno, se ci si sta a pensare, / ve l'assicura un che dice il vero, / ché doversi da tutti allontanare, / a chi non sa, può sembrar un

mistero; / pensa qualcun la morte sia uguale, / morendo, invece, termina ogni male." Ibid., 191.

189. "Molti in Italia fanno i lor commenti: / dicon facile è qua trovar lavoro; / c'è invece da passar certi momenti! . . . / Avrei piacer provassero anche loro / certamente potrebbero allor dire, / quanto quaggiù ci abbiamo da soffrire." Ibid., 209.

190. "L'America l'han vista sol di fuora: / han vissuto in un sacco rinserrati, / han lavorarato come indemoniati." Ibid., 215.

191. Antonio Andreoni, *Passaggio di Andreoni Antonio nell'America del Nord: Piccone e poesia: La cultura dell'ottava nel poema d'emigrazione di un contadino lucchese,* ed. Maria Berdinelli Predelli (Lucca: Accademia lucchese di Scienze, Lettere ed Arti, San Marco Litotipo Editore, 1997), 147–280.

192. "Amici tutti, se mi ascolterete / vi voglio un fatto vero raccontare / e son sicuro che ne resterete / contenti come a un grande desinare." Ibid., 147.

193. "Giunti alla stazione allegramente / un'eco rimbombò con voci unite, / ma io, povero misero e dolente, / stavo pensando alle grosse ferite / che aveo nel cuor, mentre colà piangente / tenea la moglie, i figli, e le partite / che faceo cogli amici e coi parenti, / e il cuor mi ritrovavo in gran tormenti." Ibid., 150–51.

194. "Venia cert'onde a tanta altessa ch'elle / perdean la forma e le sembianse di onde; / or la nave salia sopra le stelle / e su le nubi alsar parea le sponde." Ibid., 154.

195. "Io ne ringrazio il ciel di tutto cuore / che ormai quella burasca era passata." Ibid., 156.

196. "Questa è la seconda volta che la vita / mi salvò certo la Bontà infinita." Ibid., 220.

197. "Si giunse là sudati come i buoi / con certe facce come gli assassini." Ibid., 159.

198. "E' propio ver, se il gatto sta presente / il topo non può far quel che gli pare: / che quivi essendo i superiori, noi / tutti si lavorava come buoi." Ibid., 270.

199. "E mai nessuno si sente questionare / perché la ghenga mia son tutta gente / che hanno bisogno soldi guadagnare." Ibid., 274.

200. "Ho da empire più di una scodella." Ibid., 201.

201. "Par che il destino lo facci apposta / di farmi tribolar fin ch'io non mora." Ibid., 218.

202. "Io lascio fare Iddio che sempre bene, / accomoda le cose a suo piacere, / e con paziensa sopporto le pene, / che il sopportarle è propio mio dovere." Ibid., 244.

Chapter 3
Immigrant Artists

1. Giovanni Zavatti, *Cantando per il mondo: Autobiografia del tenore Giovanni Zavatti* (Chieti: La voce dell'Emigrante, no date). A copy is preserved in the Staten Island Center for Immigration Studies.

2. "Il cocchiere mi pregò di cantare qualcosa ed io cominciai timidamente a canticchiare *Silenzio cantatore*, una canzone che cantavo spesso con mio fratello Antonio. Pian piano la mia timidezza scomparve; la mia voce era gradevole e a questo punto accadde qualcosa di strano. Il cavallo che tirava la carrozza di colpo si fermò apparentemente senza nessuna ragione. Il cocchiere si mise a ridere e si complimentò con me, dicendomi che il suo cavallo si fermava solamente quando ascoltava una voce che gli piaceva." Ibid., 6.

3. "Una delle famiglie più allegre del paese." Ibid., 8.

4. "Mio padre sfortunatamente non aveva la mia passione aritstica, per cui impose la sua volontà e mi forzò a partire." Ibid., 11.

5. "La piazzetta degli spasimanti, proprio perché tutta quella gente in fila spasimava per ricevere il visto di emigrazione e non tutti erano così fortunati da riceverlo." Ibid., 7.

6. "Improvvisamente mi feci triste e mille pensieri cominciarono ad affollare la mia mente: perché lasciavo il mio paese nativo? Perché lasciavo la mia famiglia? Perché andavo così lontano? Dove andavo? Perché andavo? Sarebbe stata veramente migliore la vita lontana dalla mia bella Italia? Valeva la pena cominciare tutto da capo? Queste erano le domande che mi ponevo e non sapevo come rispondere; ad alcune di esse dopo tanti anni di vita, non ho ancora potuto rispondere." Ibid., 8.

7. "La bugia è necessaria: la vostra pubblicità deve continuare ad essere quella di un tenore scritturato dall'Italia e che in tenera età ha cantato per la chiesa e per il papa. La vostra vita da minatore a Gallup deve essere dimenticata." Ibid., 80.

8. "Ho vissuto tutta la mia vita in America e con orgoglio servo la mia patria adottiva, ma il mio sangue è italiano e resterà tale fino all'ultimo respiro." Ibid., 89.

9. "Gli si inginocchiava piangendo ai piedi, come uno scemo da manicomio." Ibid., 103.

10. "Rifiutando, commentai: Voi produttori, per l'amore del denaro date l'anima al diavolo e calpestate tutto, senza pensare alla degradazione di un popolo orgoglioso che ha dato civiltà, legge ed ordine ai vostri antenati. E' vero che l'Italia ha perso una guerra non desiderata, ma mai

l'onore in millenni di storia. Per me sarebbe stata una vera vergogna, se avessi accettato di degradare la grandezza e l'orgoglio del mio popolo." Ibid.

11. Luigi Olari, *Avventure di un emigrante* (Parma: Tip. C.E.M., 1971). Written in Italian, a copy is preserved in the National Library of Florence. Interestingly, he is the only case (besides Father Mazzuchelli) in which the autobiography is written in the third person. It is thus the exception to Lejeune's grammatical rule, even if it never denies the trust of the reader: notwithstanding grammar, the story is about himself. Lejeune considers this particular case in his article "Autobiography in the Third Person" where he writes that "naturally, this takes place within the framework of a text controlled by an autobiographical pact"; Philippe Lejeune, Annette Tomarken, and Edward Tomarken, "Autobiography in the Third Person," *New Literary History: Self-Confrontation and Social Vision* 9, no. 1 (Autumn 1977): 27–50, 27. The use of the third person signals the strength of Luigi's dream, his strong unfulfilled ambition that makes him invent his own biographer. He makes up his own biography, as a privilege reserved to successful artists—in the same way as he pays to publish his *romanze*. No one can deny the resources of this man, who *makes* himself, against all odds.

12. "Olari Luigi, figlio di Olari Francesco e di Rustici Rosa, nacque a Pagazzano, piccolo paesello dell'Appennino Parmigiano il 16 febbraio 1894." Olari, *Avventure di un emigrante*, 11.

13. "Con pala e picco nella costruzione di strade, quindi come custode nelle agenzie d'automobili. Appena finito il rimborso della sorella delle spese di viaggio dall'Europa all'America, si comprò un paio di vestiti, un orologio con catena d'oro e s'affrettò a trovare un maestro di canto." Ibid., 12.

14. "Non fu così fortunato per l'alloggio. Dovette prendere la valigetta ed andare a dormire per due o tre notti nelle stazioni ferroviarie. . . . Si vergognava un poco dovendo denaro a tutti, circa cinquecento dollari." Ibid., 13.

15. "Scrisse le lettere d'invito a giornali e riviste musicali. Fece i cartelloni di reclame, scrisse la sua biografia. Alla sera del concerto portò sua moglie al botteghino, sua figlia per mettere a posto la gente, e lui stesso alla porta per ricevere i biglietti." Ibid., 27.

16. "Aveva trovato più soddisfazione dalla sua breve visita in Italia che dai 41 anni trascorsi in America, perché in Italia c'era ancora un po' di coscienza e un po' di considerazione per le persone oneste." Ibid., 30.

17. Luigi Lombardi, *Pages of My Life by LU-L* (Fond Du Lac, WI: privately printed, 1943). A copy is preserved in the Immigration History Research Center, St. Paul.

18. Ibid., 103.

19. Ibid., 68–69.

20. Ibid., 24.

21. Ibid., 28.

22. Ibid., 43.

23. Ibid., 46.

24. Ibid., 50.

25. Ibid., 90.

26. Ibid., 97.

27. Pietro Montana, *Memories: An Autobiography* (Hicksville, New York: Exposition Press, 1977).

28. Ibid., 32–33.

29. Ibid., 33.

30. Ibid., 47.

31. Ibid., 55.

32. Ibid., 170.

33. Ibid., 183.

34. Ibid., 177.

35. Alfred D. Crimi, *A Look Back a Step Forward: My Life Story,* ed. Frank Bernard (New York: Center for Migration Studies, 1987).

36. Ibid., 180.

37. Rocco De Russo, "Papers," typescript, 1971, Immigration History Research Center, St. Paul. The microfilm includes papers, songs, and photographs.

38. "E così fra musica e canzoni, macchiette e duetti, non che lo studio della scuola, non mi restava più un minuto di tempo per divagarmi con i miei coetanei! A dodici anni anche il pianoforte lo suonavo discretamente—la musica era la mia passione, come il palcoscenico, a cui ho dato la mia intera esistenza. Per essere quel che fui, ho studiato continuamente drammi, tragedie, commedie." Ibid., 7.

39. Ibid., 30.

40. "Avrei potuto benissimo sguazzarmela in pace trionfale, ma non c'era verso di poter dimenticarme il teatro, che l'avevo nel sangue, nel cuore, nella mente! . . . una tarla che continuamente mi logorava il cervello!" Ibid., 43.

41. "Ma che ci fate in questo piccolo paesello? . . . spogliatevi della vostra divisa, e rientrate in arte . . . il palcoscenico vi aspetta." Ibid., 45.

42. "Quell'atto poco signorile, quel gesto insano, che quel disgraziato mi spinse a commettere, mi demoralizzò a tal punto da farmi decidere di abbandonare tutto. . . . Non avevo più il coraggio di presentarmi davanti a quel pubblico, a quelle brave famiglie che mi veneravano." Ibid., 59.

43. "Che bei tempi . . . che soldi!" Ibid., 65.

44. Guglielmo Emanuel Gatti, *Cinquant'anni d'arte scenica* (New York: S.F. Vanni, 1937).

45. "La fatalità che s'è giovata della mia precaria posizione economica per pormi sulla strada preventivamente destinatami. Non sarebbe spiegabile in modo diverso la mia grande passione pel teatro venuta a svilupparsi man mano, con un fascino quasi mistico." Ibid., 16.

46. "Ero, come dissi, seduto al mio solito tavolo (che molte volte era pure quello del pranzo e della cena) semisdraiato sulla sedia che qualche volta mi serviva anche da letto e da scrivania, quando un giovinetto, signoril-mente vestito e con fare distinto, dall'età presapoco la mia, mi si avvicina e mi dice; Scusi Lei è un comico? non ebbi il tempo di dire "no" che quel giovinetto proseguì: anche se è un semplici [*sic*] dilettante non importa. Il grande maestro Giovanni Toselli penserà lui a farne un artista, e poi . . . si tratta di recitare in dialetto piemontese . . . Colla rapidità che può avere il pensiero dell'amore ricordai che avevo recitato in collegio e sfacciatamente risposi: si, so recitare. Qualche volta l'audacia giova più della coscienza!" Ibid., 15.

47. "Dico teatro, così per mondo di dire. I teatri in cui recitavano gli attori italiani erano tutti confinati nella bassa città e cioè nella vecchia New York ed erano quasi tutti gestiti da ebrei russi e tedeschi." Ibid., 39.

48. "Col danaro avrei potuto mettere una musaruola [*sic*] ai cani che mi ab-baiavano, e, al ritorno in Italia, avrei potuto istituire un teatro Stabile di Arte nella mia città natale. Infatti avevo principiato assai bene; ma venne la grande guerra . . . e poi la legge restrittiva sulla emigrazione . . . ed il mio sogno è caduto come un edificio di cartone al passaggio di un tur-bine." Ibid., 45.

49. "Grande fucina fotografica il cui sole smagliante e cocente brucia le ali a tutti gli Icari che malcauti s'avvicinano." Ibid., 212.

50. "Lascio dunque riposare in pace i miei tre volumi di *scrap book* nei quali è tutto il mio patrimonio artistico e patriottico che, un giorno non lon-tano, sarà confinato in qualche cantina o venduto a qualche rigattiere per carta straccia. Requiescat in pace." Ibid., 55.

Chapter 4
The Spiritual Immigrant

1. Luigi Turco, ed. *The Spiritual Autobiography of Luigi Turco* (New York: Center of Migration Studies, 1969), 237. The work is preserved at the Immigration History Research Center, St. Paul, where it has been put on microfilm.
2. Ibid.
3. Ibid., x.
4. Ibid., 1.
5. Ibid. 1.
6. Ibid., 3.
7. Ibid., 26–27.
8. Ibid., 3.
9. Ibid., 6.
10. Ibid., 18.
11. Antonio Arrighi, *Story of Antonio, the Galley Slave: A Romance of Real Life* (New York: Fleming Revell, 1911).
12. See Rose Basile Green, *The Italian-American Novel: A Document of the Interaction of Two Cultures* (Madison: Fairleigh Dickinson University Press, 1974), 32, for the "forbidding antiquity" of the Italian background in this autobiography, especially in the chapter "Città Vecchia." The town "is so impregnated with sulfur that it gives its inhabitants tan appearance of old age" (110), even the children look old, it is called "the city of old people" (110).
13. Ibid., 193.
14. Ibid., 195, 192.
15. Ibid., 228–29.
16. Ibid., 182.
17. Constantine Panunzio, *The Soul of an Immigrant* (New York: Arno Press, 1969). The first edition is Macmillan, 1921.
18. This is what motivated William Boelhower to include immigrant Panunzio's book among his autobiographies of Americanization. See William Boelhower, *Autobiographical Transactions in Modernist America: The Immigrant, the Architect, the Artist, the Citizen* (Udine: Del Bianco, 1992).
19. William Boelhower sharply notes that this change in the narration is a shift to "antinarrative": "the compositional shift is achieved at great price, for in becoming an American somebody, his protagonist becomes, physically, a nobody. He is simply rarefied out of existence" (Ibid., 69).

20. Panunzio, *Soul of an Immigrant,* xi–xii.

21. The original title was *Memorie istoriche ed edificanti d'un missionario apostolico dell'Ordine dei Predicatori fra varie tribù di selvaggi e fra i cattolici e protestanti negli Stati Uniti d'America* (Milan, 1844); the translated edition is "Historical and Edifying Memoirs of an Apostolic Missionary of the Order of Preachers among the Various Indian Tribes and among the Catholics and Protestants in the United States of America," intro. John Ireland (Chicago: W.F. Hall Printing, 1915). I refer to the reprint: Samuel Mazzuchelli, *The Memoirs of Father Samuel Mazzuchelli, Op.P.* (Chicago: Priory Press, 1967).

22. Ibid., 303.

23. Ibid., 5.

24. Ibid., 6.

25. Ibid., 10.

26. Ibid., 13–14.

27. Ibid., 107.

28. Ibid., 59.

29. Giacomo Gambera, *A Migrant Missionary Story* (New York: Center for Migration Studies, 1994).

30. Ibid., 64.

31. Ibid., 80.

32. Ibid., 100.

33. Ibid., 105.

34. Ibid., 138.

35. Ibid., 187.

36. Ibid., 69–70.

37. Ibid., 58.

Chapter 5
Immigrant Women

1. The percentage of all female immigrants to the United States (not distinguished by race or nationality) was 31% in the 1820s, it reached a peak of 44.5% in the 1840s, and dropped again to 30.4% 1900–1909. It then picked up again and accounted for the majority of arrivals for the rest of 1900, starting from the 1930s (55.3%), with a peak in the 1940s (61.2%), and then over 50% until 1979. See the tables in Donna Gabaccia, "Women of the Mass Migration: From Minority to Majority, 1820–1930" in *European Migrants: Global and Local Perspectives,* ed. Dirk Hoerder and

Leslie Page Moch (Boston: Northeastern University Press, 1996), 90–111.

2. "Autobiography has been one of the most important sites of feminist debate precisely because it demonstrates that there are many different ways of writing the subject," wrote Linda Anderson in *Autobiography: New Critical Idiom* (London, New York: Routledge, 2001), 87. One of the most influential essays is Estelle Jelinek's in *Women's Autobiography: Essays in Criticism* (Bloomington: Indiana University Press, 1980), 1–20, where she claims that "different criteria are needed to evaluate women's autobiographies, which may constitute if not a subgenre, then an auto-biographical tradition different from the male tradition" (1). See also Judy Long, *Telling Women's Lives: Subject/ Narrator/ Reader /Text* (New York: New York University Press, 1999), for the binary distinctions: men portray themselves as separate, women as connected; men's stories are set in the public eye, women chronicle private scenes; men's lives are pruned to a terse outline, women's remain messy; men claim a destination, women record process; men universalize their experience, women set themselves in context.

3. Germaine Bree asserts that women scholars "tend merely to reverse the criteria in use: if male autobiographical writing is seen as teleological and linear, female is described as fragmented and circular; if male is defined as using a rhetoric of assertion, female is defined as using a rhetoric of seduction, and so on" Ibid., 171.

4. As Mary Frances Pipino wrote, women's individualism is not a natural condition because they are naturally subordinate: "In Italian culture, to be a woman alone was to be a person without an identity or place in the world. . . . The paradox of American individualism for Italian immigrant women and their female descendants, then, is that the opportunity of a new life in America applied only to men. The constancy of women's traditional roles and identities within the family were taken for granted, despite the 'New World' emphasis on freedom and individual achievement." Mary Frances Pipino, *I Have Found My Voice: The Italian-American Woman Writer* (New York: Peter Lang, 2000), 3–4.

5. The model for these empowered women is often the writer's illiterate peasant grandmother. For the use of grandmothers as a powerful model, or even a *strega*, for Italian American gay writers, see Ilaria Serra, "The Reappearance of *Streghe* in Italian American Queer Writings," *The Journal for the Academic Study of Magic*, 1 (2003): 131–60.

6. "Perchè nella maternità adoriamo il sacrifizio? . . . di madre in figlia, da secoli, si tramanda il servaggio. È una mostruosa catena." Sibilla Aleramo, *Una donna* (Milan: Feltrinelli, 1992), 193.

7. Sister Blandina Segale, *At the End of the Santa Fe Trail* (Milwaukee: Bruce, 1948 [1932]). On this topic of Italian American memoirs, a trend exploded in the 1980s and 1990s, see Edvige Giunta, *Writing with an Accent: Contemporary Italian American Women Authors* (New York: Palgrave, 2002). See also Caterina Romeo, *Narrative tra le due sponde: Memoir di Italiane d'America* (Roma: Carocci, 2005). The first book to gather voices of Italian American women, many of which are in first person, is Helen Barolini, *The Dream Book: An Anthology of Writings by Italian American Women* (New York: Schocken Books, 1985). These works mainly discuss second- or third-generation immigrant women for whom identity is a smoldering matter. Consequently, their style is seeped in postmodern doubts and constructions, de-constructions, and reconnections of complicated identities.

8. Rosa Cavalleri, *Rosa: The Life of an Italian Immigrant* ed. Marie Hall Ets (Minneapolis: University of Minnesota Press, 1970).

9. Fred Gardaphé, for example, assigns to her the unifying, heroic aspect of her autobiography. Fred Gardaphé, *Italian Signs, American Streets: The Evolution of Italian-American Narrative* (Durham: Duke University Press, 1996).

10. On the real identity of Rosa (Ines Ignazia), the most complete research is by Ernesto Milani, who edited the Italian translation of *Rosa* and presented his research as the talk "The Publication of the Translation of *Rosa: the Life of an Italian Immigrant*," American Italian Historical Association Conference, Boca Raton (November 6–8, 2003). Since hers is primarily an oral history, this work hardly fits my research, but given the scarcity of sources on immigrant women and since the work has been considered an autobiography in several critical essays, I have decided to include it here. Even though she claimed that her real mother was a famous actress, Milani proved she was a "wretched and penniless needlewoman" who worked for the theater in Milan. Milani, "The Publication of the Translation of *Rosa*."

11. Cavalleri, *Rosa*, 152.

12. Ibid., 38, 242, 76.

13. Ibid., 164.

14. Ibid., 187.

15. Ibid., 191.

16. Ibid., 191.

17. Ibid., 195, 171, 195.

18. Ibid., 174.

19. I include Pieracci's written testimony centered on her father, following Maria Parrino, who included it in her dissertation about autobiographies of Italian American women. Maria Parrino, "Il luogo della memoria e il luogo dell'identità: Narrazioni autobiografiche di donne dell'immigrazione italo-americana," unpublished dissertation, Università degli Studi di Genova, 1988. The text was published in Salvatore LaGumina's collection *The Immigrants Speak* (New York: Center for Immigration Studies, 1979), 33–47.

20. Bruna Pieracci, "Bruna Pieracci," in LaGumina, *The Immigrants Speak*, 33–47, 34.

21. Ibid., 35.

22. Ibid., 33.

23. Ibid., 47.

24. Ibid., 35.

25. Ibid., 35.

26. Ibid., 35.

27. Ibid., 36.

28. Ibid., 45.

29. The first time was when telling of her father's return to Scotland, the second was with his desire to move to a warmer climate.

30. Their *Memoires* are a manuscript in the Immigration History Research Center of St. Paul, Minnesota, and they cover the period 1901–71. David Yona and Anna Yona, "Memoires," transcript, 1971, Immigration History Research Center, St. Paul.

31. She was home schooled and followed some university courses as a non-degree student.

32. David's parents married on a forbidden day, for example.

33. "'Cosa significava essere una bambina ebrea in Italia al principio del secolo?' Che cosa significava? Proprio nulla, assolutamente nulla! Non c'era l'osservanza dei rituali, né la celebrazione delle festività nella casa dei miei genitori." Carla Coen Pekelis, *Memories, 1907–1941*, typescript, 1941, trans. Arianna Ascoli, Pieve Santo Stefano, Archivio Diaristico Nazionale, 1. She married a Russian exile, and in 1938 fled to France, Spain, and Portugal. In 1941, with her husband and two children, she moved to New York, where she worked as a professor of Italian at Sarah Lawrence College.

34. Yona and Yona, "Memoires," 4–5.

35. Ibid., 38.

36. Ibid., 39.

37. Ibid., 40, 34.

38. "It was one of the few times I saw David desperate. I wanted him to go immediately to the U.S., but he did not want to depart without me and the children." Ibid., 41.

39. Ibid., 50.

40. Ibid., 50.

41. Ibid., 69.

42. Ibid., 75.

43. Ibid., 70.

44. Ibid., 62–63.

45. Giuseppina Liarda Macaluso, *My Mother: Memoir of a Sicilian Woman* (New York: EPI, 1998), 240.

46. Ibid., 121.

47. Ibid., 241.

48. Ibid., 243.

49. Ibid., 68.

50. Leonilde Frieri Ruberto, *Such Is Life* (Sound Beach, NY: Pern Press, 1995), 24.

51. Ibid., 38.

52. Ibid., 52.

53. Ibid., 61.

54. Amalia Santacaterina Paguri, *Il calicanto non cresce a Chicago* (Vicenza: La Serenissima, 1992). I found this book in the house of the mayor of the little town of Chiuppano.

55. "In tutti i viaggi che ho fatto tra l'Italia e l'America, ho sempre tentato di portare a Chicago un rametto di calicanto, ma non sono mai riuscita a farlo crescere. . . . Forse, io sono come il calicanto che non cresce a Chicago." Ibid., 22.

56. "Ho in mano un rametto di calicanto che emana un soave profumo, e ridesta in me un bel ricordo della mia gioventu." Ibid., 21.

57. "Non posso dire di essermi integrata nell'ambiente. Gli alberi, se trapiantati da vecchi, attecchiscono con difficoltà," Lucia Bedarida, "Curriculum Vitae," typescript, 1995, Pieve Santo Stefano, Archivio Diaristico Nazionale, 12. Evidently she proved the expression wrong, since in 2005 she celebrated her 105th birthday by flying on a hang glider! In a letter she sent me (November 10, 2002) when she was 102, she wrote: "I know

what I will do, if I'll be alive for my 1003 [*sic*] birthday. I will be in Chamors, Valdaosta, in the Hotel Edelweis, and I'll breath the pure air that will defend me from the polluted and infected American air next winter" ("Lo so già quello che farò, se sono viva, per il mio 1003 compleanno. Sarò a Chamors in Valdaosta all'Hotel Edelweis, respirerò dell'aria pura che mi aiuterà a difendermi dall'aria polluta ed infetta di qui, durante il prossimo inverno").

58. "Ero come un uccellino strappato dal nido e portato vicino ad una pozza d'acqua, sempre in pericolo d'annegare." Santacaterina, *Il calicanto*, 29.

59. "I veneti, con qualche aiuto, si sono quasi tutti fabbricati la casa, spesso villette costruite con le proprie mani." Ibid., 95.

60. "Come in tutte le famiglie venete si vende il vino e la grappa fatta in casa. Nello scantinato c'è molto alcool pronto per essere venduto e l'alambicco per distillare." Ibid., 89.

61. "Dobbiamo adattarci alle usanze dei calabresi, gente che magari si abbassa ad andare a raccogliere il carbone con le secchie . . . sono orgogliosi di avere tra essi della gente del nord Italia che li rispetta." Ibid., 97.

62. "Come in tutte le disavventure, alla lunga subentra la rassegnazione; il cibo non manca, nemmeno il vino che il governo permette agli italiani di farsi e la grappa che si distilla clandestinamente . . . Ognuno ha un suo bel pezzo di orto dove semina le verdure. . . . Sono frequenti le cene a base di polenta ed uccelli, fagiani, lepri, funghi, si fa a gara a chi ne trova di piu." Ibid., 97.

63. "C'era il grosso problema di convincere mio marito a permettermi di andare a Milano a comperare una macchina per fare i gnocchi. . . . così decisi di partire con i miei ingredienti e con lo scarso consenso di mio marito." Ibid., 167.

64. Elvezia Marcucci, "Le memorie di una novantenne smemorata (che sarei io)," manuscript, two notebooks (A and B), 2001, Pieve Santo Stefano, Archivio Diaristico Nazionale.

65. "In quel tempo quando gli uomini erano al comando nelle situazioni famigliari, non certo come adesso nel duemila." Marcucci, "Le Memorie," 5.

66. "Se penso a tante cose che mi successero; con lui vicino le avrei evitate . . . forse . . . chissà?" Ibid., 12.

67. "Con lui sentii, come se tutto quello che mi circondava, entrasse dentro di me, lacerandomi. Subito dopo, lo vidi alzarsi, andare verso la porta e gridarmi: 'Ora mi sposerai!' Nella mia ignoranza del sesso, istintivamente pensai che mi avesse messo incinta, allora si che dovevo sposarlo!" Ibid., 54.

68. "Cercavo di essere una brava moglie invece di una brava pianista." Ibid., 62. "I tried to be a good wife instead of a good pianist."

69. "Era come se stessi sopra ad una altalena, andando in su e giù sempre con la paura di cadere e farmi del male, però dovevo rassegnarmi ora che avevo una figlia con lui." Ibid., 79.

70. "Dentro di me lo detestavo, conoscendo la sua innata violenza." Ibid., 76.

71. "Ritrovai il piacere di essere ancora giovane e libera per godermi la vita." Ibid., 111.

72. "Mi stupì quella mistura di colori, e la definii la mia prima esperienza americana." Marcucci, "Le Memorie," 4B. The page number followed by a "B" refers to Elvezia's second handwritten notebook.

73. "Notai che le persone non parlavano a voce alta e smanettando come facevano in Italia." Ibid., 4B.

74. "Digli che lo sposo ma se non andassimo d'accordo ci dovremmo divorziare." Ibid., 23B.

75. "Quando mi strinse la mano pensai facessimo un contratto d'affari." Ibid., 24B. "When he took my hand, I thought we were closing a business contract."

76. "Mi sentivo più sicura di me stessa e camminavo spedita verso l'altare." Ibid., 28B.

77. "Pensai che una cosa buona con Joe [era] che mai avrebbe avuto il coraggio di contrararmi [sic] per quanto io volevo fare." Ibid., 54B.

78. "Avevo allora sessantanove anni e li portavo bene. Sentendomi ancora giovane per vivere da sola a Grosseto, nella mia Maremma." Ibid., 99–100B.

79. "Davanti al mare del mio paese, ritornata sono da un altra sponda. Guardo nell'onda e vedo il mio passato far ritorno, scorrere sulla sabbia lasciando tracce più o meno profonde. Si ferma, si agita, poi con l'onde nel mare lontano si disperde." Ibid., 102.

80. She called this metaphor of self, "the uncertain self," which lives a battle with instincts and drives. Diane Bjorklund, *Interpreting the Self: Two Hundred Years of American Autobiography* (Chicago: University of Chicago Press, 1998).

81. "Ho la sensazione di scusarmi di esistere." Elisabeth Evans, "Un attimo una vita," typescript, 1996, Pieve Santo Stefano, Archivio Diaristico Nazionale, 3. Stopping to apologize is one of the shifts in American women's autobiography, Elizabeth Winston argues. Before 1920, in fact, women writers like Margaret Olifant, Lady Sydney Morgan, and Mary

Milford felt it necessary to apologize in some way for writing through disclaimers and words of self-deprecation: "these autobiographers express their desire to interest and entertain their readers, defend past actions, or leave a record for their children—intentions directed mainly toward satisfying others." Elizabeth Winston, "The Autobiographer and Her Readers: From Apology to Affirmation" in Jelinek, ed., *Women's Autobiography*, 93–111 (Bloomington: Indiana University Press, 1980.) 94.

82. "Amare i miei figli, la natura, le persone, gli animali, ma non me stessa, io non esisto. Sono morta così tante volte che, quando provo a cercarmi mi rendo conto che non ci sono più." Evans, "Una vita," 55.

83. "Jim e suo padre hanno ripreso a bere. Mancano i soldi e io passo parte delle notti incollata al televisore sintonizzato sul canale che preavvisa arrivi e traiettorie dei tornados." Ibid., 44.

84. "Dopo tutto quello che ho passato ho imparato che qui l'incredibile è normale e, se si parla di violenza non vi sono limiti, il bello è che tutto ciò è coperto da un tale perbenismo e bigottismo che esteriormente questo paese riesce ancora ad essere esempio di ideali per il resto del mondo." Ibid., 41.

85. "C'è un momento, quando il grande Jumbo dell'Alitalia sorvola New York e la visione della statua della Libertà si presenta illuminata nella notte davanti ai miei occhi, in cui sento quasi un rimpianto, una disperazione e, mentre la vedo sparire nel buio, piango. Sento che non rivedrò mai più questo Paese in cui, nel bene e nel male, lascio una parte della mia vita. Ho ventitre anni ed è come se ne avessi già vissuti quaranta." Ibid., 48.

86. The story of Elisabeth has many similarities with another autobiography of an Italian America woman, Louise De Salvo's *Vertigo*. They both experience depression and write to get out of it, they tell parallel events, they both hate their mothers, are not prepared for maternity, contemplate suicide and dream of independence, both live in the same turbulent period for American youth, the 1970s. Louise DeSalvo, *Vertigo* (New York: Dutton, 1997).

87. Maria Bottiglieri, "Sposa di guerra," typescript, 1986, Pieve Santo Stefano, Archivio Diaristico Nazionale.

88. "Odiavo gli alleati, come odiavo tutti quelli che avevano voluto la Guerra." Ibid., 4.

89. "Come poteva interessarmi un americano? Odiavo troppo i vincitori. A Napoli ne avevo passate tante. No, non era facile dimenticare le notti

passate nei ricoveri e sotto i tunnel per i continui bombardamenti."
Ibid., 3.

90. "Quando papà mi abbracciò ebbi l'impulso di mandare tutto al diavolo, di tornarmene a casa con lui, risedermi sulle sue ginocchia, lasciarmi ancora coccolare, ma poi, mi resi conto che un ciclo della mia vita stava per finire e ne stava iniziando un altro carico di responsabilita. Dovevo imparare ad affrontare la vita. Ecco, dovevo maturare, e con il tuo aiuto, dovevo riuscirci. Era stata una mia scelta e dovevo essere coraggiosa. . . . Malgrado i miei buoni propositi, quando la nave partì e io vedevo i miei rimpicciolirsi sempre piu, mi sentii vuota, cattiva, egoista. Quando li avrei rivisti? Avrei avuto la forza di vivere senza di loro? Piansi per quasi tutto il viaggio." Ibid., 22.

91. "Io diventavo sempre più americana. Mangiavo alla loro maniera, e qualche volta mi accorgevo di pensare addirittura in inglese." Ibid., 27.

92. "Era quasi un pellegrinaggio che dovevo compiere." Ibid., 1.

93. "Ecco, John, ora sono qui. A Firenze ho comprato un cappellino di paglia [as in their first trip together]. . . . E adesso sono qui a Napoli, sulla panchina, nel parco, dove ci siamo parlati per la prima volta. Sono qui seduta con il cappellino di paglia sulle ginocchia, mentre intorno le foglie sugli alberi, col loro stormire, mi cantano canzoni d'amore, d'amore, d'amore." Ibid., 37–38.

94. *Leggendaria* 46–47 (October 2004): 8–12, 10.

95. In the field of autobiography our women do with words what other Italian American women artists are doing in other media. In her touring exhibition *Lifeline: An Italian American Odyssey* the artist B. Amore displayed the objects of Italian immigrant women in compositions that embrace the experience of immigrant women. B. Amore, *Lifeline: An Italian American Odyssey*, exhibition, American Italian Historical Association Conference, Boca Raton, November 6–8, 2003, now a book, *An Italian American Odyssey: Lifeline—Filo della Vita: Through Ellis Island and Beyond* (New York: Fordham University Press, 2006).

Chapter 6
Toward Success

1. The same documentary value is in the book first written in 1935 by Edward Corsi, *In the Shadow of Liberty* (New York: Arno Press, 1969). The author, while not really writing an autobiography (he starts his story directly from his arrival), puts Ellis Island in the center of his narration.

He briefly speaks about his immigration and then dives into the story of the Island where he worked as an inspector, describing the people and the human cases he saw.

2. Vincenzo Grossi, "Ricordi," 1988, typescript, Pieve Santo Stefano, Archivio Diaristico Nazionale.

3. He wrote: "la famiglia De Sanctis aveva nel 1776 una proprietà che ammontava a oltre 10.000 ducati" Ibid., 1.

4. "Si sente vendicato del suo destino." Ibid., 25.

5. "Ma io quando ricordo il nostro piccolo mondo, mi domando se non valeva la pena rimanere a fare il medico a casa mia, come tutti mi consigliavano quando mori [sic] il medico Calcagni nel 1914 anno della mia laurea. E vero che oggi quando vado in villeggiatura in un bel paese d'Italia, con la nostalgia dell'emigrante, dopo pochi giorni mi annoio, ma è sempre bello sognare che forse a Santupeto sarei stato felice tutta la vita." Ibid., 39.

6. "Lasciato a me stesso, io ero disperato e così mi veniva l'idea di scappare all'estero." Ibid., 72.

7. Ibid., 76.

8. "In gran segreto se il sapore dei sorci era buono, perché la maestra a scuola le insegnava che gli italiani mangiano i topi." Ibid., 79.

9. "Pettegolezzi che poi tornavano a mio danno." Ibid., 81.

10. "Piangendo che non mi avrebbe più rivisto." Ibid., 82.

11. "In 12 anni di professione non avevo cambiato fortuna e perciò sussistevano le stesse ragioni per le quali ero venuto: fare un piccolo capitale per avere una base a Roma." Ibid., 82.

12. "Non ero da criticare perché mandavo mio figlio a studiare in Italia, quando era la mia profonda convinzione che io sarei tornato a Roma pel resto della vita." Ibid., 82.

13. "Verrò a piangere a Roma, ci sacrificheremo, faremo magari gli affittacamere, ma creperò a Roma." Ibid., 86.

14. "L'america [sic] divenne per me una ossessione e il giugno 1939 partii da roma [sic], vinto ancora dal destino." Ibid., 87.

15. "L'unico sogno svanito per me e Laura era quello di vivere a Roma. Ora che potemmo stare nella città eterna, ogni volta che la nostalgia ci tenta, guardiamo i nostri quattro nipotini che crescono sani e belli, e ci rassegniamo finalmente al destino." Ibid., 90.

16. Michele Daniele, *Signor Dottore: The Autobiography of F. Michele Daniele, Italian Immigrant Doctor (1879–1957)*, ed. Victor Rosen (New York: Exposition Press: 1959). He also published three other books: *Rime vecchie e*

nuove (Bologna: Zanichelli, 1930); *Calvario di Guerra: Diario di prigionia in Austria con 20 illustrazioni fuori testo* (Milan: Alpes, 1932); *Yankee Faith and Other Stories* (New York: Greenberg Publishing, 1935).

17. Daniele, *Signor Dottore*, 26.
18. Ibid., 33.
19. Ibid., 34.
20. Ibid., 36.
21. Ibid., 50.
22. Ibid., 51.
23. Ibid., 52.
24. Ibid., 61.
25. Ibid., 57.
26. Ibid., 137.
27. Ibid., 236.
28. Ibid., 236.
29. Giuseppe Previtali, *Doctor Beppo: An Italian Doctor in America* (privately published, 1984).
30. Ibid., 93.
31. Ibid., 94.
32. Ibid., 94.
33. Ibid., 100.
34. Ibid., 116.
35. Ibid., 119.
36. Ibid., 133.
37. Ibid., 106.
38. Ibid., 136.
39. Ibid., 135.
40. Ibid., 152.
41. Ibid., 168.
42. Ibid., 194.
43. Ibid., 214.
44. Don Peppino, *Note autobiografiche di un medico generico* (New York: Coccè Press, 1962). A copy is preserved in the Staten Island Center for Immigration Studies.
45. "Mi sembra più indicato alla mia indole, che ha una particolare attrazione per il linguaggio familiare, che dà quella dolce sensazione d'intimità, tanto cara agli esseri semplici." Ibid., 9.
46. "L'esposizione dei principii dai quali mi son fatto guidare dal giorno in cui ho iniziato la mia carriera fino al giorno in cui ho dato il mio 'addio alle armi.'" Ibid., 103.

47. "Se, non ostante la mia istintiva riluttanza, mi sono deciso a scrivere non la mia biografia, ma una modesta cronaca della mia vita, l'ho fatto solamente per appagare il desiderio della mia famiglia, di clienti e di amici per i quali ho riservato le poche copie di questa pubblicazione." Ibid., 8.

48. "In nessuna cosa gli uomini si avvicinano agli dei, come allorquando ridanno agli uomini la salute." Ibid., 8.

49. "Sono stato e sono tuttavia audace e debbo alla mia audacia i miei modesti successi. Nessuna difficoltà mi è sembrata insuperabile. Nessuna contrarietà mi ha fatto desistere nel perseverare." Ibid., 19.

50. "Dobbiamo pregare il Signore che quando ci punisce con un accidente lo faccia prima delle sette di sera!" Ibid., 30.

51. "Nel 1950 la mia posizione economica era la seguente: avevo una casa ma non ero più padrone del mio ufficio. Avevo dei titoli azionari, ma non erano sufficienti a colmare le esigenze del nostro bilancio." Ibid., 118.

52. "Ho goduto la gioventù e la maturità come ora godo la vecchiaia . . . è questa mia filosofia e questa mi convizione che mi fanno considerare la vecchiaia come il sopravvivere dello spirito individuale nello spirito dell'universo." Ibid., 120.

53. Martino Marazzi, *Voices of Italian America: A History of Early Italian American Literature with a Critical Anthology* (Madison, WI: Farleigh Dickinson University Press, 2004), 23.

54. Joseph Tusiani, *La parola difficile: Autobiografia di un italo-americano* (Brindisi: Schena Editore, 1988). The other two books have been published by the same publishing house in 1991 and in 1992. The books are written in Italian because, the author says, "I did not want to betray my characters. I had to respect their truth: I could not make my mother speak English. Besides, I wrote this autobiography for myself as a personal outburst (*sfogo*), without thinking of an audience" (personal communication with the author, October 2005).

55. "Sammarchesi venuti qui a soffrire di più per soffrire di meno"; Ibid., 205; "punito dalla vita per aver vinto al morte." Ibid., 355.

56. "Come tutti gli emigrati, a ciascuna finii col dare metà del mio cuore." Ibid., 71.

57. "Un ferro di cavallo ben visibile al centro del cancelletto, una statuetta di Sant'Antonio incastonata in una grotta di pietre policrome, un morettino di gesso con in mano una lanterna che il minimo soffio di vento faceva

oscillare, e qualche metro quadrato d'orto che sfoggiava i suoi ultimi pomodori scarlatti." Tusiani, *La parola difficile*, 15.

58. "Chi non ha mai messo piede fuori d'Italia non sa cosa sia udire all'improvviso un canto del paesello natio in terra straniera. Ti si inumidiscono gli occhi, ti passano davanti, come su uno schermo magico, tutti i volti dei vecchi amici, rivedi ogni pendio erboso, ogni vicoletto ripido, senti e distingui le campane delle chiese, e passi il dito sull'occhio per asciugare una lagrima senza vergognartene." Tusiani, *La parola difficile*, 20.

59. "Erano lì le mie radici, ma erano altrove le mie ramificazioni. Ero, insomma, in un limbo indescrivibile, tra estasi ed affanno, tra piacere e dovere. Ero io e non ero io: ero qualcosa fra due mondi, due sogni, fra due civiltà concrete e non ancor del tutto comprensibili." Tusiani, *La parola difficile*, 280.

60. Paolo Giordano, "From Southern Italian Emigrant to Reluctant American: Joseph Tusiani's *Gente Mia and Other Poems*." *From the Margin: Writings in Italian Americana*. Ed. Anthony Tamburri, Paolo Giordano, Fred Gardaphé (West Lafayette: Purdue University Press, 2000), 314–26, 317.

61. "E' una lingua brutta come un debito." Tusiani, *La parola antica: Autobiografia di un italo-americano* (Brindisi: Schena Editore, 1992), 381.

62. "Beh, quelle 'uova' che volevano significare affetto e amore, non riusciva ancora a digerirle. Ibid., 100.

63. James Craig Holte, "The Newcomer in America: A Study of Italian and Puertorican Personal Narrations" (diss. University of Cincinnati, 1978), 73–74.

64. Francesco Ventresca, *Personal Reminiscences of a Naturalized American* (New York: Daniel Ryerson, 1937), 25.

65. Ibid., 40.

66. Ibid., 165.

67. Ibid., 26.

68. Leonard Covello with Guido D'Agostino, *The Heart is the Teacher* (New York: McGraw-Hill, 1958).

69. Holte, "The Newcomer in America," 85.

70. Covello, *The Heart*, 39.

71. Ibid., 104.

72. Ibid., 129.

73. The story of an education is that of Salvatore Castagnola in his unfinished "Land Where my Father Died!" (typescript, 1909, Immigration History Research Center, St. Paul). He recounts his childhood and youth

up to his graduation at sixteen. He dedicates his story to his children "that reading it they may learn from whence came the America they now enjoy." He explains that "this is the story of an immigrant boy who, unlike most immigrants from Italy, came from a higher middle class family, leaving a home of luxury and culture. Like all other immigrants, he saw America at its worst, and by contrast to his former surroundings, felt more keenly the tribulations awaiting all foreigners of the early century and in particular of Italian origin." Born in 1883, he migrated from Messina with his mother and brothers in 1903, choosing what to bring to America: "even sentiment has to give way, however, when a life's belonging must be squeezed into one large trunk" (28). They join his father in New York. The trip occupies many pages with his expectations. He learns English, "anxious to show myself at my best, feeling toward my father, whom I had not seen for four years, as a total stranger and wanting so much to have him like me and accept me as his eldest son" (51). When they arrive he does not even recognize his father: "I had caught sight of a man in rustic working clothes, pointing and waving at me and shouting for recognition. . . . Could it be, I thought? Then with incredulity, I mused to myself, but father wore a beard, a beautiful blond beard. He was robust, immaculately dressed and cut the figure of a prince. Could this be he? And I repeated my thought aloud. 'Could this be he?' (67). His mother disillusion is equally bitter, when she sees their house with the hammock and the calico curtains for privacy: "she did not even notice the young man had gone, tears streamed down her cheeks and then she broke down, flung herself on the lowest hammock and cried. The three of us children took up the melancholy and clinging to mother's pitiful body we cried with her" (32).

74. Angelo Pellegrini, *Immigrant's Return* (New York: Macmillan, 1951). Giuseppe Prezzolini was harsh with this book and its author in *I trapiantati* (Milan: Longanesi, 1963). He called Pellegrini "l'emigrato scontento" (391): "this American professor seems to me a little professor, who is little gifted of critical spirit" (393). Prezzolini almost took it personally when Pellegrini lamented that Italy is a backward, melancholic, and sad society, and that it lacked democracy. Prezzolini answered: "it would be the same to complain that the girls of a country have blue eyes instead than black, or blond hair instead than dark. Pellegrini says the truth when he recognizes to be an American. He is really American in that characteristic that people and scholars of this country have, that of lacking *a sense of history*. It would be enough to be looking for the place

of 'spiritual values,' Italy or America. These are questions of American professors. American spiritual values are in America, and Italian ones are in Italy." Prezzolini, *I trapiantati,* 397.

75. Pellegrini, *Immigrant's Return,* 35.
76. Ibid., 50.
77. Ibid., 73.
78. Ibid., 252.
79. Angelo Massari, *The Wonderful Life of Angelo Massari,* trans. Arthur Massolo (New York: Exposition Press, 1965).
80. Ibid., 35.
81. Ibid., 236.
82. Ibid., 76.
83. Ibid., 8.
84. Ibid., 1.
85. Ibid., 21.
86. Guido Orlando, *Confessions of a Scoundrel* (Philadelphia: John Winston, 1954).
87. Ibid., 15.
88. Ibid., 9.
89. Ibid., 15.
90. Ibid., 262.
91. Fortune Gallo, *Lucky Rooster: The Autobiography of an Impresario* (New York: Exposition Press, 1967).
92. Ibid., 28.
93. Ibid., 131.
94. Vincent Sardi and Richard Gehman, *Sardi's: The Story of a Famous Restaurant* (New York: Henry Holt, 1953).
95. Ibid., 70.
96. Ibid., 83.
97. Ibid., 125.
98. Frank Capra, *The Name Above the Title: An Autobiography* (New York: Macmillan, 1971).
99. Ibid., 133–34.
100. Ibid., xi.
101. Ibid., 9.
102. Ibid., 495.

Conclusion

1. Giuseppe Prezzolini, *I trapiantati* (Milan: Longanesi, 1963), 403.

2. Luigi Fontanella saw the autobiographical element in Italian American writing as limiting and noticed that, after autobiographies, these authors did not go on to write more: "That unique book became their spiritual inheritance . . . and on the other hand, what could those immigrants—often illiterate, hungry for work and dreams—tell, if not of the disgraced experiences they lived on their skin?" (Luigi Fontanella, *La parola transfuga: Scrittori italiani in America* [Florence: Cadmo, 2003], 45–46).
3. Michele Daniele, *Signor Dottore: The Autobiography of F. Michele Daniele, Italian Immigrant Doctor (1879–1957)*, ed. Victor Rosen (New York: Exposition Press: 1959), 236.

Bibliography

Manuscripts and Published Sources with Autobiographies by Italian Immigrants

Andreoni, Antonio. "Passaggio di Andreoni Antonio nell'America del Nord." In Maria Berdinelli Predelli, *Piccone e poesia: La cultura dell'ottava nel poema d'emigrazione di un contadino lucchese.* Lucca: Accademia lucchese di Scienze, Lettere ed Arti, San Marco Litotipo Editore, 1997. 147–280.

Arrighi, Antonio. *Story of Antonio, the Galley Slave: A Romance of Real Life.* New York: Fleming Revell, 1911.

Arru, Giovanni. "Ricordo della mia infanzia." Manuscript, no date. Pieve Santo Stefano, Archivio Diaristico Nazionale.

Bedarida, Lucia. "Curriculum Vitae." Typescript, 1995. Pieve Santo Stefano, Archivio Diaristico Nazionale.

Bongiovanni, Bruno Oberdan. "Memoria autobiografica." Typescript, no date. Pieve Santo Stefano, Archivio Diaristico Nazionale.

Bordonaro, Tommaso. *La spartenza.* Milan: Einaudi, 1991.

Bottiglieri, Maria. "Sposa di guerra." Typescript, 1986. Pieve Santo Stefano, Archivio Diaristico Nazionale.

Camilletti, Giuseppe. "Autobiography of Giuseppe Camilletti." Trans. Robert Scott. Typescript, 1982. Italian Study Group of Troy, Michigan. Immigration History Research Center, St. Paul.

Campon, Peter. *The Evolution of the Immigrant.* New York: Gaus' Sons, no date. Copy in Immigration History Research Center, St. Paul

Capra, Frank. *The Name Above the Title: An Autobiography.* New York: Macmillan, 1971.

Carnevali, Emanuel. *The Autobiography of Emanuel Carnevali*. Ed. Kay Boyle. New York: Horizon Press, 1967.

Castagnola, Salvatore. "Land Where My Father Died!" Typescript, no date. Immigration History Research Center, St. Paul.

Cattarulla, Camilla. *Di Proprio pugno: Autobiografie di emigranti italiani in Argentina e Brasile*. Reggio Emilia: Diabasis, 2003.

[Cavalleri, Rosa. *Rosa: The Life of an Italian Immigrant*, ed. Mary Hall Ets. Minneapolis: University of Minnesota Press, 1970.

Chiarappa, Luigi and Nicla, "Emigranti: La storia di una vita meravigliosa." Typescript, 1995. Pieve Santo Stefano, Archivio Diaristico Nazionale.

Cianfarra, Camillo. *Diario di un Emigrato*. New York: Tipografia dell'Araldo Italiano, 1904. Copy in Immigration History Research Center, St. Paul.

Corresca, Rocco. "The Life Story of an Italian Bootblack." In *The Life Stories of Undistinguished Americans, As Told by Themselves*. Ed. Hamilton Holt. New York: Routledge, 1990. 29–38.

Corsi, Edward. *In the Shadow of Liberty* [1935]. New York: Arno Press, 1969.

Covello, Leonard, with Guido D'Agostino. *The Heart is the Teacher*. New York: McGraw-Hill, 1958.

Crimi, Alfred D. *A Look Back a Step Forward: My Life Story*. Ed. Frank Bernard. New York: Center for Migration Studies, 1987.

D'Angelo, Pascal. *Son of Italy*. New York: Macmillan, 1924.

Daniele, Michele. *Signor Dottore: The Autobiography of F. Michele Daniele, Italian Immigrant Doctor (1879–1957)*. Ed. Victor Rosen. New York: Exposition Press: 1959.

De Piero, Antonio. *L'isola della quarantina: Le avventure di un manovale friulano nei primi decenni delle grandi emigrazioni*. Florence: Giunti, 1994.

De Russo, Rocco. "Papers." Typescript, 1971. Immigration History Research Center, St. Paul.

Di Leo, Calogero. "Mai Biuriful Laif." Typescript, 2001. Pieve Santo Stefano, Archivio Diaristico Nazionale.

Dondero, Carlo. *Go West! An Autobiography of Carlo Andrea Dondero, 1842–1939*. Eugene, OR: Garlic Press, 1992.

Evans, Elisabeth. "Un attimo una vita." Typescript, 1996. Pieve Santo Stefano, Archivio Diaristico Nazionale.

Federico, Pio. *An Autobiography*. Ed. and trans. Helen Federico. Privately printed, 1966. Staten Island Center for Immigration Studies.

Gaja, Giuseppe. *Ricordi di un giornalista errante*. Turin: Editore Bosio & Accame, no date. Found in Immigration History Research Center, St. Paul.

Gallo, Fortune. *Lucky Rooster: The Autobiography of an Impresario*. New York: Exposition Press, 1967.

Gambera Giacomo. *A Migrant Missionary Story*. New York: Center for Migration Studies, 1994. Staten Island Center for Immigration Studies.

Gatti, Emanuel Guglielmo. *Cinquant'anni d'arte scenica*. New York: S. F. Vanni, 1937.

Greco, Pietro. *Ricordi d'un immigrato, Brooklyn, 3 Maggio 1965*. Typescript, 1965. Immigration History Research Center, St. Paul.

Grossi, Vincenzo. *Ricordi*. Typescript, 1988. Pieve Santo Stefano, Archivio Diaristico Nazionale.

Iacocca, Lee. *Iacocca: An Autobiography*. New York: Bantam Books, 1984.

Iamurri, Gabriel. *The True Story of an Immigrant*. Boston: Christopher Publishing House 1951 [1945].

Iannace, Carmine Biagio. *La Scoperta dell'America: Un'autobiografia*. West Lafayette: Bordighera Press, 2000.

Lamont, Michael. "Michael Lamont." *Italian American Autobiographies*. Ed. Maria Parrino. Providence: Italian Americana Publications, University of Rhode Island, 1993. 41–54.

Lombardi, Luigi. *Pages of My Life by LU-LO*. Fond du Lac, WI: Luigi Lombardi, 1943.

Lombardo, Guy, with Jack Altshul. *Auld Acquaintance*. New York: Doubleday, 1975.

Lugnani Raffaello. *Sulle orme di un pioniere*. Ed. Aquilio Lugnani. Massarosa (Lucca): Tipografia Offset, 1988. Copy found in Tuscany, in his son's house.

Macaluso, Giuseppina Liarda. *My Mother: Memoir of a Sicilian Woman*. Trans. and ed. Mario Macaluso. New York: EPI, 1998.

Marcucci, Elvezia. "Le memorie di una novantenne smemorata (che sarei io)." Manuscript, 2001. Pieve Santo Stefano, Archivio Diaristico Nazionale.

Margariti, Antonio. *America! America!* Salerno: Galzerano, 1983.

Marzani, Carlo. *The Education of a Reluctant Radical*. New York: Topical Books, 1992.

Massari, Angelo. *The Wonderful Life of Angelo Massari*. Trans. Arthur Massolo. New York: Exposition Press, 1965.

Mattia, Peter. "The Recollections of Peter B. Mattia. Assembled and edited by Kenneth J. Rosa." Typescript, no date. Immigration History Research Center, St. Paul.

Mazzuchelli, Samuel. *The Memoirs of Father Samuel Mazzuchelli, Op.P.* Chicago: The Priory Press, 1967.

Montana, Pietro. *Memories: An Autobiography*. Hicksville, New York: Exposition Press, 1977.

Musci, Lorenzo, "Storia di famiglia." Manuscript, 1956. Pieve Santo Stefano, Archivio Diaristico Nazionale.

Olari, Luigi. *Avventure di un emigrante*. Parma: Tip. C.E.M., 1971. Copy in Florence, Biblioteca Nazionale.

Orlando, Guido. *Confessions of a Scoundrel*. Philadelphia: John Winston, 1954.

Pantatello, Michele. *Diario-biografico, l'ultimo immigrante della Quota, 25 nov. 1922*. Privately printed, 1967. Immigration History Research Center, St. Paul.

Panunzio, Constantine. *The Soul of an Immigrant*. New York: Macmillan, 1921. Reprinted, New York: Arno Press, 1969.

Pekelis, Carla Coen. "Memories. 1907–1941." Trans. Arïanna Ascoli. Typescript, no date. Pieve Santo Stefano, Archivio Diaristico Nazionale.

Pellegrini, Angelo. *Immigrant's Return*. New York: MacMillan, 1951.

Peppino, Don. *Note autobiografiche di un medico generico*. New York: Coccé Press, 1962.

Piacenza, Aldobrando. "Memories." Typescript, 1956. Immigration History Research Center, St. Paul.

Pieracci, Bruna. "Bruna Pieracci." LaGumina, Salvatore. In *The Immigrants Speak*. New York: Center for Immigration Studies, 1979. 33–47.

Previtali, Giuseppe. *Doctor Beppo. An Italian Doctor in America*. Privately printed, 1984.

Quartaroli, Antenore. "Grande Disastro della Mina di Cherry, Ills. 13 Novembre 1909 scritto da Quartaroli Antenore, Uno dei Superstiti, Otto giorni Sepolto vivo nella Mina." Manuscript, no date. Pieve Santo Stefano, Archivio Diaristico Nazionale.

Riccobaldi, Pietro. *Straniero indesiderabile*. Milan: Rosellina Archinto, 1988.

Rosasco-Soule, Adelia. *Panhandle Memoirs: A Lived History*. Ed. Ron Cannon. Pensacola, FL: West Florida Literary Federation and Pensacola Press Club, 1987.

Rossi, Adolfo. *Nel paese dei dollari: Tre anni a New York*. Milan: Max Kantorowics Editore, 1893.

———. *Un italiano in America*. Treviso: Buffetti: 1907.

Ruberto Leonilde, Frieri. *Such Is Life*. Trans. Laura Ruberto. Sound Beach, New York: Pern Press, 1995.

Santacaterina Amalia, Peguri. *Il calicanto non cresce a Chicago*. Vicenza: La Serenissima, 1992.

Sardi, Vincent with Richard Gehman. *Sardi's: The Story of a Famous Restaurant*. New York: Henry Holt, 1953.

Scaia, Gregorio. "Un pezo di pane dale sete cruste: Diario di Gregorio Scaia (1881–1971)." *Judicaria*, May–August, 1991. 1–71. Found in Archivio Storico di Trento.

Segale, Sister Blandina. *At the End of the Santa Fe Trail* [1932]. Milwaukee: Bruce, 1948.

Sodano, Daniele. "Ricordi di una lunga vita (1914–1992)." Manuscript, no date. Pieve Santo Stefano, Archivio Diaristico Nazionale.

Stagi, Divo. "Quaderno di Divo Stagi." Manuscript, no date. Pieve Santo Stefano, Archivio Diaristico Nazionale.

Toffolo, Pietro. *Alla ricerca del nido: Pensieri e testimonianze di un emigrante*. Pordenone: Ente Autonomo Fiera di Pordenone, 1990.

Tosi, Humbert Federico. *My Memoir: Le mie memorie*. Ed. Humbert Renzo Tosi. Renzo Tosi, 1968. Staten Island Center for Immigration Studies.

Tresca, Carlo. "Autobiography." Typescript, no date. New York Public Library.

Triarsi, Emanuele. "La solitudine mi spinge a scrivere." Typescript, 1986. Pieve Santo Stefano, Archivio Diaristico Nazionale.

———. *Piccole storie e poesia scritte da Emanuele Triarsi*. Typescript, no date. Pieve Santo Stefano, Archivio Diaristico Nazionale.

Turco, Luigi. *The Spiritual Autobiography of Luigi Turco*. Ed. Lewis Turco. New York: Center of Migration Studies, 1969.

Tusiani, Joseph. *La parola difficile: Autobiografia di un italo-americano*. Brindisi: Schena Editore, 1988.

———. *La Parola N. Autobiografia di un italo-americano*. Brindisi: Schena Editore, 1992.

Vanzetti, Bartolomeo. *Una vita proletaria*. Salerno: Galzerano, 1987.

Veltri, Giovanni. *The Memories of Giovanni Veltri*. Ed. John Potestio. Ontario: Multicultural History Society Ontario Heritage Foundation, 1987.

Ventresca, Francesco. *Personal Reminiscences of a Naturalized American*. New York: Daniel Ryerson Inc., 1937.

Viarengo, Gioanni. "Memoriale di Gioanni Viarengo. Partenza d'Europa ed arrivo in S. U. d'America." Manuscript, no date. Pieve Santo Stefano, Archivio Diaristico Nazionale.

Yona, Anna, and David Yona. "Memoires." Transcript, 1971. Immigration History Research Center, St. Paul.

Zavatti, Giovanni. *Cantando per il mondo. Autobiografia del tenore Giovanni Zavatti*. Chieti: La voce dell'Emigrante, no date. Found in Staten Island Center for Immigration Studies.

Secondary Sources

Aaron, Daniel. "The Hyphenate American Writer." *Rivista di Studi Angloamericani* 3, nos. 4–5 (1984–85): 11–28.

———. "The Hyphenate Writer and American Letters." *Smith Alumnae Quarterly*, July 1964, 213–17.

Ahmad, Aijad. "Jameson's Rhetoric of Otherness and the 'National Allegory.'" *Social Text* 17 (Autumn 1987): 3–25.

Aleramo, Sibilla. *Una donna.* Milan: Feltrinelli, 1992.

Amfitheatrof, Erik. *The Children of Columbus. An Informal History of the Italians in the New World.* Boston: Little, Brown, 1973.

Anderson, Benedict. *Imagined Communities: Reflections on the Origin and Spread of Nationalism.* New York: Verso, 1991.

Anderson, Linda. *Autobiography: New Critical Idiom.* London, New York: Routledge, 2001.

Antonelli, Quinto. "'Io o' comperato questo libro . . .' Lingua e stile nei testi autobiografici popolari." In *Pagine di scuola, di famiglia, di memorie. Per un indagine sul multilinguismo nel Trentino Austriaco.* Ed. Emanuele Banti and Patrizia Bordin. Trento: Museo Storico di Trento, 1996. 209–63.

Baily, Samuel. *Immigrants in the Lands of Promise: Italians in Buenos Aires and New York City, 1870–1914.* Ithaca: Cornell University Press, 1999.

———, and Franco Ramella. *One Family, Two Worlds: An Italian Family's Correspondence across the Atlantic, 1901–1922.* London: Rutgers University Press, 1988.

Banfield, Edward. *The Moral Basis of a Backward Society.* Glencoe: The Free Press, 1958.

Barolini, Helen. *Chiaroscuro. Essays of Identity.* West Lafayette: Bordighera, 1997.

———, ed. *The Dream Book: An Anthology of Writings by Italian American Women.* New York: Schocken Books, 1985.

Bartoletti, Efrem. *Emozioni e ricordi.* Bergamo: La Nuova Italia Letteraria, 1959.

Barzini, Luigi. *The Italians.* New York: Atheneum, 1965.

Basile Green, Rose. *The Italian-American Novel: A Document of the Interaction of Two Cultures.* Madison: Fairleigh Dickinson University Press, 1974.

Battistini, Andrea. *Lo specchio di Dedalo: Autobiografia e biografia.* Bologna: Il Mulino, 1990.

Bec, Christian. "Mercanti e autobiographia a Firenze tra '300 e '400." Paper read at the XXXVI Corso di aggiornamento e perfezionamento per italianisti "Verita' e finzioni dell'io' autobiografico." Venice, Fondazione Giorgio Cini, 9–26 July 2002.

Benveniste, Emile. *Problemes de linguistique generale*. Paris: Gallimard, 1966.

Berdinelli Predelli, Maria. *Piccone e poesia: La cultura dell'ottava nel poema d'emigrazione di un contadino lucchese*. Lucca: Accademia lucchese di Scienze, Lettere ed Arti, San Marco Litotipo Editore, 1997.

Bernardi, Adria. *These Hands Have Done a Lot*. Highwood, Ill: privately printed, no date.

Berschin, Walter. "Biografie ed autobiografie nel Medioevo." *L'Autobiografia nel Medioevo* (Atti del XXXIV Convegno storico nazionale, Todi, 1997). Spoleto: Centro Italiano di Studi sull'Alto Medioevo, 1998.

Bevilacqua, Piero, Andreina De Clementi, and Emilio Franzina, eds. *Storia dell'emigrazione italiana: Partenze*. Rome: Donzelli Editore, 2001.

———. *Storia dell'emigrazione italiana: Arrivi*. Rome: Donzelli Editore, 2002.

Bizzell, Patricia, and Bruce Herzberg, ed. *The Rhetorical Tradition: Readings from Classical Times to the Present*. Boston: Bedford/St. Martin's Press, 2001.

Bjorklund, Diane. *Interpreting the Self: Two Hundred Years of American Autobiography*. Chicago: University of Chicago Press, 1998.

Boelhower, William. Afterword. *La Scoperta dell'America*. Iannace, Carmine Biagio. 193–231.

———. *Autobiographical Transactions in Modernist America: The Immigrant, the Architect, the Artist, the Citizen*. Udine: Del Bianco, 1992.

———. *Immigrant Autobiographies in the United States*. Verona: Essedue Edizioni, 1982.

———. "Immigrant Novel as Genre." *Melus* 8, no. 1 (Spring 1981): 3–13.

———. "The Making of Ethnic Autobiography in the United States." Ed. John Paul Eakin. *American Autobiography: Retrospect and Prospect*. 123–41.

———. *Through a Glass Darkly: Ethnic Semiosis in American Literature*. Oxford: Oxford University Press, 1984.

Bottrall, Margaret. *Personal Records. A Gallery of Self Portraits*. London: Rupert Hart-Davis, 1961.

Bourdieu, Pierre. *Distinction: A Social Critique of the Judgement of Taste*. Trans. Richard Nice. Cambridge: Harvard University Press, 1984.

Bree, Germaine. "Autogynography." Ed. Olney James. *Studies in Autobiography*. New York: Oxford University Press, 1988. 171–79.

Bugiardini Sergio. "L'autobiografia di un anarchico fra l'Italia e gli Stati Uniti." Unpublished paper. *Esuli pensieri. Scritture migranti*. Arezzo, November 14–15, 2003.

Burnett, John, David Vincent, and David Mayall. *The Autobiography of the Working Class: An Annotated, Critical Bibliography. Vol. I 1790–1900.* New York: New York University Press, 1984.

Cacioppo, Marina. "Se i marciapiedi di questa strada potessero parlare: Space, Class, and Identity in Three Italian American Autobiographies." Ed. Boelhower, William, and Rocco Pallone. *Adjusting Sites: New Essays in Italian American Studies.* New York: Forum Italicum, 1999. 73–88.

Cascaito, James, and Douglas Radcliff-Umstead. "An Italo-English Dialect." *American Speech,* 50, 1–2, 1975. 5–17.

"Il Carroccio." *The Italian Review* 16, no. 1 (July 31, 1922).

Colacicchi, Piero, ed. *Davanti alla sedia elettrica: Come Sacco e Vanzetti furono ammazzati.* Santa Maria Capua Vetere (Caserta): Edizioni Spartaco, 2005.

Conway, Jill. *In Her Own Words: Women's Memories from Australia: New Zealand, Canada and the United States.* New York: Vintage Books, 1999.

Covino, William. *Magic, Rhetoric, and Literacy: An Eccentric History of the Composing Imagination.* Albany: State University of New York Press, 1994.

Cox, James. *Recovering Literature's Lost Ground. Essays in American Autobiography.* Baton Rouge: Louisiana State University Press, 1989.

De Man, Paul. "Autobiography as De-facement." *MLN* 94, no. 5 (December 1979): 919–30.

Derrida, Jacques. *The Ear of the Other: Autobiography, Transference, Translation. Texts and Discussions with Jacques Derrida.* Trans. Peggy Kamuf and Avital Ronell. Ed. Christie McDonald. Lincoln: University of Nebraska Press, 1988.

De Salvo, Louise. *Vertigo.* New York: Dutton, 1997.

Dos Passos, John. "La trappola in cui cadono Sacco e Vanzetti." *La Repubblica,* August 27, 2005. 30–33.

Douglass, Frederick. "From My Bondage and My Freedom." In *The Rhetorical Tradition: Readings from Classical Times to the Present.* Ed. Patricia Bizzell and Bruce Herzberg. Boston: Bedford/St. Martin's Press, 2001. 1075–78.

Dubuffet, Jean. "Anticultural Positions." In *Dubuffet and the Anticulture.* Ed. Richard Feigen. New York: Richard L. Feigen & Co, 1969.

Durante, Francesco. *Italoamericana: Storia e Letteratura degli italiani negli Stati Uniti.* Milan: Mondadori, 2005.

Eakin, Paul John, ed. *American Autobiography: Retrospect and Prospect.* Madison: University of Wisconsin Press, 1991.

———. "Narrative and Chronology as Structures of Reference and the New Model Autobiographer." In *Studies in Autobiography.* Ed. James Olney. New York: Oxford University Press, 1988. 32–41.

Elbaz, Robert. *The Changing Nature of the Self: A Critical Study of the Autobiographic Discourse.* Iowa City: University of Iowa Press, 1987.

Fabian, Ann. *The Unvarnished Truth: Personal Narratives in Nineteenth-Century America.* Berkeley: University of California Press, 2000.

Falaschi, Giovanni. *La letteratura partigiana in Italia 1943–45.* Milan: Editori Riuniti, 1984.

Ferlinghetti, Lawrence. "The Old Italians Dying." *From the Margin: Writings in Italian Americana.* Ed. Anthony Tamburri, Paolo Giordano, Fred Gardaphé. 135–38.

Fontanella, Luigi. *La parola transfuga. Scrittori italiani in America.* Florence: Cadmo, 2003.

Forgacs, David, and Geoffrey Nowell-Smith, eds. *Antonio Gramsci: Selections from Cultural Writings.* Trans. William Boelhower. Cambridge: Harvard University Press, 1991.

Fortis-Lewis, Angelica. *L'Italia autobiografica.* Rome: Bulzoni, 1986.

Franzina, Emilio. *Dall'Arcadia in America: Attivita letteraria ed emigrazione transoceanica in Italia (1850–1940).* Turin: Edizioni della Fondazione Giovanni Agnelli, 1996.

———. *L'immaginario degli emigranti.* Treviso: Pagus, 1992.

Freire, Paulo. *Education for Critical Consciousness.* New York: Seabury Press, 1973.

Friedman, Susan. "Women's Autobiographical Selves: Theory and Practice." Benstock, Shari. *The Private Self.* London: Routledge, 1988.

Gabaccia, Donna. *Militants and Migrants: Rural Sicilians Become American Workers.* New Brunswick, NJ: Rutgers University Press, 1988.

———, and Fraser Ottanelli, eds. *Italian Workers of the World: Labor Migration and the Formation of Multiethnic States.* Chicago: University of Illinois Press, 2001.

———. "Women of the Mass Migration: From Minority to Majority, 1820–1930." *European Migrants: Global and Local Perspectives.* Ed. Dirk Hoerder, and Leslie Page Moch. Boston: Northeastern University Press, 1996. 90–111.

Gallo, Patrick. *Ethnic Alienation: The Italian-Americans.* Rutherford: Farleigh Dickinson University Press, 1974.

Gardaphé, Fred. "A Class Act: Understanding the Italian/American Gangster." In *Screening Ethnicity: Cinematographic Representations of Italian Americans in the United States.* Ed. Camaiti Hostert Anna, and Anthony Tamburri. Boca Raton, FL: Bordighera Press, 2002. 48–68.

———. "The Evolution of Italian American Autobiography." *The Italian American Heritage: A Companion to Literature and Arts*. Ed. Pellegrino D'Acierno. New York: Garland Publishing, 1999. 289–321.

———. *Italian Signs, American Streets: The Evolution of Italian-American Narrative*. Durham: Duke University Press, 1996.

Giannini, Giovanni. *Teatro popolare lucchese*. Turin: Carlo Clausen, 1895.

Gilmore, Leigh. *The Limits of Autobiography: Trauma and Testimony*. Ithaca, NY: Cornell University Press, 2001.

Ginsborg, Paul. *A History of Contemporary Italy: Society and Politics, 1943–1988*. London, New York: Penguin Books, 1990.

Ginzburg, Carlo. *The Cheese and the Worms*. Baltimore: Johns Hopkins Press, 1980.

Giordano, Paolo. "From Southern Italian Emigrant to Reluctant American: Joseph Tusiani's *Gente Mia and Other Poems*." In *From the Margin: Writings in Italian Americana*. Ed. Anthony Tamburri, Paolo Giordano, Fred Gardaphé. West Lafayette: Purdue University Press, 2000. 314–26.

Giunta, Edvige. *Writing with an Accent: Contemporary Italian American Women Authors*. New York: Palgrave, 2002.

———, and Caterina Romeo. "Memoir e scrittura: il viaggio delle parole." *Leggendaria* 46–47 (October 2004): 8–12.

Goldman, Anne. *Take My Word: Autobiographical Narratives of Ethnic American Working Women*. Berkley: University of California Press, 1996.

Gramsci, Antonio. *Quaderni del Carcere*. Ed. Valentino Gerratana. Turin: Einaudi, 1977.

Gusdorf, Georges. "Conditions and Limits of Autobiography." In *Studies in Autobiography*. Ed. James Olney. New York: Oxford University Press, 1988. 28–48.

Hicks, Emily. *Border Writing: The Multidimensional Text*. Minneapolis: University of Minnesota Press, 1991.

Holte, James Craig. "The Newcomer in America: A Study of Italian and Puertorican Personal Narrations." Diss. University of Cincinnati, 1978.

———. "The Representative Voice: Autobiography and the Ethnic Experience." *Melus* 9, no. 2 (1982): 25–46.

Hostert, Anna Camaiti, and Anthony Tamburri, eds. *Screening Ethnicity: Cinematographic Representations of Italian Americans in the United States*. Boca Raton, FL: Bordighera Press, 2002.

Hunsaker, Steven. *Autobiography and National Identity in the Americas*. Charlottesville: University of Virginia Press, 1999.

Iorizzo, Luciano, and Salvatore Mondello. *The Italian Americans*. Rev. ed. Boston: Twayne, 1980.

Jelinek, Estelle. "Women's Autobiography and the Male Tradition." In *Women's Autobiography: Essays in Criticism*. Ed. Estelle Jelinek. Bloomington: Indiana University Press, 1980. 1–20.

LaGumina, Salvatore. *Wop! A Documentary History of Anti-Italian Discrimination in the United States*. San Francisco, Straight Arrow Books, 1973.

La Sorte, Michael. *La Merica: Images of Italian Greenhorn Experience*. Philadelphia: Temple University Press, 1985.

Lang, Candace. "Autobiography in the Aftermath of Romanticism." Diacritics 12 (1982): 2–16.

Lejeune Philippe. *On Autobiography*. Trans. Katherine Leary. Ed. John Paul Eakin. Minneapolis: University of Minnesota Press, 1989.

Lejeune, Philippe, Annette Tomarken, and Edward Tomarken. "Autobiography in the Third Person." *New Literary History*. Self-Confrontation and Social Vision 9, no. 1 (Autumn 1977): 27–50.

Leopardi, Giacomo. *Leopardi: Selected Poems*. Trans. Eamon Grennan. Princeton: Princeton University Press, 1997.

Long, Judy. *Telling Women's Lives: Subject/ Narrator/ Reader /Text*. New York: New York University Press, 1999.

Lopreato, Joseph. *Italian Americans*. New York: Random House, 1970.

Loriggio, Francesco, ed. *Social Pluralism and Literary History: The Literature of the Italian Emigration*. Toronto, New York: Guernica, 1996.

Macchione, Pietro. "Diario di un emigrante della Valcuvia." *Tracce: Rivista trimestrale di storia e cultura del territorio varesin* 4 (1990): 245–79.

Mangione, Jerry, and Ben Morreale. *La Storia: Five Centuries of the Italian American Experience*. New York: Harper Collins, 1992.

Masters, Edgar Lee. *Spoon River Anthology*. New York: Barnes & Noble Books, 1993.

Milani, Ernesto. "The Publication of the Translation of Rosa, the Life of an Italian Immigrant." Unpublished paper read at AIHA Conference of Boca Raton (November 6–8, 2003).

Minh-ha, Trinh T. *Woman, Native, Other: Writing Postcoloniality and Feminism*. Bloomington: University of Indiana Press, 1989.

Misch, Georg. *A History of Autobiography in Antiquity*. Trans. E. W. Dickes. Cambridge: Harvard University Press, 1951.

Murray, Donald. "All Writing is Autobiography." *College Composition and Communication* 42, no. 1 (February 1991): 66–74.

Neppi, Enzo. *Soggetto e fantasma: Figure dell'autobiografia*. Pisa: Pacini Editore, 1991.

Niccolini, Lapo. "Libro degli affari proprii di casa." Vittore Branca, ed. *Mercanti e scrittori, Ricordi nella Firenze tra Medioevo e Rinascimento*. Milan: Rusconi, 1986. 567–570.

Nishime LeiLani. "Engendering Genre: Gender and Nationalism in *China Men* and *The Woman Warrior*." *Melus* 20, no. 1 (Spring 1995): 67–82.

Olney, James. *Metaphors of Self: The Meaning of Autobiography*. Princeton: Princeton University Press, 1972.

Ong, Walter. *Orality and Literacy*. London: Metheun, 1981.

Parrino, Maria. *Il luogo della memoria e il luogo dell'identita: narrazioni autobiografiche di donne dell'immigrazione italo-americana*. Unpublished dissertation, Genoa, 1988.

Pascal, Roy. *Design and Truth in Autobiography*. Cambridge, Harvard University Press, 1960.

Pascoli, Giovanni, *Poesie*. Ed. Mario Pazzaglia. Rome: Salerno Editrice, 2002.

Pastore Passaro, Maria. "L'autobiografia di Joseph Tusiani." *To See the Past More Clearly: The Enrichment of the Italian Heritage, 1890–1990*. Ed. Harral Landry. A.I.H.A. XXIII Conference, 1990, 1994. 145–52.

Payne, James Robert, ed. *Multicultural Autobiography: American Lives*. Memphis: University of Tennessee Press, 1992.

Pipino, Mary Frances. *I Have Found My Voice: The Italian-American Woman Writer*. New York: Peter Lang, 2000.

Pitto, Cesare, ed. *Per una storia della memoria: Antropologia e storia dei processi migratori*. Cassano Ionico: Jonica Editrice, 1990.

Prezzolini, Giuseppe, *I trapiantati*. Milan: Longanesi, 1963.

Pritchett, V. S. "All About Ourselves." *The New Statesman*, May 26, 1956. 601–902.

Rayson, Ann. "Beneath the Mask: Autobiographies of Japanese-American Women." *Melus* 14, no. 1 (Spring 1987): 43–57.

Renza, Louis. "The Veto of Imagination: A Theory of Autobiography." *New Literary History* 9, no. 1 (1977): 2–26.

Rickman, H. P. "Wilhelm Dilthey and Biography." *Biography* 2 (1979): 218–29.

Riley Fast, Robin. "Brothers and Keepers and the Tradition of the Slave Narratives." *Melus* 22, no. 4 (Winter 1997): 3–20.

Rodriguez, Barbara. *Autobiographical Inscriptions: Form, Personhood, and the American Woman Writer of Color*. Oxford: Oxford University Press, 1999.

Sandage, Scott. *Born Losers: A History of Failure in America*. Cambridge: Harvard University Press, 2005.

Sayad, Abdelmalek. *La doppia assenza: Dalle illusioni dell'emigrato alle sofferenze dell'immigrato*. Ed. Salvatore Palidda. Milan: Raffaello Cortina Editore, 2002.

Scarlini, Luca. *Equivoci e miraggi: Pratiche d'autobiografia oggi*. Milan: Rizzoli, 2003.

Severgnini, Beppe. *Un italiano in America*. Milan: Rizzoli, 2001.

Shell, Marc, and Werner Sollors, ed. *The Multilingual Anthology of American Literature: A Reader of Original Texts with English Translations*. New York: New York University Press, 2000.

Shirinian, Lorne. "David Kherdian and the Ethno-Autobiographical Impulse: Rediscovering the Past." *Melus* 22, no. 4 (Winter 1997): 77–89.

Sillanpoa, Wallace, and Mary Capello. "Compagno/Compagna." Capone Giovanna (Janet), Nico Leto Denise, Avicolli Mecca Tommi, eds. *Hey Paesan! Writings by Lesbians and Gay Men of Italian/Sicilian Descent*. Oakland: Three Guineas Press, 1999. 290–302.

Smith, Sidonie. "Self, Subject, Resistance: Marginalities and Twentieth-Century Autobiographical Practice." *Tulsa Studies in Women's Literature* 9, no. 1, Women Writing Autobiography (Spring 1990): 11–24.

Sollors, Werner. *Beyond Ethnicity: Consent and Descent in American Culture*. New York: Oxford University Press, 1986.

Spadaro, Antonio. "Il caso del poeta-spaccapietre, Pascal D'Angelo (1894–1932)." *La Civilta Cattolica* 1 (January 2004): 130–42.

Spectrum 4, no. 2 (Summer 1983): 4–7.

Spengemann, William. *The Forms of Autobiography: Episodes in the History of the Literary Genre*. New Haven: Yale University Press, 1980.

Stella, Gian Antonio. *L'Orda: Quando gli albanesi eravamo noi*. Milan: Rizzoli, 2003.

Stuart Bates, Edward. *Inside Out: An Introduction to Autobiography*. New York: Sheridan House, 1937.

Swindells, Julia. *The Uses of Autobiography*. London: Taylor & Francis, 1995.

Tamburri, Anthony. "Lo scrittore italo-americano: Nuove definizioni per una vecchia tradizione." Giordano, Paolo and Anthony Tamburri, ed. *Esilio Migrazione, Sogno Italo-Americano*. West Lafayette: Bordighera Press, 2001.

———. *To Hyphenate or Not to Hyphenate*. Toronto: Guernica, 1991.

Tamburri, Anthony, Paolo Giordano, and Fred Gardaphé, ed. *From the Margin: Writings in Italian Americana*. West Lafayette: Purdue University Press, 2000.

Thompson, Becky, and Sangeeta Tyagi, eds. *Names We Call Home: Autobiography on Racial Identity*. New York: Routledge, 1996.

Turner, Sarah. "Spider Woman's Grandaughter": Autobiographical Writings by Native American Women. *MELUS*, Vol. 22, No. 4 (Winter 1997): 109–132.

Tusiani, Bea. *Con Amore: A Daughter-in-Law's Story of Growing Up Italian-American in Bushwick*. Boca Raton: Bordighera, 2004.

Tusiani, Joseph. *Envoy from Heaven*. New York: Obolensky, 1965.

———. *Gente Mia and Other Poems*. Stone Park, Ill.: Italian Cultural Center, 1978.

Verga. Giovanni. *The House by the Medlar Tree*. Trans. Raymond Rosenthal. Berkeley: University of California Press, 1983.

Vincent, David. *Bread, Knowledge and Freedom: A Study of Nineteenth-Century Working Class Autobiography*. London: Europa Publication Limited, 1981.

Ward, Martha. *A Sounding of Women: Autobiographies from Unexpected Places*. Boston: Allyn and Bacon, 1998.

Watson, Martha. *Lives of Their Own: Rhetorical Dimensions in Autobiographies of Women Activists*. Columbia: University of South Carolina Press, 1999.

Yans-McLaughlin, Virginia. "Metaphors of Self in History: Subjectivity, Oral Narrative, and Immigration Studies."

———. ed. *Immigration Reconsidered: History, Sociology, and Politics*, New York: Oxford University Press, 1990. 254–90.

Zeitlin, Steven, Amy Kotkin, and Holly Cutting Baker. *A Celebration of American Family Folklore*. Cambridge, MA: Yellow Moon Press, 1982.

Index

language, 5, 14, 16, 17, 44, 49, 63, 77,
   78, 79, 86, 112, 115, 122, 140, 147,
   148, 149, 159n17, 18; barrier 19,
   26, 142, 144, 158n15, 169n71
Liguria, 1, 37, 62, 69
Lomanto, Michael, 41, 42. *See also*
   Lamont, Michael
Lombardi, Luigi, 90, 94–95
Lopreato, Joseph, 30
Los Angeles, 57, 91, 137, 153
Lucania, 140
Lucca, 88, 191n172
Lugnani, Raffaello, 83, 86–87, 88,
   191n172

Macaluso, Giuseppina Liarda, 116,
   122–23
Mangione, Jerre, 3, 32, 167n55,
   169n72
Manzoni, Alessandro, 69
Marazzi, Martino, 142
Marcucci, Elvezia, 17, 116, 117,
   126–28
Margariti, Antonio, 19, 44, 45, 65–
   66, 184n84
Marzani, Carlo, 184n83
Massachussetts, 67, 68, 70, 122
Massari, Angelo, 28, 140, 149–50,
   161n14
Mattia, Peter, 49, 177n3
Mazzuchelli, Samuel, 111–13, 194n11
Messina, 98, 211
metaphor of self, 12–13, 27, 50, 54,
   111, 124, 145, 205n80
Migliaccio, Eduardo, 100
Milan, 102, 111, 118, 126, 201n10
Milani, Ernesto, 118
Minnesota, 70, 95
Misch, Gorge, 162n28

Modena, 57, 119
Molise, 135
Montana, Pietro, 90, 95–97
Morreale, Ben, 3
Musci, Lorenzo, 19, 164n39

name, significance of, 1, 13, 18, 20,
   21, 52, 53, 58, 88, 97, 99, 110, 128,
   139, 140, 152, 163n32
Naples, 60, 77, 90, 91, 100, 127, 129,
   130, 136, 141
Native Americans, 112
New Jersey, 70, 71, 106
New Orleans, 114
New York, 20, 32, 42, 44, 51, 54, 55,
   56, 58, 61, 63, 65, 68, 70, 71, 72,
   76, 78, 79, 80, 82, 83, 86, 91, 93,
   95, 96, 97, 100, 101, 102, 108,
   109, 114, 121, 123, 125, 127, 128,
   129, 134, 135, 137, 139, 141, 145,
   146, 147, 153, 172n96, 202n33,
   211n73
Niccolini, Lapo, 36

Ohio, 109, 135, 137, 164n39
Oklahoma, 92, 129
Olari, Luigi, 90, 92–94, 194n11
Olney, James, 12, 13, 14, 166n49
Ong, Walter, 39, 40, 42, 43
orality, 6, 23, 25, 26, 32, 37–43, 44,
   53, 84, 85, 86, 156, 168n60,
   176n6, 201n10. *See also*
   storytelling
ordinary people, 4, 6, 24–25. *See also*
   quiet individual
Orlando, Guido, 28, 32, 150–51

Palermo, 62, 77, 123
Pantatello, Michele, 50–52, 54, 177n8